MW00997732

HARNESSING WINNERS

HARNESSING WINNERS

THE COMPLETE GUIDE TO HANDICAPPING HARNESS RACES

DAVE BROWER

DRF Press

New York

Copyright 2009 © by Dave Brower
All rights reserved.

No part of this book may be reproduced or transmitted in any form or by any means,
including electronic, photocopying, recording, or by any information or storage-and-retrieval
system, without prior permission, in writing, from the publisher.

Published by
Daily Racing Form Press
100 Broadway, 7th Floor
New York, NY 10005

ISBN 10: 1-932910-72-7
ISBN 13: 978-1-932910-72-8

Library of Congress Control Number: 2009925898

Jacket and Text designed by Chris Donofry

Printed in the United States of America

Due to the technical constraints involved in re-creating past performances for
races used as examples, some statistics pertaining to career and single-season
records of horses, drivers, and trainers may differ from those that appeared on
the original date referenced.

Past performances and result charts courtesy of *Harness Eye*

HARNESS EYE

Statistical data and related information provided by:
UNITED STATES TROTTING ASSOCIATION
WWW.USTROTTING.COM
750 MICHIGAN AVE COLUMBUS, OH 43215 (877) 800-USTA (8782)

ACKNOWLEDGMENTS

I'd like to thank all the good folks at DRF Press for giving me this opportunity to share my love for harness racing and show what an exciting game it can be. In particular, Robin Foster for her creative editing abilities, Chris Donofry for putting the entire layout and production together, and Sarah Feldman for keeping us all on the straight and narrow.

A lot of work was done by the guys over at *Harness Eye* as well. Editor Derick Giwner not only wrote a chapter for me, but also was instrumental in procuring the past performances and race-result charts. Matt Rose did the dirty work not once, but twice, as we changed the format of the past-performance lines. I thank them both, and they've been great friends and press-box colleagues over the years.

I'd also like to thank "the Giss"—Keith Gisser—for providing us with an insider's view of Northfield Park. They get a lot of good betting action there and the racing has always been lively and exciting. There was no better person to provide that critical insight.

Thanks as well to the number one harness driver in the world, Brian Sears, for letting us know how he thinks and how he prepares for his "day at work." Obviously, it's a little different from anybody else's nine-to-five grind. His is a lot more exciting and he gave us a taste of what it's like.

I'd also like to recognize my dear friends and colleagues at the Meadowlands Racetrack, who keep me going, even on those slow Wednesday nights in the winter. Without Ken Warkentin, Bob Heyden, and Sam McKee, the job just wouldn't be any fun. They are undoubtedly the best in the business and together, I feel we make a great team.

To my mom, who put up with a son going to the racetrack a lot, I say thank you for letting me do what I had to do. To my dad, who never got to see my name in the program, or my face on TV, I hope I made you proud. And to Dean Keppler, who was the first to think of me for this project, I am grateful for the confidence and the opportunity to become a published author. Maybe I've finally put my journalism degree to good use.

Thanks to the horsemen and women. Many have worked in harness racing their entire lives. They put on a great show and without them, there would be no fun for the rest of us.

And last, my enduring gratitude to the bettors and fans that keep the game alive. A wise old racetracker once told me that without betting, there would be no racing. He was right. Sometimes, I think the people who run racetracks forget that, and need a refresher course. Good luck and good racing!

INTRODUCTION

Harness racing in the United States has a long and rich tradition, but let's be honest: The sport suffers from an image problem. A lot of people think it's boring. Worse, many think it's fixed. They think drivers are in complete control of the outcome of any race. They think trainers can rig horses' equipment so they won't perform at their best. And they think "insiders" make all the money.

That's just not true. I am an insider—about as inside as you can get—and I still find the process of picking winners extremely difficult and challenging. I've been at this since age 10. I'm now 40 and I still haven't figured it all out, and probably never will.

As for the people who think harness racing isn't exciting, I can guarantee they've never attended a Hambletonian Day on the first Saturday in August, or the Little Brown Jug on the third Thursday in September.

The buzz and electricity of a Hambo Day crowd has to be felt to be believed. Think 25,000 people on a beautiful summer day enjoying sun, picnics, family activities, and the thrill of the sport's greatest race, with a purse of $1.5 million. And I haven't even mentioned the $8 million or so that gets bet on the 15-race card.

Jug Day in Ohio is practically a state holiday. Fifty thousand spectators show up at the Jug and the Delaware County Fair on a Thursday. A big tradition there is chaining your chair to the racetrack's outside fence a year in advance to guarantee a good view.

I am a fan of all horse racing and have attended 10 editions of the Breeders' Cup and several runnings of the Belmont Stakes. In my opinion, the Thoroughbreds have got nothing on us in terms of excitement.

First, let me give you a little background. I work at the mecca of harness racing, the Meadowlands Racetrack in East Rutherford, New Jersey. "The Big M" is indisputably the number one harness track in the world, and has been since its first meet in 1976. The horses and drivers that race there are the very best in the business, and more money is handled on a nightly basis than at many other tracks combined.

I am the morning-line oddsmaker, track-program handicapper, and part of a television team that produces both simulcast and on-track presentations. I've been fortunate enough to watch the best horses, drivers, and trainers compete at the highest level for a long time. Many people tell me I have a dream job. For the most part, they're right, but it takes a lot of effort and a lot of hours. Like any other job, it is work, and if you don't enjoy it, you won't be able to do it.

I've done just about everything involved in the sport, including grooming and training the horses themselves. I've driven in amateur races. (I wish every harness fan could jog a pacer or trotter just once. Believe me, after two minutes they would have a whole new feeling of respect for the trainers and drivers who do it every day and night. It's not as easy as it looks.)

I've interned and worked in media relations, writing stories and press releases. I've charted races and literally done hundreds of broadcasts, including many that were available on an international level. I've even operated the race teletimer. Remember the infamous dead-heat Hambo of 1989 between Park Avenue Joe and Probe? I timed that race and helped in making that photofinish image. We were making prints for weeks!

My goal in writing this book is threefold. I want to debunk some of the age-old stereotypes about harness racing. I want to show you just how exciting the sport can be. And I want to guide you in finding the situations where you have an edge in picking winners. It's not easy, and it requires a fair amount of work, but if you are intrigued by Standardbreds, then read on. I promise it will be worth it.

With the advent of two round-the-clock horse-racing networks, TVG and HRTV, many new fans have been introduced to harness racing, and they need a primer. For them, and other novices, I will explain some of the basics involved, starting with the horse, the driver, and the trainer. We'll look at different-size racetracks and analyze post positions and strategies. We'll then get into more complex handicapping situations, such as equipment changes, class drops and hikes, and claimers versus conditioned races. We'll also examine things like qualifiers, trip handicapping, and barn changes by citing specific examples of horses that raced in the past year, using the past performances, charts, and my own pre-race comments, which were published in the official track program.

I'll also introduce you to the sport's current top driver, Brian Sears, who will tell us how he handicaps a race before he drives in it.

For some, horse racing isn't fun without betting, so the ultimate goal of this book is to get you the information you need to pick more winners and have more fun. I hope you enjoy it.

CONTENTS

1

THE BASICS/
INTERVIEW WITH BRIAN SEARS

Any discussion of horse racing must begin with the horse. In harness racing, we're dealing with the Standardbred breed. The Standardbred is very different from the Thoroughbred in terms of actual size, speed, and durability. There is a reason that a Standardbred can race just about every seven days while healthy, whereas most Thoroughbreds require substantially more time between races to recover.

Standardbreds have been around since the late 1700s and are known to be durable, well-mannered workhorses. They are adaptable to more than just racing, and they make great pleasure horses, show horses, and even police horses.

Ever wonder why some track records for Thoroughbreds have stood for decades, while the trotters and pacers seem to get faster every year? I have no scientific explanation for that, but my theory is that the Standardbred breed has improved significantly over the past 30 years or so. The same is true of the equipment used and the racetrack surfaces themselves.

During the actual one-mile race, which usually lasts less than two minutes, the most important person involved is a horse's driver. He or she is responsible for formulating a plan that gives a horse its best chance to win. Some drivers are more aggressive, some a bit more passive. It's all about the strategy.

Every track has its star drivers, and these are the names you need to pay attention to. If you're betting the Meadowlands, you want to see Brian Sears, Ron Pierce, George Brennan, or John Campbell. If it's Yonkers, you want names like Stephane Bouchard, Jeff Gregory, Jason Bartlett, and Greg Grismore. In Canada, pay attention to Mark MacDonald, Jody Jamieson, Rick Zeron, and Paul MacDonell. In Pennsylvania, whether you're betting the Meadows, Chester Downs, or Pocono, you need to know Tim Tetrick, Tony Morgan, and Dave Palone. In Florida, the top guns are Bruce Ranger and Wally Hennessey. These are just a few of the names that deserve extra consideration.

For the entire week leading up to a race, the trainer is the most important person involved in a horse's preparation. He or she maps out a regimen that will result in the most effective performance. Since every horse is different, needing varying types of conditioning, coddling, and overall good health decisions, you want to look at the track program and see who's winning all the races. It sounds simple, but most people don't do it. A wise old handicapper once told me that 10 percent of the trainers out there win 90 percent of the races. That goes for both harness and Thoroughbred racing. Without doing the years of research necessary to prove that, I believe it.

Most trainers have specific strengths and weaknesses. Some do well with claiming and lower-level stock; others have predominantly stakes horses. In harness racing, some trainers condition only trotters, while their counterparts focus solely on pacers. It's difficult to get a handle on it, but if you pay attention, you will figure out what those strengths are.

At the Meadowlands in 2008, the top three trainers for the main meet were Ross Croghan, Ken Rucker, and Mark Kesmodel. All are fine horsemen and all deserve the extra look when you are handicapping a race, especially if a horse is making its first start for one of those barns. Other trainers that I pay specific attention to at "the Med" are Mark Silva, Larry Remmen, Ron Burke, Carmine Fusco, and Casie Coleman. I haven't even mentioned trainers who excel in certain situations; we'll get to that later. These names are the ones that race all year and put the most horses in the entry box. If you play other tracks, I suggest you pull up the leaderboards and see who is successful. There is a reason for that success.

In North America, we have harness-racing tracks in four different sizes. There are half-mile tracks, such as Yonkers and Freehold; five-eighths tracks such as the Meadows and Chester Downs; seven-eighths tracks such as Woodbine and Mohawk; and one-mile tracks, such as the Meadowlands and the Red Mile. They are all very different, and not just in terms of the surface or size. Drivers calculate strategies to fit each track and drive accordingly. The style of racing at each venue has its own flavor and is constantly changing. That's why handicapping harness racing is so difficult and intriguing. The way Dave Palone drives a favorite at his home track, the Meadows, doesn't necessarily translate to the way Brian Sears guides the chalk at the Meadowlands. A one-mile race up at Woodbine has a distinctly different flow from the way it unfolds at Yonkers. Being able to recognize those differences is paramount to your success.

The importance of post position on any size track is monumental. It can't be emphasized enough. It takes an exceptional horse, or a monster effort, to overcome the 10 hole at the Meadowlands or the 8 hole at Yonkers. When the trotters convene in Delaware, Ohio, for Little Brown Jug Week, it's practically a death sentence to draw post 7 or 8 unless your horse possesses blazing early speed. Even then, it still might not work out. One of the little angles I like to use concerns horses that have been saddled with a string of outside posts for the past several starts. When those horses finally draw inside, watch out, because they will be more aggressively driven. They also usually offer quite a bit of value, since their lines look rather ordinary. If one of those horses is dropping in class, then the angle gets even stronger.

Drivers themselves tend to downplay post positions, and a perfect example of that is given every time John Campbell draws post 10 in a big stakes race. At every press conference, he utters the words we have come to expect: "The post is just a starting point."

It works for him, and many other top pilots have adopted that phrase simply to deflect the pressure associated with driving in a big race. Campbell and a few others are superb at turning that inconvenience into a golden opportunity.

THE WHITE KNIGHT

In any discussion of the top drivers in modern-day harness racing, the first name that comes up is Brian Sears. Sears, who is just 41, has accomplished more in the past five years than any driver in harness-racing history.

In that span, horses driven by Sears have earned more than $60 million in purses. In 2008 alone, he was the regular pilot behind four of the sport's division champions: Mister Big, Muscle Hill, My Little Dragon, and Major In Art.

MICHAEL LISA / LISA PHOTO

The third-generation horseman has captured nine straight driving titles at the Meadowlands, considered the premier venue in the sport. Perhaps his most amazing feat occurred between March 3 and May 18 of 2006, when he won a race over 48 consecutive programs, eclipsing a 20-year-old track record set by the great John Campbell.

That consistency makes him a fan favorite and an asset to the betting public, and was one of the reasons I sought his input for a handicapping book. Who better than the top driver at the sport's greatest racetrack to give out a few tips on trying to pick a winner?

DB: Before you go to the track, do you look at the program?
BS: Yes, I always try to look at the program. I look at it the night before, before I go to bed. I want to get a look at what I've got in. I like to get an idea what my night might look like for tomorrow. Then I like to glance at it again in the morning. I usually have a routine that I like to go through, and then I like to be back in my bed by about 3:30 to take a little nap and kind of hang out with the program. Get an idea of what my chances look like that night.

DB: How do you handicap a race?
BS: Well, it's nice when you have races where you know these horses inside and out. It's like having Mister Big, or Falls For You, where it's the same horses week in and week out. It makes my job a lot easier because I know what those other horses are capable of, and I know what my horses are capable of. In the claimers or the conditioned races, you've got a lot of horses coming from different tracks. You really don't know what they're capable of doing sometimes. You are sometimes shocked and you get some surprises. It does make it a little tougher. But, if I do have a live horse, I know there are horses that I can't have between them and me, and the horses I have to beat. I try not to put myself too far away from the horses that I have to beat.

DB: How much does your pre-race handicapping affect your strategy behind the gate?
BS: My handicapping definitely helps me behind the gate, but there are too many times behind the gate when you look over and see somebody blasting out with a horse and you think, 'Who is that, again?' By then, it's a little too late. Especially in a 10-horse field. You have to try and know them all. Some people are just going to take their shots and they're going to blast and you have to know what you're going to do with them from that point on.

DB: How important are the choices you make when the entries come out?

BS: Choices are very important and there's no question about it. The more choices you have, the more opportunities you're going to have. There are horses you want to drive, and there are ones you just can't get away from. Sometimes I hope I've got one in against them, so I can pick off, but sometimes it doesn't happen for weeks in a row. But, the more opportunities you have, the more successful you're going to be.

DB: Do you always take the horse you feel has the best chance to win, and if not, why?

BS: No, I don't always take the horse that has the best chance to win that night, but sometimes the horse has an upside, like a 3-year-old with stakes potential. I took one the other day because I thought she would win, but then she went out and raced poorly. I missed out on one that's going to be competitive in the sire stakes later on.

DB: How hard is it to make some of those decisions?

BS: It's definitely painful, especially Tuesday night when the sheet comes out for the weekend. I don't even go to the computer with the sheet. I just don't want to deal with it on Tuesday night, which is my night off. I'll just wait and deal with it Wednesday morning.

DB: How do you deal with the trainers or owners that you turn down?

BS: There are often times when I will give them a call to see how they're taking it. I'll call up George Teague or Ronnie Burke. They are guys that I drive a lot of horses for. I don't really want to rub them the wrong way. I tell them I really want to drive this other horse, but if you twist my arm and really want me to do it, I'll do it for you, but in my heart, I'd really like to go with the other horse. Sometimes, I can be persuaded, but I always tell them not to be mad at me after the program comes out, because by then, it's already too late.

DB: What do you feel are your strengths as a driver?

BS: I try to race horses like they're horses. I was always a big fan of Brett Pelling and loved the way he kept horses mentally sharp. I loved the way he never thought of horses as just racing machines. He knew how to have them mentally and physically fit and he knew you couldn't race them on their toes every week. He had a lot of respect for the horses, and that makes them last longer and stay a lot sharper. I like that and that's the way I like to race horses. I like to have them finishing. If you have a horse that's finishing his miles, sometimes he's going to be out of position and not be able to win, but he will stay sharp a lot longer than the horse that has to race up front every week. I know you have to race horses up front so often, especially nowadays. But if you can race one from off the pace, they will be good horses for a longer time.

DB: How do you get the most out of a horse on any particular night?

BS: It just depends how the horse has done. If the horse is feeling good and you score him down and he feels really good, I will want to stretch his legs and he might throw up some numbers that he's not really used to. Sometimes, he'll carry it farther than he's used to. When I start driving on a horse, it's usually over. I want to make him think that he's not really doing it. When a horse is relaxed and going easy and confidently, he will always give you more and go a lot farther. When I call on him, he knows he's already tired and then they pack it in.

DB: How do you deal with outside posts?

BS: Outside posts aren't that big a deal on a mile track, as long as you've got the power. But if you've got a horse that's just trying to get a check, you've only got so much gas in the tank, so I try to get him into a spot where he might be able to get a check. Sometimes when you use him too hard to get into that spot, the tank is already empty. Then, it's just not going to happen for you, so you're damned if you do and damned if you don't. I know some people just want their horses to have a shot and I understand that, but I'd much rather come back with a horse that's a little bit fresher and had a little more pace on the end. Then, next week, I might be able to get you some money.

DB: Do you feel you drive any differently on a mile track, as opposed to a half-mile or five-eighths?

BS: There is definitely a difference. A half-mile track is usually a speed track. You have to be up close and you can finish with tired horses. It's a short stretch. But on the mile track, if my horse is walking at the wire, somebody's usually going to pick you up, because there's no place to hide. There's always going to be a fresh one slipping out and he's going to run you down.

DB: Which do you like better, trotters or pacers?

BS: I don't really have a preference, per se, but there's nothing like driving a great trotter. There are so few of them that can go as fast as an Arch Madness or a Sand Vic, or something like that. They're few and far between, so it's more special to drive a fast trotter.

DB: How important is it for a fan or handicapper to watch the post parade, the scoredown, or even the warm-ups? What should we be looking for?

BS: I think watching horses warm up or post parades is really key for people that want to be successful handicappers, especially when you watch young horses, first- or second-time starters coming out of these baby races. You can just tell the ones that look mature and good-gaited. How they get over the ground. I think people make a living watching those post parades and seeing the way horses are acting. At a horse show, you can always tell who's Best in Show, and a lot of times that shows up when you go behind the gate.

DB: What is the secret to finding a Brian Sears-driven $20 winner?

BS: Lately, with the recession and Tim Tetrick around, I think there's a lot of value in Brian Sears. Over the last couple of years, I would go to the gate and see horses that I was driving were 4-5 and wonder why. A horse would be 4-5 and I just knew I couldn't drive him like a 4-5 shot. I wish I could drive him like a 4-5 shot, because it would make my life so much easier. But, I knew I couldn't be that aggressive. I'd have to sit fourth at the rail and hope to slide out second or third over and that would be the only trip where he could win. Sometimes, I'd try to sneak up the rail to get him across and sometimes that helps, but that's no value to have somebody run around there to try and get a 4-5 shot. I don't think that's the value we're looking for.

DB: How can I spot a bad favorite, or conversely, a horse that's too big a price?
BS: There are definitely some horses that I can't believe are so overbet, and some that are underbet. There are a lot of reasons why. Just last week, John Campbell won a final with Southwestern Dream. He faced the same horses the week after that incredible trip and somehow pays $10 again. He could not have gotten a worse trip than he did the first time.

DB: What's the best way to spot a live longshot?
BS: There's a lot of research into true handicapping and people know these horses and follow them for a couple of weeks at a time. They look at the tapes and follow the qualifiers and they kind of know [who] to tab for later. They take a horse and realize he's progressing. He hasn't had a good spot. He's had bad posts. It's only his second or third start. Now, finally he's getting a class break. It also helps when these horses get in week in and week out. Earlier in the meet, when these horses are getting in once every three weeks, you just don't know what you have. They're inconsistent. Sometimes the weather is bad. They're not getting enough work into them and they're just not getting in. But when you see a horse that's finally getting a little rhythm and he finally gets a spot he needs, all he needs is the opportunity. Maybe he draws the 4 or 5 hole, where he won't get used too hard early and there might be some value there.

DB: You make a pretty nice living as a driver. Do you think you could do as well if you had to handicap and bet for a living?

BS: No. Definitely not. There are rare occasions, though, that I wish I was up there, because I come back and wonder how they let this horse pay 12-1. But hindsight is always 20/20. It's easy to see that horses are paying too little or too much . . . after the race. My gamble is trying to put the horse in the right spot, giving him the best chance to win. I make the best educated decision, based on what I know the horse can do. Sometimes, the odds don't reflect that properly.

DB: What do you make of the recent brouhaha over whipping?

BS: I don't think it's that big a deal. If you see someone that's abusing the whip, you pull him aside and say, 'If you want to keep driving horses, you better calm it down.' Even if you want to set him down for a few days, that's fine. I don't think that I abuse the whip at all. I think it's a necessary thing and I'd hate to see somebody take it away from me when I've driven horses for 20 years and learned how to make them go and do things that make them go, but I know you can't make them go by hurting them. I try to make them go by asking them. Not too many of them will go just by hurting them. That's for sure.

DB: If there were one thing in the sport you could change, what would it be?

BS: I would like to see a little less racing . . . maybe a lot less racing. I'd like for the racing to be more special, more eventful, and not like we're going to a factory every night and just grinding it out. I think it needs to be more of an event.

DB: What's the one race you want to win?

BS: I'd love to win the Hambletonian and the Jug. I'd love to win them all, and I've been fortunate enough to win a lot of big races and some of them multiple times in a short period of time. But if I don't win any of them, it shouldn't define me as a driver. It shouldn't define my career. I don't want to be the Dan Marino that never won a Super Bowl. And that's not to say that Dan Marino wasn't one of the greatest quarterbacks ever. If people want to look at that, they can, but with the body of work and job that I do, I'm happy with the way I race horses. As long as people are still happy with the way I do it, I'll get work. That's fine by me.

DB: What about your nickname, the White Knight? Do you like it?
BS: I didn't pick "the White Knight." I don't think you should get to pick your nickname. I know one thing, it's a lot better than some of the other names out there. If I'm the savior for some of those bettors out there, I'll be your white knight. I don't have a problem with it.

DB: Is there anything else that can help the bettors?
BS: I think it's really important to just watch the horses. Take a look at how much equipment they wear. If a horse acts like they're really too hot and appear out of control, that's really not a good sign. You want them lively, but not overzealous. That's a good sign. You can do all right by watching the warm-ups and things like that. And those people that warm up, those trainers are out there because they want to win. They mean it. If they've got some Joe Schmo out there warming them up, it's not the way I want to see it done.

2

TRIPS, REPLAYS, AND TRACK BIAS

Hopefully, everybody is now familiar with the basic principles regarding harness racing, so it's time to delve into more detail, examining specific instances where you can find an edge. Unfortunately, it's not as easy as it used to be. With the advent of more information in programs, available race replays on the Internet and at racetracks, plus the ability of fans to watch qualifying races, the job of picking winners is a lot tougher. It's also much harder to find true value nowadays, and I don't mean the hardware store. Some of the following examples include horses that paid $5 or $6 to win. Ten or 15 years ago, they would have paid $10 or $20. Nobody knew about them. Nobody saw them, except for the very few sharp handicappers that did their homework.

TRIP HANDICAPPING

Trip handicapping is probably the most overrated of angles in modern harness handicapping. It is no longer the edge it used to be. Years ago, very few people watched races closely and took notes. Now, when a horse has a bad trip, everybody sees it and it's simply not worth betting that horse at even money or less when he comes back the next week. It's almost worth betting against him.

The obvious examples of horses getting blocked or locked in no longer offer proper value, so you must watch races even more closely for the subtle signs that hint at future improvement. With a little practice, you'll learn what to look for. Following are a few examples of what I'm talking about.

On April 5, 2008, at the Meadowlands in the night's final race, I latched on to Joey Rico, a horse I absolutely loved for many reasons. When you look at the horse's past performances in the program, below, you might question my sanity. Believe me, this was the right spot for Joey Rico, and something that trainer Mark Capone had had in mind for a while.

Green **JOEY RICO** — br h 4, by Bettor's Delight, Sparkling Hanover by Abercrombie — 1:51.2 M1 08 28 5 3 3 $79,4

Arabest Racing Stables,Syracuse,Ny — 1:52.0 Wbn 7/8 07 15 4 3 3 $85,3

4 George Brennan (150) (0-0-0-0 .000) — Tr.Mark Silva(273-37-31-27 .136) — Last 6 Sts-$9,620 — 4 1:51.2 (1) — Lifetime $189,

	3-28 08	M1	1	fst	26^{3}	56	1.25^{3}	1.52^{2}	NW4 2-4YO	26000	8	9^{10}	$9^{7\frac{1}{2}}$	9^{5}	9^{6}	$6^{4\frac{3}{4}}$	26^{4}	1.53^{2}	27.80	BrennanG	CndrllGy$\frac{3}{4}$,ProvnLvr$1\frac{3}{4}$	inside,clear,r
	3-22 08	M1	1	fst	27^{1}	56	1.23^{4}	1.51	NW4 2-4YO	26000	1	$3^{2\frac{3}{4}}$	$3^{o1\frac{3}{4}}$	$2^{o\frac{1}{2}}$	3^{2}	$7^{5\frac{1}{4}}$	28^{1}	1.52	21.20	BrennanG	FreeDeVi$1\frac{3}{4}$,Allmrcnldl nk	uncovered,ti
	3-15 08	M1	1	fst	27^{2}	54^{3}	1.22^{1}	1.51^{2}	NW4 2-4YO	26000	4	$6^{6\frac{1}{4}}$	$6^{o7\frac{1}{4}}$	$6^{o5\frac{3}{4}}$	4^{4}	$5^{2\frac{3}{4}}$	28^{3}	1.52	12.60	GingrasY	RcknrllnNw2,RckHrdTn hd	rally mid lane,fl
	3-1 08	M1	1	fst	27^{3}	55^{3}	1.24^{2}	1.52^{1}	NW4 2-4YO	27000	3	$5^{4\frac{1}{4}}$	$5ix^{5\frac{1}{2}}$	7^{11}	$7^{9\frac{1}{4}}$	$7^{8\frac{3}{4}}$	27^{2}	1.54	45.30	GingrasY	Allmrcnldl$\frac{3}{4}$,RckHrdTn$\frac{3}{4}$	p.6,wiped
9-2	2-16 08	M1	1	fst	27^{2}	54^{3}	1.23	1.50^{4}	NW3 2-4YO	26000	3	7^{9}	7^{7}	$8^{6\frac{1}{2}}$	9^{10}	9^{11}	28^{4}	1.53	72.30	GoodellE	WstrnSmchr$1\frac{3}{4}$,TheManic nk	no ra
	2-7 08	M1	1	fst	28^{1}	57	1.27^{1}	1.55^{1}	Qua 4YO		6	8^{14}	8^{18}	$7^{6\frac{3}{4}}$	$7^{4\frac{3}{4}}$	5^{10}	28^{3}	1.57^{1}	nb	BrennanG	ArtstsVw$2\frac{1}{4}$,FrnscZTm$\frac{3}{4}$	passed tiring fo

On paper, Joey Rico looked to be out of form. However, if you watched his race on March 28, you knew otherwise. Against a field where Joey Rico was seemingly overmatched, driver George Brennan took back from post 8 and simply saved ground from the back of the pack. Although the line looks bad, Joey Rico was absolutely loaded with plenty of pace—even though he finished sixth. You also needed to keep in mind that Joey Rico was still relatively fresh off a layoff from October. His first several starts saw him outclassed in spots where he wasn't able to seriously threaten. But once he got some money off his card, he would find the right spot, and this was it.

As expected, the usually aggressive Brennan brushed Joey Rico to the lead by the half-mile pole and the horse drew away to an easy victory in a lifetime-best time of $1{:}51\frac{2}{5}$. The only thing wrong with this picture was the price. Joey Rico paid a whopping $5 to win. No one is going to get rich on $5 mutuels, but if you used your trip-handicapping skills in the previous race, the 11th, you could have had a cold late double that returned $18.40. In the 11th, Hennessy Hanover was one of those obvi-

TWELFTH RACE: MEADOWLANDS, APR. 5-1 Mile Pace. Non-winners of $12,500 in last 6 starts. Winners over $115,000 in 2007-08 ineligible. Purse $23,500.

3-28-2M1	Joey Rico	G.Brennan	3	$3^2\frac{1}{4}$	1^onk	1^2	$13\frac{1}{4}$	$1\frac{1}{2}$	274	274	274	28	1.51^2	M.Capone	★1.50
3-26-6M1	Little Mister	R.Pierce	5	$6\frac{3}{4}$	$6^o1\frac{3}{4}$	$4^o\frac{1}{2}$	4^2	$22\frac{1}{2}$	284	272	28	271	1.51^2	J.DeCarlo	12.40
3-29-9M1	Mata Harry	A.Miller	7	$1\frac{1}{2}$	$3\frac{1}{2}$	$51\frac{1}{4}$	5hd	3nk	271	28^3	28^2	274	1.52	T.Fanning	L 33.40
3-29-9M1	Art Rulz N	Y.Gingras	9	$7^o1\frac{1}{4}$	$8^o1\frac{3}{4}$	$6^o\frac{3}{4}$	$6\frac{3}{4}$	4nk	29	27^3	28	27^2	1.52	Pe.Fusco	L 12.40
3-26-4M1	Thats Justice	M.Lancaster	6	8hd	7hd	9	$81\frac{1}{2}$	$51\frac{1}{4}$	291	272	28^2	27	1.52	K.Lancaster	L 12.70
3-29-11M1	Dont Fool Me Now	B.Sears	4	$51\frac{3}{4}$	$4^o\frac{3}{4}$	$3^o1\frac{1}{2}$	2hd	6nk	28^2	27^3	274	28^3	1.52^2	G.Anthony	1.80
3-22-11YR	Dudinkas Cullen N	Dv.Miller	8	9°	9°	$8^o\frac{1}{2}$	71	$73\frac{1}{2}$	291	274	274	27^3	1.52^2	Ri.Norman	L 11.60
3-15-8M1	Kathryn Dancer A	Ti.Tetrick	2	$2^o2\frac{1}{4}$	$21\frac{1}{4}$	$2\frac{1}{2}$	3hd	8^{13}	271	28^2	281	291	1.53	A.Salerno	L 7.20
3-20-qM1	Our Man Hammer	Jo.Campbell	1	$41\frac{1}{2}$	$5\frac{1}{2}$	$73\frac{1}{4}$	9	9	281	28	28^2	311	1.55^4	L.Iordan	L 53.70

Scratched: Adams Mate A -lame.
Lasix: Mata Harry, Art Rulz N, Thats Justice, Dudinkas Cullen N, Kathryn Dancer A, Our Man Hammer.
Off: 10:51 Time: 0:27.1, 0:55.3, 1:23.2, 1:51.2. Mutuel Pool: $335,613. Temp. 50°
MUTUELS: **Joey Rico** $5.00, 4.00, 2.80; **Little Mister** $8.20, 5.40; **Mata Harry** $10.60
LATE DD (6-4) $18.40. EXACTA (4-6) $38.00. TRIFECTA (4-6-8) $269.70.
10 CENT SUPER (4-6-8-10) $210.23. PICK 3 (1-6-4) $30.20. PICK 3 CONS (1-6-1) $7.70.

JOEY RICO made a quick brush to reach the front past the half, sailed through a solid third panel, opened a lead big lead midstretch and needed all of it to hold off a hard-charging LITTLE MISTER. The latter made a second-over bid on turn two and found his best stride a few yards too late to reel in the winner. MATA HARRY made the front easy on turn one, got shuffled to third in on the backstretch, lost action on turn two, giving up several lengths, but came on again in the lane to pick up the show. ART RULZ N followed the outer flow third-over, fanned wide and closed well from a difficult spot. THATS JUSTICE skimmed the cones, lost some ground behind his roughgaited rival on turn two and came on in the lane for the final check. DONT FOOL ME NOW was left first-over entering the final turn, offered token pressure and faded. DUDINKAS CULLEN N got into the flow late and last over and offered no response in the lane. KATHRYN DANCER A made two moves to the front, yielded to the favorites brush before the half and stopped at the top of the stretch. OUR MAN HAMMER made no moves.

br h 4 by Bettor's Delight, Sparkling Hanover by Abercrombie
Owners: 1. Arabest Racing Stables,Syracuse,Ny, 2. M D K Racing Stable Llc,Ballston Spa,NY, 3. Elliot Misshula,Manchester,NH, 4. Dreamland Farms,Cream Ridge,NJ, 5. Kelly A Lancaster,Columbus,NJ;Paul M Epstein,Great Neck,NY, 6. Darryl O Gombert,Rutherford,NJ;Hankook Stable,Fort Lee,NJ, 7. Neven N Botica,Wembley Perth Wa,AS, 8. Trezza Partners #37,Twp Of Washington,NJ, 9. Edward P De Rosa,Carlsbad,CA;Leo T Iordan,Toms River,NJ;Matthew J Iovaldi,Eureka,MO.

ous trip horses that was locked in and loaded the prior week. At least he followed up on the promise.

Joey Rico provides us with an excellent example of subtle trip handicapping, and I like to think that one of the reasons he paid so little was my analysis in the official Big M program that night.

RACE 12 REVIEW Saturday, April 5, 2008
By David Brower

1 **ADAMS MATE A** - Over from Yonkers and into a similar spot. Gets a new pilot in Dube, so let's see if Danny can make some speed with this guy.

2 **OUR MAN HAMMER** - Tough to make a strong case here. Let's pass now.

3 **KATHRYN DANCER A** - Last seen on March 15th, so that's a mild issue. However, this is a good-size class drop and a good effort wouldn't surprise.

4 **JOEY RICO** - I believe this is the spot they've waited for. Joey had more pace than you think in that last one, so tonight's the night to hop on board.

5 **DON'T FOOL ME NOW** - Might end up the fave, provided Joey doesn't take ALL the tote action. Needed his last and finished up smartly. Use.

6 **LITTLE MISTER** - Pierce put a perfect steer on this fella last time. Steps up now and I doubt things will work out that well again. It's your call, folks.

7 **THAT'S JUSTICE** - If the race sets up for a closer, then he has a chance. If not, he'll be too far back. Horse is deceptively sharp, but this post hurts.

8 **MATA HARRY** - Where's he going from this slot? Unfortunately not very far. If he tries to leave again, he might get parked out again. Not for me.

9 **DUDINKAS CULLEN N** - The wild card in here! Miller's choice of three. Won here earlier and is best as a one move horse. Can he get close?

10 **ART RULZ N** - The final pass of the crew, but I will caution this one will be ready shortly. Take a good, long look and watch for future consideration.

TOP CONTENDERS 4-5-3-9

Another good example of subtleties in trips came with Palmer's Z Tam on June 18, 2008, in the evening's fifth race, but in order to capitalize on this one you needed to exercise patience and wait for the right spot.

Red **PALMER'S Z TAM** — br g 3, by Mcardle, Born To Be Best by Cambest — 1:52.4 M1 — 08 26 5 6 1 $42,810
Z Tam Racing LLC,Nanuet,NY;Patrick D Lachance,Manalapan,NJ — 07 0 0 0 0 -
1 Patrick Lachance (140) (0-0-0-0 .000) — Tr.Patrick Lachance(40-1-2-4 .025) — Last 6 Sts-$10,500 — 3 1:52.4 (1) — Lifetime $50,810

	6-11$_{08}$	M1	1	fst	27^4	55^2	1.23^4	1.51^1	NW1 3YO	12500	5	2^1	3^3	$4^{2\frac{3}{4}}$	$6^{2\frac{1}{2}}$	$5^{3\frac{1}{4}}$	27^2	1.51^4	9.90	LachanceP	MajrGnrl^{no},MajorHtt$^{2\frac{3}{4}}$	yld,shuff,boxed,hung
	6-4$_{08}$	M1	1	fst	29^2	58^3	1.27^2	1.53^4	NW1 3YO	12500	1	$2^{1\frac{3}{4}}$	$2^{1\frac{1}{4}}$	$2^{1\frac{1}{4}}$	1^{nk}	2^{hd}	26^1	1.53^4	*1.10	LachanceP	GldStrSmkn^{hd},PlmrsZTm^{nk}	trip,tip fnl,urge,cght
	5-21$_{08}$	M1	1	fst	28	55^2	1.24^1	1.52^1	NW1 3YO	12500	3	$5^{4\frac{3}{4}}$	$5^{5\frac{1}{2}}$	$5^{2\frac{3}{4}}$	$4x^{1\frac{1}{4}}$	$4^{5\frac{3}{4}}$	28^3	1.53^2	5.00	LachanceP	ThnksFrStppn$^{1\frac{1}{4}}$,Lvfrrdhrd$^{1\frac{1}{4}}$	plnty,hit by wnr's whp
	4-30$_{08}$	ChD $\frac{5}{8}$	1	fst	28	57^3	1.26	1.55	NW2PMCdHG	11000	1	3^2	1^1	$1^{2\frac{1}{2}}$	$1^{\frac{1}{2}}$	$2^{\frac{1}{2}}$	29	1.55	*.80	LachancoP	RlyWstrn,PlmrsZTm	failed to menace
5-2	4-24$_{08}$	M1	1	fst	28^4	58	1.27^3	1.54^4	Qua 3YO		6	6^{11}	$6^{6\frac{1}{4}}$	$6^{6\frac{3}{4}}$	$6^{3\frac{1}{2}}$	4^1	26	1.55	nb	PierceR	ChstrSqr^{nk},Arterosa$^{\frac{1}{2}}$	sat in,late gain
	4-1$_{08}$	YR	1	gd	29^1	58^2	1.27^1	1.56^1	NW3000	6000	3	4^5	$4^{\circ 4\frac{1}{2}}$	$2^{\circ no}$	2^{nk}	$2^{\frac{1}{2}}$	29	1.56^1	*1.45	LachanceP	BJsTsunm$^{\frac{1}{2}}$,PlmrsZTm^1	blew final,aim,hung

The story starts with the race on May 21, where Palmer's Z Tam and his driver, Pat Lachance, were searching desperately for room in the stretch. Once they found it, Palmer's Z Tam got smacked in the face with an opposing driver's whip. He shied, almost stumbled, and was officially charted with a break. Yes, that was obvious, but his follow-up effort was outstanding. On June 4, he lost by a head to a well-meant first-time starter. The time of that race was quick, and even though he was beaten, the effort was there.

Palmer's Z Tam's following start is a great example of something I like to call "strength of field." On June 11, he was in against a much stronger bunch, even though the race condition was the same. The winner of that race, Major General, went on to compete against the best 3-year-olds in the country in stakes races, so the loss there was no disgrace.

Finally, we get to the night of June 18. Palmer's Z Tam drew the rail and was clearly facing a softer grouping for this nonwinners-of-one condition. This was the right spot, and if you had been patient enough to follow him, this was the night to unload!

Palmer's Z Tam overcame a difficult trip that night to break his maiden, prevailing by a head in $1{:}52\frac{4}{5}$. Unfortunately, he paid only $4.80, but a 45-1 shot finished second to complete a nice exacta.

In our final example, we come to a situation in which we got slightly more value from a trip-handicapping situation. The third race on July 16, 2008, featured Rustyaholic, a 3-year-old trotter who started out at 7-2 on the morning line.

Blue	**RUSTYAHOLIC**							**b c 3, by Conway Hall, Coast Road by Lindy Lane**								**1:57.2 M1**	**08 15 1 4 2**			**$18,369**
								Carter Racing Stable LLC,Greenville,DE								**2:01.0 RcR 5/8**	**07 2 1 0 0**			**$1,650**
2	**Michel Lachance (152) (0-0-0-0 .000)**							**Tr.Francisco Del Cid**							**Last 6 Sts-$4,775**	**3 1:57.2 (1)**	**Lifetime**			**$25,864**
	7-2 08	M1	1 fst	28^4	58^1	1.27^2 1.55	NW1 3YO	12500	5	6°7½	6°8¼	7°5¾	7 8½	6^{12}	28^4 1.57^2	5.60 LachanceM	SpamSpad 9,ChezBell¾			dull flow,no rally
	6-23 08	PcD 5/8	1 fst	28	57^3	1.26^1 1.56^2	NW2	7500	scr	sk				scr						scratched-sick
	6-15 08	M1 (A)	1 fst	29^4	59^4	1.29 1.57^3	NW1 3YO	12500	1	3 3¼	2°nk	1°1¼	1 1¼	2 1½	28^4 1.57^4	15.60 DelCidF	Crazed1½,Rustyhlc3½			unc,duel,clear,wknd
	6-5 08	M1	1 fst	29^2	58^3	1.25^3 1.54	Qua 3YO		5	2 1½	4 6¾	3^{15}	3^{15}	3^{16}	28^3 1.57^1	nb LachanceM	Dwychtmnhw10,HelnsClt6			steady late
7-2	5-13 08	ChD 5/8	1 fst	30^3	1.00^3	1.30^3 2.00^4	Qua		5	4^3	4 5½	4°8	3^4	4^3	29^1 2.01^2	nb MyersR	BLAKEISLE,Davner			1st over,evenly
	9-22 07	RcR 5/8	1 fst	30	1.00^4	1.30^4 2.01	NW1	3000	1	1	1 1½	1^2	1 4½	1^{11}	30^1 2.01	4.00 MyersR	Rustyahlc,XiaoHan,ChinaRoad			

Rustyaholic's race on June 15 was a standout performance, even though he got beat. On that afternoon, Rustyaholic was driven by his trainer, Francisco Del Cid, in his seasonal debut, indicating that he might need a race. (Trainers at the Meadowlands rarely drive in races, although the first start off a layoff can be an exception.) The colt was parked almost the entire mile and dug in tenaciously through the stretch, eventually losing to Crazed. Just six weeks later, Crazed went on to finish second in the Hambletonian behind Deweycheatumnhowe, the eventual Harness Horse of the Year. Talk about a key race!

Eight days later at Pocono Downs, Rustyaholic was scratched due to illness, then returned at one mile against another eventual stakes winner in Spam Spade. The latter won that race on the front end by more than nine lengths, so Rustyaholic had absolutely no chance from his position in the outer tier at the back of the pack.

When Rustyaholic showed up in the entries on July 16 and I checked out his competition, I knew this was the time to bet. There were no potential stakes winners that night, and Rustyaholic proceeded to romp in 1:57⅖ for Mike Lachance, to the tune of $7.80. At least he wasn't the favorite.

The bottom line here is that trip handicapping can be useful, but you have to look beyond the obvious situations.

RACE REPLAYS

Trip handicapping is now much easier than it used to be, thanks to the accessibility of race replays. The ability to easily watch replays has completely changed the way modern harness handicapping is done. In the old days, professional handicappers used to videotape the recap shows every night and keep files. That was a real pain, because the Meadowlands recap show rarely aired at exactly the same time every night.

Over the years, *Racing From the Meadowlands* has been shown on Madison Square Garden Network, Sportschannel, Fox Sports New York, and now Sportsnet New York. If the Mets are playing that night, or a college-basketball game runs long, the show might not air until 2:00 or 3:00 in the morning. Some of the current pros pay to have the show taped by our television department and then FedExed to them at home. That might give you an idea how important it is to actually watch the races.

Race replays are also available at kiosks at the track and on the Internet at sites such as RaceReplays.com. In other words, almost everybody has access to them, but you have to do the work.

I feel the best way to utilize race replays is if you can establish the existence of a track bias on a particular night. When you watch an entire card, you get a feel for how the track was playing. Most of the time, it will play fairly, but every once in a while you get a special night when a bias truly existed. May 16, 2008, at the Meadowlands was one of those nights, as you can see in the race-result charts on the following pages. It was a rainy, sloppy Friday, and speed was absolute death. Not a single horse that turned for home in front won the race. That's what I call a bias!

OFFICIAL HARNESS EYE CHARTS

MEADOWLANDS CHARTS: Chartcaller: Peter Iovino and Ben Medich.
Charts Copyright Daily Racing Form, LLC. All Rights Reserved. Official Finish.

Friday, May 16, 2008
Weather: Steady Showers; Track: Sloppy; Temp: 48°;
Track Variant & Bias: -1, 0w; Attendance: 4,763;
Track Handle: $358,138; Off Track Handle: $2,522,412; Total Handle: $2,800,550.

FIRST RACE: MEADOWLANDS, MAY 16-1 Mile Trot. Non-winners of $12,500 (F&M $15,000) in last 6 starts. Winners over $125,000 in 2007-08 ineligible. Purse $26,000.

5-9-9M1	‡Nepp Hanover	G.Brennan	6	9$\frac{1}{2}$	8$\frac{3}{4}$	6°$\frac{3}{4}$	4$\frac{1}{2}$	1hd	30	28^3	28^4	29^2	1.56^4	A.Skultety,Jr.	L 20.00
5-8-8M1	Local Girl	D.Beaulieu	5	6$\frac{1}{2}$	6°1$\frac{3}{4}$	4°°1	2no	2$\frac{1}{4}$	29^2	28^3	29	29^4	1.56^4	D.Beaulieu	L 10.70
5-9-9M1	Sudden Susan	D.Dube	4	7hd	7$\frac{1}{2}$	7$\frac{1}{2}$	5$\frac{1}{2}$	3$\frac{1}{2}$	29^3	28^4	29	29^3	1.57	R.Croghan	22.80
5-9-9M1	A Gentleman	Jo.Campbell	2	3$\frac{1}{2}$	1°$\frac{1}{2}$	1^2	13$\frac{1}{2}$	4$\frac{1}{4}$	28^3	28^1	29^1	31^1	1.57^1	J.Duer	*1.20
5-7-15Har	dq--Maid To Command	B.Sears	7	4$\frac{1}{4}$	5$\frac{1}{2}$	5^1	3xnk	x5x^{16}	29	28^3	29^3	30^1	1.57^2	R.Shahan	L 28.60
5-2-9M1	Futile Qwest	Y.Gingras	8	5°1	4°no	3°1$\frac{1}{2}$	ix6x3$\frac{1}{4}$	62	29^1	28^2	29	34^1	2.00^4	T.Griffith	L 5.90
5-11-4M1	dq--Rose Run Fastball	Dv.Miller	3	12$\frac{3}{4}$	22$\frac{1}{4}$	2$\frac{1}{2}$	x7x^{12}	x7x^7	27^4	29	29^3	34^4	2.01^1	S.Cunmulaj	2.20
5-9-9M1	Designable	J.Marmarou	10	8°1$\frac{1}{2}$	93$\frac{1}{4}$	9°1$\frac{1}{4}$	81$\frac{3}{4}$	88$\frac{1}{4}$	29^3	29^1	30^2	33^2	2.02^3	J.Marmarou	L 45.80
5-8-qM1	Play Time	R.Pierce	9	10	10	10°	94$\frac{3}{4}$	9^{17}	30^2	29	30	34^4	2.04^1	J.Doherty,Jr.	L 51.50
5-9-7M1	‡Hes A Blizzard	A.Miller	1	2$\frac{1}{2}$	3$\frac{1}{4}$	x8ir^1	x10	10	28^2	29	31^3	38^3	2.07^3	W.Carroll	L 19.50

Lasix: Nepp Hanover, Local Girl, Maid To Command, Futile Qwest, Designable, Play Time, Hes A Blizzard.
  dq-Rose Run Fastball was disqualified for violation of the breaking rule in the stretch & finish and was placed 10th. dq-Maid To Command was disqualified for violation of the breaking rule in the stretch & finish and was
placed 6th.
Off: 7:02 Time: 0:27.4, 0:56.0, 1:26.0, 1:56.4. Mutuel Pool: $190,620. Temp. 48°
MUTUELS: **Nepp Hanover** $42.00, 14.60, 8.20; **Local Girl** $8.20, 4.40; **Sudden Susan** $8.80
EXACTA (6-5) $438.60. TRIFECTA (6-5-4) $2,035.70.

NEPP HANOVER sat the wood to the final turn, came out into open space, moved freely down the lane, took over the front and held driving to the wire. LOCAL GIRL was stuck behind dull cover, moved wide final turn, took aim from afar in the lane and closed well to just miss. SUDDEN SUSAN sat in all the way, angled free in the lane and came with mild trot to the wire. A GENTLEMAN brushed to the front down the backside, opened up the lead final turn, tried to get away in the stretch but came to a walk late. MAID TO COMMAND left for early position, sat to the lane, angled out and made a break taking out a rival, came back to a trot and then broke again. FUTILE QWEST floated away from the car searching for cover then never came, grinded weakly on the rim and was broken into while tiring in the lane. ROSE RUN FASTBALL left to the front, yielded for a pocket, gapped out final turn and broke in the stretch. DESIGNABLE wanted to leave but had to sit on the rim near the back, stayed out in no mans land the rest of the way and tired. PLAY TIME never had any fun. HES A BLIZZARD gapped in a three-hole and broke.

b g 7 by Lindy Lane, Nook Hanover by Sierra Kosmos
Owners: 1. Kyle Wendy Skultety,Hightstown,NJ, 2. Marilyn Singer,Island Park,NY;Michael Singer,Baldwin,NY, 3. Ole Bach Nielsen,E Windsor,NJ, 4. Carter H Duer,Lexington,KY;William B Weaver III,Freehold,NJ, 5. Diana L Harrison,Houston,DE, 6. Judith Ann Couture,Harrisville,RI;Donald E Couture,Pascoag,RI, 7. Ameer Najor,W Bloomfield,MI, 8. Marcos Ameralis,Bergenfield,NJ, 9. John Regina Stables Inc,Bedminster,NJ, 10. Meadow Drive Stable,Hewlett,NY;Jonathan R Klee,East Rockaway,NY;Andrew B Woolf,New York,NY.

SECOND RACE: MEADOWLANDS, MAY 16-1 Mile Pace. New Jersey Sire Stakes - 1st Leg. 3 Year Old Fillies. Purse $38,900.

5-10-7Fhd	Knock Three Times	Dv.Miller	3	9	9	7°°$\frac{3}{4}$	3hd	13$\frac{1}{4}$	29^4	27^1	28	27^1	1.52^1	R.Croghan	L 9.80
5-10-9Fhd	Best Place	G.Brennan	3	6$\frac{1}{2}$	6°1$\frac{1}{4}$	3°$\frac{1}{2}$	42$\frac{1}{2}$	2^2	28^4	27^3	28^1	28^1	1.52^4	G.W.Sholty	7.00
5-10-12Fhd	Cartniverous	E.Goodell	1	5$\frac{1}{2}$	4°no	1°hd	1$\frac{3}{4}$	3^1	28^3	28	28^1	28^4	1.53^1	Js.Green	13.40
4-30-5M1	Ideal Newton	R.Pierce	2	4°1$\frac{3}{4}$	11$\frac{1}{4}$	2^1	2hd	4^2	28^1	27^1	29	29	1.53^2	N.Daley	*1.40
5-7-6M1	Ideal Justice	Ti.Tetrick	4	3$\frac{1}{2}$	51$\frac{1}{4}$	8^1	7nk	5$\frac{3}{4}$	28	27^3	28^1	28^3	1.53^4	Ji.Campbell	L 13.70
5-7-8M1	Ideal Morning	D.Dube	7	8$\frac{1}{4}$	8$\frac{1}{2}$	9°°	9	61$\frac{3}{4}$	29^3	27^1	28^3	28^3	1.54	P.Kleinhans	L 18.60
5-7-8M1	Sweet Work Of Art	Jo.Campbell	5	72$\frac{1}{4}$	7°1	5°$\frac{1}{2}$	6^1	7$\frac{3}{4}$	29	27^3	28^1	29^2	1.54^1	S.Elliott	24.90
5-7-qM1	Miss Scarlett	A.Miller	6	2°1$\frac{1}{4}$	21$\frac{1}{4}$	4^1	5nk	8nk	29	27^4	29	29^4	1.54^2	Ju.Miller	L 2.10
4-25-8Mw	Pembroke Swifty	Y.Gingras	9	1hd	31$\frac{1}{4}$	6$\frac{1}{2}$	8nk	9	27^4	28	29^1	29^2	1.54^2	D.M.Smith	21.10

Lasix: Knock Three Times, Ideal Justice, Ideal Morning, Miss Scarlett.
Off: 7:25 Time: 0:27.4, 0:55.2, 1:24.2, 1:52.1. Mutuel Pool: $254,337. Temp. 48°
MUTUELS: **Knock Three Times** $21.60, 9.00, 7.00; **Best Place** $8.20, 5.80; **Cartniverous** $8.00
DD (6-8) $426.20. EXACTA (8-3) $188.00. TRIFECTA (8-3-1) $785.90.

KNOCK THREE TIMES was out fourth over in a very live flow, moved wide final turn, took aim in the lane and swept on by in easy fashion. BEST PLACE worked out a perfect cover trip, tipped in the lane for aim, came with pace but proved no match for the winner. CARTNIVEROUS was out uncovered to the half, grinded up to apply heavy pressure final turn, took over in the lane but was no match for the fresh foes. IDEAL NEWTON brushed to the front down the backside, faced stiff pressure final turn and gave way early in the lane. IDEAL JUSTICE left first to the front, raced from a four-hole down the backside, angled free in the lane and lacked rally. IDEAL MORNING improved rail position down the backstretch, came out to follow the winner final turn but had no pace when it counted. SWEET WORK OF ART was out third over in good position but never rallied. MISS SCARLETT took a brief tuck on the first turn, drove up to the front past the quarter, yielded for a pocket, angled in the lane but had nothing left to offer. PEMBROKE SWIFTY took the front before the quarter, yielded for a three-hole, sat in and tired.

b f 3 by Western Ideal, Deer Valley Miss by Artsplace
Owners: 1. Mentally Stable Inc,Delray Beach,FL;Robert Cooper Stables LLC,Boca Raton,FL, 2. DM Stables LLC,Naples,FL;William J Rufenacht,Archbold,OH, 3. Leonard R Hubbard,Cambridge,MD, 4. Adam Victor&Son Stble LLC,New York,NY, 5. Arlene L & Jules J Siegel,New Hope,PA, 6. P Kleinhans Racing Inc,Flemington,NJ, 7. Spring Haven Farm,Utica,OH;Miller's Stable Inc,Deleon Springs,FL, 8. Charles & Julie R & Francene Nash,Lexington,KY, 9. William L Varney,Bangor,ME;Randall B Bendis,Bridgeville,PA.

THIRD RACE: MEADOWLANDS, MAY 16-1 Mile Pace. $30,000 Clm. Alw. Fillies & Mares. Purse $20,500.

5-9-8M1	Swarde	Dv.Miller	2	5^{1}	$5^{\circ 2\frac{1}{4}}$	$4^{\circ\frac{1}{2}}$	$3^{2\frac{1}{2}}$	$1^{1\frac{1}{4}}$	28^{1}	27^{2}	28^{2}	29	1.53	M.Kesmodel	L 2.50
5-9-9YR	Laura Lane N	C.Manzi	6	$4^{1\frac{1}{2}}$	$3^{\circ\frac{1}{2}}$	$2^{\circ 1}$	2^{1}	2^{hd}	28	27^{2}	28^{1}	29^{3}	1.53^{1}	E.Annunziata	L 20.60
5-9-8M1	A And Gs Rockette	Jo.Campbell	1	$1^{1\frac{1}{4}}$	$4^{\frac{3}{4}}$	5^{1}	7^{1}	$3^{\frac{1}{2}}$	27^{2}	28^{1}	28^{2}	29^{1}	1.53^{1}	M.Capone	18.40
5-8-6M1	Allamerican Happy	Ti.Tetrick	9	9	$8^{\frac{3}{4}}$	$7^{\frac{3}{4}}$	$8^{1\frac{1}{2}}$	4^{nk}	29	27^{2}	27^{4}	29^{1}	1.53^{2}	S.Didomenico	L 14.50
5-9-8M1	Makin A Statement	G.Brennan	4	2^{hd}	$1^{\circ 1\frac{1}{2}}$	1^{2}	1^{1}	$5^{1\frac{1}{4}}$	27^{3}	27^{2}	28^{1}	30^{1}	1.53^{2}	K.Mcdermott	L 5.40
5-9-8M1	Tu Tu Twain	Y.Gingras	8	$7^{\circ\frac{3}{4}}$	$7^{\circ\frac{1}{2}}$	$8^{\circ\circ 1\frac{3}{4}}$	6^{hd}	6^{1}	28^{3}	27^{4}	28	29^{1}	1.53^{3}	M.Burke	L 6.10
5-8-6M1	Harmony Oaks Quest	A.Miller	5	$8^{1\frac{1}{2}}$	9°	9	9	$7^{\frac{1}{2}}$	28^{4}	27^{4}	28^{1}	29	1.53^{4}	S.Rollins	L 33.20
4-18-7Wbn	Blessednbeloved	D.Dube	7	$3^{\circ 1\frac{1}{2}}$	$2^{\frac{3}{4}}$	$3^{\frac{3}{4}}$	4^{nk}	$8^{\frac{3}{4}}$	27^{3}	27^{3}	28^{3}	30^{1}	1.54	R.Banca	14.10
5-9-8M1	Lady Jay	B.Sears	3	$6^{\circ 1}$	$6^{\circ 1\frac{1}{4}}$	$6^{\circ nk}$	5no	9	28^{2}	27^{4}	28	29^{4}	1.54	K.Rucker	L *1.60

Scratched: Lye Creek Betty -sick.
Lasix: Swarde, Laura Lane N, Allamerican Happy, Makin A Statement, Tu Tu Twain, Harmony Oaks Quest, Lady Jay.

Off: 7:49 Time: 0:27.2, 0:55.0, 1:23.1, 1:53.0. Mutuel Pool: $232,325. Temp. 48°
MUTUELS: **Swarde** $7.00, 4.60, 4.20; **Laura Lane N** $13.20, 9.00; **A And Gs Rockette** $6.80
EXACTA (2-7) $155.00. TRIFECTA (2-7-1) $597.20. PICK 3 (6-8-2) $1,062.90.

SWARDE worked out a cover trip, tipped clear in the lane and used a late surge to get up under an all out drive. LAURA LANE N left for a first turn spot, came uncovered by the half, grinded her way into position in the la but was outkicked to the wire. A AND GS ROCKETTE left around the corner to the front, yielded for a three-hole, was badly shuffled final turn, came for room in the lane and closed with good pace to the wire. ALLAMERIC HAPPY sat in gapping most of the way, angled to a seam in the lane and closed with very good late pace. MAKIN A STATEMENT left into an early pocket, took command passing the half, rated the rest of the w unchallenged but couldnt last once tested in the lane. TU TU TWAIN was out from the back with no chance, moved wide final turn and came mildly to the line. HARMONY OAKS QUEST sat in all the way and never show any life. BLESSEDNBELOVED was used hard to grab the front past the quarter, yielded for a pocket by the second call, gapped badly final turn and clogged the rail flow. LADY JAY set it up third over but lacked response

b m 6 by Oh Fore, Which Way by Storm Damage
Claiming Prices: 1. $36,000, 2. $36,000, 3. $36,000, 4. $36,000, 5. $42,000, 6. $36,000, 7. $36,000, 8. $42,000, 9. $42,000.
Owners: 1. Jeffrey P Bamond,Brick,NJ, 2. Richard R Annunziata,Mahopac,NY, 3. Willie J Tomlin,Bronx,NY, 4. Larry J Fischer,Syosset,NY, 5. Joseph Pennacchio,New York,NY, 6. Sylvia A Burke,Fredericktown,PA;Howard A Taylor,Penn Valley,PA;Bethann Palone,Houston,PA, 7. John J Foti Jr,Center Beach,NY;John J Foti Sr,Center Beach Li,NY, 8. Canamerica Capital Corp,ON;David S Ramsay,ON;Hyatt Holdings Inc,ON, 9. Engel Stable LLC,Buffalo Grove,IL;Centaur Stable,Oak Lawn,IL;Jordon M Sklut,Chesterton,IN.

FOURTH RACE: MEADOWLANDS, MAY 16-1 Mile Pace. New Jersey Sire Stakes - 1st Leg. 3 Year Old Fillies. Purse $39,500.

5-10-9Fhd	Cheyenne Trish	G.Brennan	8	$7^{1\frac{1}{2}}$	$8^{\circ 1\frac{1}{2}}$	$6^{\circ\frac{1}{2}}$	2^{hd}	$1^{\frac{1}{2}}$	29^{4}	28^{2}	28^{2}	27^{1}	1.53^{4}	R.Siegelman	L 11.00
5-1-3ChD	Erma La Em	Dv.Miller	9	1no	$2^{1\frac{1}{4}}$	$3^{\frac{3}{4}}$	$4^{\frac{3}{4}}$	$2^{2\frac{1}{2}}$	28	29^{1}	29	27^{3}	1.53^{4}	S.Leblanc	5.40
5-8-qM1	Jk Getupngo	Ti.Tetrick	6	$8^{2\frac{3}{4}}$	$9^{\circ hd}$	$8^{\circ\frac{3}{4}}$	7^{nk}	3^{1}	30	28^{3}	28^{1}	27^{3}	1.54^{2}	L.Toscano	12.80
5-8-qM1	Good News Lady	A.Miller	3	4^{2}	$5^{1\frac{1}{4}}$	$7^{\frac{3}{4}}$	$8^{\frac{1}{2}}$	$4^{\frac{3}{4}}$	28^{4}	29	29	27^{4}	1.54^{3}	J.Takter	4.00
5-8-qM1	Mcarts N Crafts	M.Lachance	1	$3^{2\frac{1}{4}}$	$3^{\frac{3}{4}}$	$5^{\frac{3}{4}}$	6^{hd}	$5^{\frac{1}{2}}$	28^{1}	29^{2}	28^{4}	28^{2}	1.54^{4}	H.Giannoulis	52.30
5-8-5Mhk	Santa Fe Yankee	Jo.Campbell	2	$2^{\circ 1\frac{1}{2}}$	$1^{1\frac{1}{2}}$	$1^{\frac{1}{2}}$	1^{hd}	$6^{\frac{3}{4}}$	28	29	29	28^{4}	1.54^{4}	R.Coyne,Jr.	5.70
5-10-7Fhd	Valmctorian	C.Manzi	10	10	10	10°	10	$7^{\frac{1}{2}}$	31^{1}	27^{2}	28^{3}	27^{4}	1.55	L.Remmen	45.20
5-1-7M1	Chocolate Art	B.Sears	4	$5^{1\frac{3}{4}}$	$4^{\circ\frac{1}{2}}$	$2^{\circ\frac{3}{4}}$	3no	$8^{\frac{3}{4}}$	29^{1}	28^{2}	28^{2}	29	1.55	N.Daley	*1.40
5-10-12Fhd	Alices Restaurant	Y.Gingras	7	$9^{2\frac{3}{4}}$	$7^{\frac{1}{2}}$	9^{1}	9^{1}	$9^{1\frac{1}{2}}$	30^{3}	27^{3}	28^{4}	28^{1}	1.55^{1}	Mi.Hall	L 54.60
5-7-8M1	Diamond Jubilee	R.Pierce	5	$6^{1\frac{1}{2}}$	$6^{\circ\frac{3}{4}}$	$4^{\circ\frac{1}{2}}$	$5^{\frac{1}{2}}$	10	29^{2}	28^{3}	28^{2}	29^{1}	1.55^{3}	R.Croghan	11.90

Lasix: Cheyenne Trish, Alices Restaurant.

Off: 8:12 Time: 0:28.0, 0:57.0, 1:26.0, 1:53.4. Mutuel Pool: $304,372. Temp. 48°
MUTUELS: **Cheyenne Trish** $24.00, 8.60, 6.80; **Erma La Em** $5.80, 4.40; **Jk Getupngo** $5.40
EXACTA (8-9) $111.60. TRIFECTA (8-9-6) $546.60. 10 CENT SUPER (8-9-6-3) $178.65.
PICK 3 (8-2-8) $497.10.

CHEYENNE TRISH was out third over in good position, moved wide for a clear shot in the lane and went by easily under a mild drive. ERMA LA EM left hard out to the front, yielded for a pocket, ducked inside down the lan to the front but couldnt hold off the winner all out. JK GETUPNGO was out fourth over behind the winner, faltered early in the lane but did come on late to get up for the show dough. GOOD NEWS LADY sat in buried near th back, angled in the lane and came past the rest with mild late rally. MCARTS N CRAFTS sat a three-hole trip, angled for a clear shot up the inside but never showed any kick. SANTA FE YANKEE brushed to the front passin the quarter, rated out the action, faced pressure final turn and gave way willingly. VALMCTORIAN was out from the back final turn and never fired. CHOCOLATE ART was out uncovered down the backside, grinded up t apply pressure final turn but ran out of steam in the lane. ALICES RESTAURANT sat buried on the cones, became stuck behind a wall in the lane and never became clear. DIAMOND JUBILEE followed cover down th backside, angled into traffic in the lane but had no kick once free.

b f 3 by Artiscape, Falconstor
Owners: 1. Lessee-The Cheyenne Gang LLC,Port Washington,NY, 2. Joseph Barbera,Huntington Station,NY, 3. 3 Brothers Stables,New York,NY, 4. Brittany Farms,Versailles,KY;Val D'Or Farms,Millstone,NJ;Christina Takter,East Windsor,NJ, 5. Haralabos Giannoulis,New Milford,NJ, 6. Robert B Young,ON;David R Garrett,ON;Stan Klemencic,ON;Premier&Associates Farm,Howell,MI, 7. John Lichtenberger,N Bergen,NJ;Saverio Spagnolo,Potsdam,NY;James D Chambers,Annapolis,MD, 8. Patricia Stable,Massapequa,NY, 9. Mitchell S Rosenthal,Dallas,TX;Daniel J Pallay,Bridgeport,CT, 10. Mentally Stable Inc,Delray Beach,FL.

FIFTH RACE: MEADOWLANDS, MAY 16-1 Mile Pace. Non-winners of $12,500 in last 5 starts. Winners over $50,000 in 2008 ineligible. Fillies & Mares. Purse $23,500.

5-7-5M1	Born Storyteller	G.Brennan	7	$7^{1\frac{1}{2}}$	$7^{\circ nk}$	$6^{\circ\frac{3}{4}}$	4^{nk}	1no	29^{1}	27^{2}	27^{4}	28	1.52^{2}	K.Harrison	5.50
5-9-6M1	Ciela Hanover	Jo.Campbell	4	$5^{1\frac{1}{2}}$	$4^{\circ no}$	$2^{\circ 1\frac{1}{4}}$	$1^{\frac{3}{4}}$	2^{1}	28^{3}	27^{2}	27^{4}	28^{3}	1.52^{2}	K.Mcdermott	L 19.20
5-9-9PcD	Up Front Jan E Lu	D.Dube	1	$3^{1\frac{1}{4}}$	$5^{1\frac{1}{2}}$	$7^{\frac{1}{2}}$	$7^{\frac{1}{2}}$	$3^{1\frac{1}{2}}$	28	28	28^{3}	28	1.52^{3}	M.Ford	L 10.90
5-9-3M1	Gro	Dv.Miller	3	$4^{1\frac{1}{2}}$	$1^{\circ hd}$	1^{nk}	2^{1}	4^{nk}	28^{2}	27^{1}	28^{1}	29	1.52^{4}	F.Calcagni	L 5.80
5-2-6M1	U All Bb	Ti.Tetrick	6	$1^{\circ 1}$	$2^{1\frac{1}{4}}$	3^{hd}	3^{nk}	5^{nk}	27^{3}	28	28^{2}	29	1.53	M.Gelrod	L *1.30
5-9-3M1	The Queen Of Trash	R.Pierce	5	9	9	$8^{\circ 1}$	8^{1}	6^{nk}	29^{4}	27^{2}	27^{2}	28^{2}	1.53	O.Greene	L 6.70
5-8-12ChD	Sees Alookin	E.Goodell	2	$2^{1\frac{1}{2}}$	$3^{1\frac{1}{4}}$	5^{nk}	6^{hd}	7^{nk}	27^{4}	28	28^{3}	28^{3}	1.53	S.Cunmulaj	L 31.90
5-5-8ChD	Queens Gambit N	B.Sears	8	$8^{1\frac{1}{2}}$	$8^{2\frac{1}{4}}$	9	9	$8^{3\frac{1}{4}}$	29^{2}	27^{2}	28	28^{1}	1.53	M.Silva	L 22.50
5-2-1M1	Delightful Hope	Y.Gingras	9	$6^{1\frac{1}{4}}$	$6^{\circ 1\frac{1}{2}}$	$4^{\circ 1\frac{1}{4}}$	$5^{\frac{1}{2}}$	9	29	27^{2}	27^{3}	29^{4}	1.53^{4}	Pe.Fusco	L 5.50

Lasix: Ciela Hanover, Up Front Jan E Lu, Gro, U All Bb, The Queen Of Trash, Sees Alookin, Queens Gambit N, Delightful Hope.

Off: 8:35 Time: 0:27.3, 0:55.3, 1:23.4, 1:52.2. Mutuel Pool: $287,156. Temp. 48°
MUTUELS: **Born Storyteller** $13.00, 7.00, 5.20; **Ciela Hanover** $13.40, 6.60; **Up Front Jan E Lu** $5.60
EXACTA (7-4) $228.20. TRIFECTA (7-4-1) $737.60. PICK 3 (2-8-7) $355.20.

BORN STORYTELLER was out third over in yet another live flow, moved for a clear shot in the lane and was just up on the wire under an all out drive. CIELA HANOVER was out uncovered down the backside, moved into position final turn, took over in the lane but was nailed on the money in a very game try. UP FRONT JAN E LU sat the cones all the way, angled out wide down the lane and came willingly to the wire. GRO was headstrong early and moved to the front past the quarter, faced heavy pressure final turn and gave way in the drive. U ALL BB left to the front passing the quarter, yielded for a pocket, angled for shot in the lane but lacked rally. THE QUEEN OF TRASH was off the gate as she usually is, came out from the back final turn and picked off a few in the lane. SEES ALOOKIN sat a three-hole journey, angled in the lane for room, came with a brief move bu flattened out quickly. QUEENS GAMBIT N was totally buried at the back, angled in the stretch and came with a mild late flurry. DELIGHTFUL HOPE worked out a perfect cover trip but came up empty.

b m 6 by Badlands Hanover, Fictionals Filly by Run The Table
Owners: 1. Ronald J Mario,Longboat Key,FL, 2. Joseph R Zicchino,Point Pleasant,NJ, 3. C Ed Mullinax,Amherst,OH, 4. Jerry P & Frank Calcagni,Pine Bush,NY, 5. Fred Monteleone Stbl LLC,Pompano Beach,FL, 6. Nanticoke Racing Inc,Seaford,DE;Brandon A Givens,Seaford,DE;Donna M Messick,Delmar,DE, 7. Ameer Najor,W Bloomfield,MI, 8. Bell Valley Farms Inc,Frankfort,IL, 9. Dreamland Farms,Cream Ridge,NJ.

SIXTH RACE: MEADOWLANDS, MAY 16-1 Mile Trot. Non-winners of $25,000 in last 6 starts. A.E.: Non-winners of 5 ext. pari-mutuel races or $275,000 lifetime. Purse $37,500.

5-9-5M1	Likeabatoutahell	C.Manzi	2	4¹	5°1½	5°1¼	41¾	1¾	28^{4}	28^{3}	28^{3}	28^{2}	1.54^{2}	T.Smedshammer	L 7.60
5-9-2M1	dq--Mystical Ryan	D.Dube	3	5°1½	1°1½	1½	1¼	2nk	29	27^{2}	29	29^{1}	1.54^{3}	A.Montini	L *1.40
4-25-9M1	‡Hope Reins Supreme	G.Brennan	4	8½	7¼	6¾	7½	3½	29^{4}	27^{4}	28^{3}	28^{2}	1.54^{3}	J.Hartline	L 17.50
5-2-7M1	One Man Show S	Dv.Miller	10	2°hd	2½	2nk	3i¾	4½	28^{2}	28^{1}	29	29	1.54^{3}	N.Daley	L 3.10
5-9-5M1	Angelo Kosmos	R.Pierce	5	3½	4°1¼	3°1¼	2no	53¼	28^{2}	28^{4}	28^{3}	29	1.54^{4}	A.Viens	L 7.70
5-7-6Har	Fivedollarsforsox	G.Dennis	8	10°	10°	9°11	8no	6hd	30^{1}	28	28^{3}	28^{3}	1.55^{2}	G.Dennis	L 80.60
5-2-7M1	Just A Con Man	B.Sears	6	9nk	9½	8¼	9dis	7hd	30^{1}	28	28^{2}	28^{4}	1.55^{2}	M.Silva	L 7.90
5-9-5M1	‡Smooth Muscles	Jo.Campbell	1	6¾	6°hd	7°½	6no	8¹	29^{1}	28^{2}	28^{4}	29	1.55^{2}	J.Duer	L 38.70
5-9-2M1	The Federalist	Y.Gingras	7	1°1¼	3¾	4nk	5½	9dis	28^{1}	28^{4}	29	29^{3}	1.55^{3}	M.Ford	L 30.70
5-9-2M1	‡Focus	Ti.Tetrick	9	7½	8°1¼	x10x	10	10	29^{3}	28^{2}	31			J.Raymer	L 10.00

Lasix: Likeabatoutahell, Mystical Ryan, Hope Reins Supreme, One Man Show S, Angelo Kosmos, Fivedollarsforsox, Just A Con Man, Smooth Muscles, The Federalist, Focus.

dq-Mystical Ryan was disqualified for causing interference in the stretch and was placed 4th.

Off: 8:58 Time: 0:28.1, 0:56.2, 1:25.2, 1:54.2. Mutuel Pool: $315,977. Temp. 48°

MUTUELS: **Likeabatoutahell** $17.20, 9.60, 5.40; **Hope Reins Supreme** $15.40, 8.80; **One Man Show S** $4.20

EXACTA (2-4) $250.60. TRIFECTA (2-4-10) $717.40. PICK 3 (8-7-2) $872.40.

LIKEABATOUTAHELL set it up in perfect cover position, moved off in the stretch and powered on by late for the score. MYSTICAL RYAN brushed to the front down the backside, rated out the fractions, was put to a drive early in the lane, shut off a rival while lugging in but did hang on the place before being disqualified. HOPE REINS SUPREME sat the cones all the way, angled for a shot in the stretch and came flying to the wire. ONE MAN SHOW S left to the front at own pace, yielded for a pocket, tried to get to the rail in the lane but never cleared a path with plenty of trot. ANGELO KOSMOS left for an early spot, came uncovered to the half, grinded at own pace on the lane and tired late. FIVEDOLLARSFORSOX was out from the back with excess cover, moved wide down the lane and came by the rest. JUST A CON MAN sat in all the way and never fired. SMOOTH MUSCLES was out third over but never found any rally. THE FEDERALIST left to the front passing the quarter, raced from a three-hole, angled in the lane but was empty. FOCUS was out fourth over and lost focus final turn.

b g 5 by Sj's Caviar, Miss Molly Tamale by Final Score

Owners: 1. Michael D Andrew,Gorham,ME, 2. Frank Cirillo,Kleinburg,ON, CA, 3. Stephen W Demeter,Tarrytown,NY;Thomas George Aquilino,Yonkers,NY, 4. Matsocholoveriksson Ab,Sandviken,SD, 5. Andre Viens,Coral Springs,FL, 6. George&Tina Dennis Inc,Wyoming,DE;Ask W Stables Inc,Wyoming,DE, 7. Barnik Racing Stable,Schenectady,NY, 8. L&L Devisser LLC,Holland,MI, 9. Martin Scharf,Lawrence,NY, 10. Trillium Racing Stable,New Holland,PA.

SEVENTH RACE: MEADOWLANDS, MAY 16-1 Mile Pace. Non-winners of $37,500 in last 6 starts. A.E.: 5 Year Olds & Under that are non-winners of 5 ext. pari-mutuel races or $175,000 lifetime. Fillies & Mares. Purse $37,500.

5-9-6M1	Marietta Hall	G.Brennan	4	2½	22½	2¾	2hd	1no	27^{3}	28^{1}	28^{3}	27^{3}	1.52	S.Elliott	5.50
5-9-6M1	Jadah Rose A	Ti.Tetrick	6	4°1	4°1¼	3°nk	3¹	2¾	28^{1}	28^{1}	28^{1}	27^{2}	1.52	P.Walsh	L *.60
5-2-6M1	Postmark	Dv.Miller	8	9°1¾	9°1½	9°°1¼	4no	3½	29^{1}	28	28^{1}	26^{4}	1.52^{1}	N.Daley	L 5.00
5-9-6M1	Mind Boggling	Jo.Campbell	10	10	10	10°°	8hd	4nk	29^{3}	28	28	26^{3}	1.52^{1}	R.Croghan	40.60
5-5-12ChD	Cruzin Foralivin N	R.Pierce	2	3½	3¼	4¼	5nk	5¾	27^{4}	28^{2}	28^{2}	27^{3}	1.52^{1}	V.Morgan,Jr.	L 13.10
5-9-6M1	Ms Maggie	A.Miller	7	1³	1¾	1¼	1¹	6hd	27	28^{2}	28^{4}	28^{1}	1.52^{2}	Ju.Miller	L 49.70
5-9-6M1	Twin B Tiara	E.Goodell	1	5½	5nk	5no	7nk	7¾	28^{2}	28^{2}	28	27^{3}	1.52^{2}	M.Stanislao	L 23.30
5-9-6M1	Cowgirls N Indians	B.Sears	5	8°1¾	7°nk	7°nk	9½	8nk	28^{4}	28^{1}	28^{1}	27^{2}	1.52^{3}	J.Dunning	26.40
5-9-3M1	Seamstresforthepan	D.Dube	3	7½	8¹	8¾	10	9¹	28^{4}	28^{1}	28^{1}	27^{2}	1.52^{3}	Ma.Davis	L 74.40
4-26-5M1	Kg Katriona	Y.Gingras	9	6°1¼	6°1¼	6°1¼	6¾	10	28^{2}	28^{2}	28	28	1.52^{4}	C.Coleman	15.50

Lasix: Jadah Rose A, Postmark, Cruzin Foralivin N, Ms Maggie, Twin B Tiara, Seamstresforthepan.

Off: 9:23 Time: 0:27.0, 0:55.2, 1:24.1, 1:52.0. Mutuel Pool: $341,028. Temp. 48°

MUTUELS: **Marietta Hall** $13.00, 3.80, 3.40; **Jadah Rose A** $2.60, 2.20; **Postmark** $2.80

EXACTA (4-6) $35.00. TRIFECTA (4-6-8) $50.00. 10 CENT SUPER (4-6-8-10) $70.08.

PICK 3 (7-2-4) $517.60.

MARIETTA HALL left into pocket position, tracked from there all the way, angled to the lead in the lane and held life and death to the wire. JADAH ROSE A was uncovered down the backside, moved into contention at own pace, took aim in the lane but was just denied all out. POSTMARK was out from the back fourth over, circled up wide final turn, moved with slight aim in the lane and came with plenty to the wire. MIND BOGGLING was out wide from the back final turn and came willingly to the line. CRUZIN FORALIVIN N sat a live three-hole trip, angled free but lacked rally. MS MAGGIE left quickly to command, calmed down to the half, rated the rest of the way at own clip but gave way once confronted. TWIN B TIARA sat in all the way, angled in the lane and came evenly to the wire. COWGIRLS N INDIANS was out third over, became blind final turn, freed up in the lane but lacked serious rally. SEAMSTRESFORTHEPAN was locked in at the back and never had a chance. KG KATRIONA floated away waiting for cover, found live protection, followed to the lane but tired.

b m 4 by Cambest, Mib Hanover by Tyler B

Owners: 1. Bulletproof Enterprises,Boca Raton,FL, 2. Peter V Walsh,Allentown,NJ, 3. Charles Stillings,Indianapolis,IN;Dean E Ehrgott,Indianapolis,IN, 4. Let It Ride Stables Inc,Delray Beach,FL;Mentally Stable Inc,Delray Beach,FL, 5. Joseph V Muscara,Huntingdon Valley,PA, 6. James Alan Geis,Chicago,IL;Bert J Hochsprung,Elburn,IL, 7. Robin Bruce Batcho,North Plainfield,NJ;Monico P Stanislao,No Plainfield,NJ, 8. Ian P Fromowitz,Richmond Hill,ON, CA;John D Fielding,Toronto,ON, CA, 9. Kathleen Davis,Smyrna,DE, 10. Mac T Nichol,Burlington,ON, CA;Casie Coleman,Cambridge,ON, CA.

EIGHTH RACE: MEADOWLANDS, MAY 16-1 Mile Trot. $35,000/$42,500 Clm. Alw. Hcp. Post positions drawn to base price. Purse $26,000.

5-2-2M1	Bail Jumper	A.Miller	9	1°½	2¼	3¼	3¼	1½	28^{3}	29^{1}	29^{2}	29	1.56^{1}	K.Rucker	L 10.30
5-9-7M1	Rockome Vic	Jo.Campbell	1	2¾	3nk	4½	4¾	2¾	28^{3}	29^{3}	29^{2}	28^{4}	1.56^{2}	C.Fusco	8.90
5-2-2M1	New Dice Please	Dv.Miller	10	3°¾	1½	1hd	2½	3½	28^{4}	28^{4}	29^{2}	29^{3}	1.56^{3}	A.Montini	*2.00
5-9-7M1	Braggin Rights	E.Goodell	2	4½	4°1½	2°1½	1hd	4hd	29	29^{1}	28^{4}	29^{4}	1.56^{4}	C.Gillespie	L 32.50
5-2-2M1	Mighty Moses	R.Pierce	3	6¼	7°1¼	8°1¼	8¾	5hd	29^{3}	29^{1}	29	29	1.56^{4}	E.Ell	L 3.00
5-9-7M1	‡Autumn Victory	D.Dube	5	8nk	6¼	6no	6½	6¹	30^{1}	28^{1}	29^{2}	29	1.56^{4}	M.Sorentino,Jr.	L 14.80
5-2-2M1	‡Stonetag	G.Brennan	4	7°1¼	8°no	7°°nk	5hd	7¹	29^{4}	29^{1}	28^{4}	29^{1}	1.57	J.Hartline	L 5.80
5-8-3M1	Farmer Jones	Y.Gingras	8	5°1¾	5°hd	5°¹	7¹	83½	29^{1}	29^{1}	29^{1}	29^{3}	1.57^{1}	J.Mcdermott	L 15.80
4-25-2M1	Heart Of Shovey	B.Sears	6	9°1¾	10°	10	10	9¾	30^{1}	29	29^{1}	29^{2}	1.57^{4}	Ri.Johnson	L 10.20
5-9-7M1	Close Encounter	Ti.Tetrick	7	10	9½	9°°1¼	9¾	10	30^{3}	28^{2}	29^{1}	30	1.58^{1}	G.Anthony	L 17.00

Lasix: Bail Jumper, Braggin Rights, Mighty Moses, Autumn Victory, Stonetag, Farmer Jones, Heart Of Shovey, Close Encounter.

Claimed: Mighty Moses by Cataway Racing Stable & Pat Caturano, N.Y..

Off: 9:46 Time: 0:28.3, 0:57.3, 1:27.0, 1:56.1. Mutuel Pool: $287,545. Temp. 48°

MUTUELS: **Bail Jumper** $22.60, 10.40, 6.00; **Rockome Vic** $7.60, 4.20; **New Dice Please** $3.40

EXACTA (9-1) $174.20. TRIFECTA (9-1-10) $312.30.

BAIL JUMPER made the front passing the quarter, yielded for a pocket, angled in the lane for dead aim and went by rather easily for the score. ROCKOME VIC sat a three-hole, angled out wide in the drive and came with trot to grab the place spot near the wire. NEW DICE PLEASE left under own power to the front well past the quarter, rated down the backside, faced pressure final turn and gave way in the lane after a minor skirmish. BRAGGIN RIGHTS was out uncovered to the half, grinded into contention final turn, moved to the front in the lane but ran out gas shortly after. MIGHTY MOSES was out fourth over, moved to a clear path in the lane and came with mild trot to the wire. AUTUMN VICTORY sat in all the way and was even. STONETAG was out from the back with excess cover, tried to circle up final turn, took aim in the lane but had nothing left to offer. FARMER JONES gapped off very live cover and clogged. HEART OF SHOVEY was out briefly from the back but never had a chance. CLOSE ENCOUNTER followed wide from the back final turn but had no stretch rally.

b g 5 by Jailhouse Jesse, We Got Next by Overcomer

Claiming Prices: 1. $35,000, 2. $35,000, 3. $42,500, 4. $35,000, 5. $35,000, 6. $35,000, 7. $35,000, 8. $35,000, 9. $42,000, 10. $35,000.

Owners: 1. Engel Stable LLC,Buffalo Grove,IL;Rucker Stable Inc,Beecher,IL, 2. Todd P Stone,Larksville,PA, 3. Bill G Manes,ON;Robert W Little,ON;Paul Sabourin,ON;William G Cripps,ON, 4. Carolyn & Irving Atherton,Bronxville,NY, 5. W Kenneth & B L Wood,Denton,MD;W J Dittmar Jr,Langhorne,PA;S J Iaquinta,Havertown,PA, 6. Michael Sorentino Jr,Bronxville,NY, 7. Jackson Street Stable,Jackson,NJ, 8. Richard Moreau,Lachenaie,PQ, CA, 9. Exit 67 Racing LLC,Boynton Beach,FL, 10. Darryl O Gombert,Rutherford,NJ;Jeffrey Rose,Brooklyn,NY;Hankook Stable,Fort Lee,NJ.

NINTH RACE: MEADOWLANDS, MAY 16-1 Mile Pace. Non-winners of $15,000 in last 6 starts. A.E.: 4 Year Olds & Under that are non-winners of 4 ext. pari-mutuel races or $100,000 lifetime. A.E.: Opt. $50,000 Clm. Alw. Fillies & Mares. Purse $29,500.

5-9-1M1	Im Warning U	Ti.Tetrick	8	$4^{2\frac{3}{4}}$	$4^{\circ 1\frac{3}{4}}$	2^3	$2^{4\frac{1}{4}}$	1^2	28^2	28^4	28^2	27	1.52^3	C.Coleman	*1.50
5-9-3M1	Jessalilmixup	Jo.Campbell	5	$1^{\circ 2}$	$1^{1\frac{1}{2}}$	$1^{1\frac{3}{4}}$	1^{nk}	$2^{\frac{1}{2}}$	27^2	29	28^4	27^4	1.53	K.Lancaster	L 2.00
5-9-6Fhd	Sleazebiscuit	R.Pierce	6	$7^{1\frac{1}{2}}$	$7^{\circ 1\frac{1}{4}}$	$5^{\circ\circ no}$	3^2	$3^{3\frac{1}{4}}$	29^3	28^1	28^3	26^3	1.53	K.Rucker	L 11.40
5-9-1M1	O Narutac Bella	G.Brennan	7	$8^{1\frac{3}{4}}$	$8^{\circ 2\frac{1}{4}}$	$7^{\circ no}$	4^1	$4^{3\frac{1}{4}}$	30	28^1	28^2	27^1	1.53^4	B.Saunders	3.80
5-9-3M1	Jm Dancing Star	Y.Gingras	1	3^2	3^1	$6^{1\frac{1}{2}}$	6^{nk}	$5^{\frac{3}{4}}$	28	29	29^2	28	1.54^2	J.Dunning	54.80
5-9-1M1	Striptease Hall	B.Sears	2	$5^{1\frac{3}{4}}$	5^{nk}	$8^{1\frac{1}{4}}$	8^{nk}	$6^{1\frac{3}{4}}$	29	28^3	29	28	1.54^3	M.Burke	9.90
5-9-8M1	Julies Shadow	D.Dube	9	9	9	9	9	7^5	30^2	28^1	28^1	28	1.54^4	F.Bisaccia	L 32.20
5-8-12ChD	Flannel Yankee	E.Goodell	3	$2^{1\frac{1}{2}}$	$2^{1\frac{1}{2}}$	3^{hd}	$7^{\frac{3}{4}}$	8^{nk}	27^4	28^4	29^3	29^3	1.55^4	K.Harrison	L 61.10
5-9-3M1	Before Dawn	Dv.Miller	4	$6^{1\frac{1}{2}}$	$6^{\circ 1\frac{1}{2}}$	$4^{\circ 1}$	$5^{\frac{3}{4}}$	9	29^2	28^1	28^3	29^4	1.56	P.Kleinhans	L 23.20

Scratched: Final Renee -sick.
Lasix: Jessalilmixup, Sleazebiscuit, Julies Shadow, Flannel Yankee, Before Dawn.

Off: 10:09 Time: 0:27.2, 0:56.2, 1:25.1, 1:52.3. Mutuel Pool: $316,937. Temp. 48°
MUTUELS: **Im Warning U** $5.00, 3.00, 2.60; **Jessalilmixup** $3.20, 2.80; **Sleazebiscuit** $3.80
EXACTA (8-5) $18.40. TRIFECTA (8-5-6) $49.70. 10 CENT SUPER (8-5-6-7) $13.65.
PICK 3 (4-9-8) $145.30. PICK 4 (2-4-9-8,10) $1,607.20. PICK 6 (4 OF 6) $20.10.
PICK 6 CARRYOVER $2,198.47.

IM WARNING U left for solid early position, came uncovered down the backside, ducked into a wide open pocket final turn, angled for dead aim in the lane and went by easily for the score. JESSALILMIXUP moved to command passing the first marker, rated the pace up front, tired to get away final turn but was no match for the winner. SLEAZEBISCUIT was stuck behind dull cover, moved wide final turn, took aim on the rest in the lane and came with solid late pace. O NARUTAC BELLA was also caught out in the dull flow fourth over and did what she could to get up for minor spoils. JM DANCING STAR sat a three-hole trip, was shuffled badly final turn, angled free in the lane and came with even pace to the wire. STRIPTEASE HALL gapped along the cones to the half, moved under urge to catch the field but never got involved in the lane. JULIES SHADOW never responded at the back. FLANNEL YANKEE left out to the front, yielded for a pocket, gapped badly final turn and stopped the rail flow. BEFORE DAWN lost live cover final turn and hit a wall shortly after.
br m 5 by As Promised, Tsunami Warning by Scruffy Hanover
Claiming Prices: 1. $60,000, 2. , 3. , 4. , 5. $60,000, 6. $70,000, 7. , 8. , 9. $70,000.
Owners: 1. Steve W Calhoun,Chatham,ON, CA, 2. Larry H Asher,Bellmore,NY;Kelly A Lancaster,Columbus,NJ, 3. Engel Stable LLC,Buffalo Grove,IL, 4. Cataway Racing Stable,Smithtown,NY;Pat C Caturano,North Merrick,NY, 5. Michael J Mitchell,Lindenwold,NJ, 6. S Burke,Frdrcktwn,PA;Weaver Bruscemi,Cnsbrg,PA;J Koechlin,Blftn,SC;W Haas Jr,Pt Orng,FL, 7. Raymond J McDonough,Mahopac,NY, 8. Ronald J Mario,Longboat Key,FL, 9. P Kleinhans Racing Inc,Flemington,NJ;Let It Ride Stables Inc,Delray Beach,FL.

TENTH RACE: MEADOWLANDS, MAY 16-1 Mile Trot. Non-winners of $7,500 in last 6 starts. Winners over $40,000 in 2008 ineligible. A.E.: 4 Year Olds & Under that are non-winners of 3 (F&M 4) ext. pari-mutuel races or $75,000 lifetime. Purse $22,000.

5-3-11PcD	Im A Cool Breeze	Ti.Tetrick	5	$1^{1\frac{3}{4}}$	$2^{2\frac{1}{2}}$	$2^{2\frac{3}{4}}$	$2^{3\frac{3}{4}}$	1no	28^3	29^2	29^1	28^2	1.55^3	J.Bobby	L 13.00
5-1-6M1	‡Summertime Yankee	A.Miller	2	$3^{\circ 1\frac{1}{2}}$	$1^{1\frac{1}{2}}$	$1^{1\frac{1}{2}}$	$1^{\frac{3}{4}}$	$2^{1\frac{1}{2}}$	29	28^4	29^1	28^3	1.55^3	J.Raymer	*1.80
5-8-qM1	Aisling	Dv.Miller	7	7^{hd}	$6^{\frac{1}{2}}$	$5^{\circ 1\frac{1}{4}}$	$3^{1\frac{3}{4}}$	3^8	30^3	28^3	28^4	27^4	1.55^4	R.Bencal	29.20
5-8-qM1	‡Four Starz Credit	B.Sears	1	$2^{\frac{3}{4}}$	$4^{1\frac{1}{2}}$	4^{nk}	$4^{\frac{3}{4}}$	4^{nk}	29	29^3	29^2	29^2	1.57^2	E.Schulman	23.40
5-8-8M1	‡Shutter Boy	Jo.Campbell	10	$8^{\circ 1\frac{1}{2}}$	$7^{\circ 1\frac{1}{2}}$	$7^{\circ 4\frac{1}{4}}$	6^{nk}	$5^{1\frac{1}{2}}$	30^3	28^3	29^1	29^1	1.57^3	G.Dennis	10.20
5-8-3M1	‡Huckster	E.Goodell	8	9^{dis}	$8^{1\frac{1}{2}}$	$6^{\frac{1}{2}}$	7^7	$6^{3\frac{1}{4}}$	30^4	28^4	28^3	29^3	1.57^4	R.Croghan	L 19.60
5-8-3M1	Mamalu N	G.Brennan	9	$4^{4\frac{1}{2}}$	$3^{\circ hd}$	$3^{\circ\frac{3}{4}}$	$5^{\frac{3}{4}}$	7^{13}	29^2	29^1	29^1	30^3	1.58^2	R.Sharpe	L 4.20
5-8-3M1	Julius Secret	Y.Gingras	3	x6x$^{\circ 1\frac{1}{4}}$	9^{dis}	8^{12}	8^{18}	8^{21}	30^2	29^2	29^2	32	2.01^1	M.Ford	L 23.80
5-7-7M1	Sing Me To Sleep	R.Pierce	6	5^{nk}	$5^{\circ 1\frac{1}{4}}$	x9^{dis}	9^{25}	9^{14}	30^1	28^3	32^4	33^4	2.05^2	S.Elliott	2.60
5-8-8M1	‡Silverado Hall	D.Dube	x4x	10	10	10	10	10	38^4	29^2	30	30	2.08^1	P.Kleinhans	L 14.40

Lasix: Im A Cool Breeze, Huckster, Mamalu N, Julius Secret, Silverado Hall.

Off: 10:32 Time: 0:28.3, 0:57.4, 1:27.0, 1:55.3. Mutuel Pool: $350,251. Temp. 48°
MUTUELS: **Im A Cool Breeze** $28.00, 6.80, 5.20; **Summertime Yankee** $3.80, 2.80; **Aisling** $10.40
LATE DD (8-5) $86.60. EXACTA (5-2) $97.00. TRIFECTA (5-2-7) $664.90.
10 CENT SUPER (5-2-7-1) $934.46. PICK 3 (9-8-5) $577.60.

IM A COOL BREEZE left to the front, yielded for a pocket, angled in the lane with dead aim and was just up on the wire under an all out drive. SUMMERTIME YANKEE brushed to the front down the backside, rated out the trot, braced for pressure in the lane and was just nailed in the last stride. AISLING was out from midpack final turn and came with a strong late rally to nail down the show dough. FOUR STARZ CREDIT sat a three-hole, lost touch final turn and came better than the tired rest for a check. SHUTTER BOY was out from the back and never threatened. HUCKSTER sat in all the way and never moved. MAMALU N left for a first turn tuck, came uncovered down the backside and tired without making a bid. JULIUS SECRET broke first turn and was done for the night. SING ME TO SLEEP left for a tuck, came out third over and broke final turn. SILVERADO HALL broke before the start and was far back throughout.
b g 7 by E N S Talisman, E N S Born Free by Brilliant Yankee
Owners: 1. Julianne Bobby,McDonald,PA;Scott D Woogen,Mechanicsville,VA, 2. Trillium Racing Stable,New Holland,PA;Tyler J Raymer,New Holland,PA, 3. Little E LLC,New York,NY, 4. Four Starzzzz Stable LLC,Hauppauge,NY, 5. North State Street Stable,Dover,DE;George&Tina Dennis Inc,Wyoming,DE, 6. D W Snyder,Meadow Lands,PA;T D Nurmi,Washington,DC;Stake Your Claim Stb,Secaucus,NJ, 7. Ray A Sharpe,Howell,NJ, 8. Jean Picard,Orford,PQ, CA, 9. Steve M Elliott,New Symrna Beach,FL;Paul L Bordogna,Fair Lawn,NJ, 10. P Kleinhans Racing Inc,Flemington,NJ.

I was working the *Drive Time* show on TVG that night, as I did most Fridays in 2008, and kept hammering the point home as the night wore on. Since I was on the air, I couldn't exactly take advantage of the anti-speed bias at that time, but I knew it would provide me with later opportunities over the next few weeks.

The first example came the following Thursday, May 22. In the ninth race, U All Bb stood out for several reasons.

nk	**U ALL BB(L)**									**b m 4, by Allamerican Ingot, U Neek B B by Cams Magic Trick**										**1:49.3 PcD 5/8**	**08 21 4 1 2**	**$70,965**
										Fred Monteleone Stbl LLC,Pompano Beach,FL										**1:50.2 Lx1**	**07 16 5 3 2**	**$177,395**
7	**Tim Tetrick (160) (0-0-0-0 .000)**									**Tr.Monte Gelrod**									**Last 6 Sts-$6,495**	**4 1:49.3 5/8**	**Lifetime**	**$272,560**
	5-1608	M1	1 sly	273	553	1.234	1.522	NW12500FM		23500	6	1°1	2hd	31½	31¾	52¾	29	1.53 L	★1.30 TetrickTi	BrnStrytllrno,CielHnvr1		spd,pckt,ang,no punch
	5-208	M1	1 fst	272	55	1.232	1.51	NW25000FM		37500	3	56¾	45¼	4°2¼	41¼	63¾	28	1.514 L	10.80 TetrickTi	Guestimthd,Postmark1¼		cover,no rally
	4-2608	M1	1 fst	271	541	1.22	1.504	Strada		75000	1	1nk	32	42¾	43	68¼	294	1.522 L	13.30 BrennanG	IdelWthr1¼,EnhncThNght1½		inside,little
	4-1808	M1	1 fst	274	554	1.242	1.512	NW25000FM		37500	1											scratched-sick
-1	4-1108	M1	1 fst	28	56	1.234	1.512	NW27500FM		37500	8	107½	10°6½	10°6	84¾	42½	264	1.514 L	45.30 MillerDv	LisleaPhno,MarttHll½		no chance,plenty
	4-308	M1	1 fst	28	56	1.254	1.542	Qua			9	46¾	44¼	2°½	11	2½	283	1.542 L	nb MillerDv	DrlnsDlght½,UAllBb2¾		1st over,gamely

U All Bb was hard-used in an early pace battle on May 16 and paid the price for it late, with almost no stamina for the stretch drive. The effort was particularly disappointing for the mare, who was dropping in class for the second straight time and had been sent off as the 6-5 favorite, but weakened to finish fifth. When you took into account the fact that she had raced against the bias, however, and was subject to yet another class drop the next time out, she shaped up as a most likely winner.

TH RACE: MEADOWLANDS, MAY 22-1 Mile Pace. Non-winners of $7,500 in last 5 starts. Fillies & Mares. Purse $15,000.

-5M1	U All Bb	Ti.Tetrick 7	41½	4°1½	1°¾	11¼	1½	273	28	273	272	1.503	M.Gelrod	L ★1.10
-11Fhd	Stratus	Y.Gingras 1	51½	5°hd	3°½	22¼	23¾	28	274	273	271	1.503	D.Cassar	L 38.10
-5M1	The Queen Of Trash	Jo.Campbell 2	61½	7°1¼	5°¾	3hd	31	281	28	273	273	1.512	O.Greene	L 2.70
-3M1	A And Gs Rockette	Dv.Miller 10	3°1¾	11½	2¾	41½	4¾	272	272	283	281	1.513	M.Capone	7.60
-qM1	Daydream Believer	R.Pierce 3	71¼	61¼	7½	6¾	5nk	283	271	282	273	1.514	S.Rollins	L 20.40
3M1	L Dees Rosemel	E.Goodell 6	11½	21½	41	51¼	61½	264	281	283	281	1.514	Ri.Johnson	L 11.20
3M1	Phyleon	D.Dube 9	10	9nk	9½	8¾	76¾	292	271	274	274	1.521	M.Silva	L 13.30
-3M1	Love Card	B.Sears 8	2°1¼	31	61	71	82¼	27	282	283	292	1.532	J.Drolet	34.10
-6M1	Above The Starz	A.Miller 4	81¼	8°¾	8°¾	92¼	96½	284	273	274	294	1.54	S.Didomenico	L 14.10
-3M1	Pacific Dazzle	G.Brennan 5	91½	10°	10°	10	10	29	273	274	304	1.551	M.SimonJr.	25.80

ix: U All Bb, Stratus, The Queen Of Trash, Daydream Believer, L Dees Rosemel, Phyleon, Above The Starz.

Off: 10:01 Time: 0:26.4, 0:54.4, 1:23.1, 1:50.3. Mutuel Pool: $416,005. Temp. 60°
MUTUELS: **U All Bb** $4.20, 3.00, 2.60; **Stratus** $18.00, 11.00; **The Queen Of Trash** $3.20
LATE DD (2-7) $17.00. EXACTA (7-1) $104.20. TRIFECTA (7-1-2) $113.90.
10 CENT SUPER (7-1-2-10) $65.02. PICK 3 (6-2-7) $47.80. PICK 4 (3-6-2-7) $274.30.
PICK 6 (6 OF 6) $2,256.80. PICK 6 (5 OF 6) $10.40.

LL BB left for good early position, came uncovered down the backside, challenged to take the lead late final turn, opened up enough in the lane and held safe under a drive. STRATUS was out with cover from the winner, k aim in the lane but was unable to go by under a constant drive. THE QUEEN OF TRASH followed up third over and was simply best of the rest. A AND GS ROCKETTE was used hard to the front, faced heavy pressure l turn and gave way headstretch. DAYDREAM BELIEVER shot a gap along the cones down the backside, angled in the lane and came with even pace to the wire. L DEES ROSEMEL left to the front, yielded for a pocket, s shuffled out final turn but didnt show any life once free in the lane. PHYLEON saved ground all the way and came best of the rest. LOVE CARD left hard but had to settle for a pocket, lost ground as the lead changed l turn and tired. ABOVE THE STARZ was out from the back with nothing to offer. PACIFIC DAZZLE was overmatched tonight.
1 4 by Allamerican Ingot, U Neek B B by Cams Magic Trick
ners: 1. Fred Monteleone Stbl LLC,Pompano Beach,FL, 2. Pace To Place Stable Com Inc,Plainsboro,NJ, 3. Nanticoke Racing Inc,Seaford,DE;Brandon A Givens,Seaford,DE;Donna M Messick,Delmar,DE, 4. Willie J Tomlin,Bronx,NY, 5. ott A Dillon,Anson,ME, 6. Patrick Harley,Dumont,NJ, 7. Lightning Stable,Manalapan,NJ, 8. Michael J Kessler,New Hartford,NY;David L Van Slyke,Westdale,NY, 9. Steve J & Robert A Bevilacqua,Oswego,IL, 10. Triple S Stables, LLC,New nswick,NJ.

Again, we are not going to get rich on horses that pay $4.20, but with a little imagination, anyone could have hit the exacta with 38-1 longshot Stratus for second—or, the late double, with the favorite in the eighth race, Twin B Navigator, which returned a healthy $17.

One night later, Erma La Em provided a similar opportunity in the third race, an elimination for the Miss New Jersey Stakes. Like U All Bb, Erma La Em flashed strong speed on May 16 and actually finished well to end up second that night. That was an extra-good performance, hinting that she would come back with another strong one.

Yellow **ERMA LA EM** — b f 3, by Cam's Card Shark, I'm Prime Time by Kentucky Spur — Joseph Barbera,Huntington Station,NY — 1:53.0 M1 08 26 6 5 4 $97,867 — 1:58.2 Fhd 07 11 1 4 1 $52,481

6 Ron Pierce (160) (0-0-0-0 .000) — Tr.Steven LeBlanc(51-6-3-5 .118) — Last 6 Sts-$47,393 — 3 1:53.0 (1) — Lifetime $175,918

	5-16 08	M1	1 sly	28	57	1.26	1.53^{4}	NJSS 3YO F	39500	9	1no	$2^{1\frac{1}{2}}$	$3^{1\frac{1}{4}}$	4^{nk}	$2^{\frac{1}{2}}$	27^{3}	1.53^{4}	5.40 MillerDv	ChynnTrsh$^{\frac{1}{2}}$,ErmaLaEm$^{2\frac{1}{2}}$	top,pckt,led,2nd best
	5-1 08	ChD 5/8	1 fst	26^{3}	56	1.23^{3}	1.53^{1}	NW6PMCdFM	17000	3	6^{4}	$5^{\circ 3\frac{1}{2}}$	$4^{\circ 1\frac{1}{4}}$	$3^{1\frac{1}{2}}$	$1^{\frac{1}{2}}$	29^{2}	1.53^{1}	★.40 TetrickTi	ErmaLaEm,WldNWndr	uncovered,steadily
	4-16 08	M1	1 fst	29^{3}	57^{2}	1.26^{2}	1.53	BlossomFnl-D	68900	3	$4^{3\frac{3}{4}}$	$4^{4\frac{1}{2}}$	$2^{\circ 1}$	2^{1}	3^{4}	27^{1}	1.53^{4}	9.20 PierceR	TgRvrPrncss$^{3\frac{1}{4}}$,ChynnTrsh$^{\frac{3}{4}}$	took shot,wknd late
	4-9 08	M1	1 fst	28^{3}	58	1.27	1.54^{1}	Blossom	22500	4	$4^{4\frac{3}{4}}$	4^{4}	$2^{\circ 1}$	$2^{\frac{3}{4}}$	1^{hd}	27	1.54^{1}	★1.20 PierceR	ErmaLaEm^{hd},Cartnvrs$^{\frac{1}{2}}$	unc,top,held driving
7-2	4-2 08	M1	1 fst	29	59^{2}	1.28^{3}	1.55	Blossom	22500	1										scratched-sick
	3-25 08	DD 5/8	1 fst	27^{2}	57^{3}	1.27	1.55	NW3 FM	10500	5	$2^{\circ\frac{1}{4}}$	$1^{1\frac{1}{2}}$	1^{1}	1^{5}	$1^{6\frac{3}{4}}$	28	1.55	★.50 TetrickTi	ErmaLaEm,Seasatinl,BelkaHnv	

I must admit that Erma La Em wasn't my top choice on that occasion, but my program analysis did point out her strong performance against the bias. Erma La Em worked out a perfect trip behind the attacking favorite and romped home a two-length winner for Ron Pierce in 1:53, a new lifetime mark. She paid $6.20 to her backers, who were smarter than I was.

Our final example of the anti-speed bias came a week later, on May 30, with Mystical Ryan in the sixth race. On May 16, Mystical Ryan had the trip of the night, setting all the fractions and eventually losing by less than a length.

Blue **MYSTICAL RYAN(L)** — b g 6, by Striking Sahbra, Eclectia by Mr Vic — Frank Cirillo,Kleinburg,On — 1:52.3 M1 08 32 9 4 4 $195,070 — 1:55.3 Wbn 7/8 07 31 3 6 7 $79,500

2 Daniel Dube (150) (0-0-0-0 .000) — Tr.Anthony Montini — Last 6 Sts-$44,682 — 6 1:52.3 (1) — Lifetime $342,812

	5-16 08	M1	1 sly	28^{1}	56^{2}	1.25^{2}	1.54^{2}	NW25000	37500	3	$5^{\circ 3\frac{3}{4}}$	$1^{\circ 1\frac{1}{2}}$	$1^{1\frac{1}{2}}$	$1^{1\frac{1}{4}}$	$2^{\frac{3}{4}}$	29^{1}	1.54^{3} L	★1.40 DubeD	Lkbtthll,*HpRnsSprm	dq,p.4,brsh,prs,lug in
	5-9 08	M1	1 sly	27^{2}	55^{3}	1.24^{2}	1.53^{4}	NW25000	37500	9	$8^{\circ 11}$	$9^{\circ 9}$	$6^{\circ 7\frac{3}{4}}$	$3^{5\frac{1}{4}}$	$1^{\frac{3}{4}}$	27^{4}	1.53^{4} L	3.00 DubeD	MystclRyn$^{\frac{3}{4}}$,Focus$^{3\frac{1}{2}}$	tough trip,powerful
	5-2 08	M1	1 fst	27^{4}	56^{2}	1.25	1.53^{1}	NW25000	37500	4	$7^{9\frac{3}{4}}$	$7^{\circ 8\frac{1}{4}}$	$8^{\circ 6\frac{1}{2}}$	$8^{6\frac{3}{4}}$	7^{6}	28^{1}	1.54^{2} L	8.80 DubeD	OnMnShwS$^{1\frac{3}{4}}$,InstntPht$^{2\frac{1}{4}}$	too far,no threat
	4-4 08	FlD	1 gd	28^{3}	57^{3}	1.26^{4}	1.56^{1}	Prf	16000	1	$2^{1\frac{1}{2}}$	$2^{1\frac{1}{2}}$	2^{4}	$2^{1\frac{1}{4}}$	$1^{1\frac{1}{2}}$	28^{3}	1.56^{1} L	2.00 CoulterR	MysticalRyan,LocofocoN,WildMagic	
3-1	3-28 08	FlD	1 fst	28	57	1.26	1.56^{2}	Prf	16000	3	$4^{2\frac{3}{4}}$	4^{4}	$4^{\circ 3}$	$4^{3\frac{1}{2}}$	3^{2}	30^{1}	1.56^{4} L	3.55 CoulterR	LocofocoN,WildMagic,MysticalRyan	
	3-14 08	Wbn 7/8	1 fst	27^{2}	56^{4}	1.25^{3}	1.54	NW27500L6C	26260	5	$4^{7\frac{1}{4}}$	$4^{\circ 5}$	$1^{4\frac{1}{4}}$	$1^{4\frac{1}{2}}$	$1^{1\frac{1}{2}}$	28^{2}	1.54 L	★1.40 BallrgeonM	MysRyan,BrkngBnj	tuck,chall,took off

By now the pattern from May 16 had been established and verified, and it boded very well for Mystical Ryan on this night. I was on *Drive Time* once again, and since this race kicked off the pick four, we had a bit of extra time to talk about it. I'm sure I didn't use the words "mortal lock," but I was quite enthusiastic about his chances.

SIXTH RACE: MEADOWLANDS, MAY 30-1 Mile Trot. Non-winners of $25,000 in last 6 starts. A.E.: Non-winners of 5 ext. pari-mutuel races or $175,000 lifetime. Purse $37,500.

Date	Horse	Driver	PP										Time	Handler	Odds
5-16-6M1	Mystical Ryan	D.Dube	2	$4\frac{1}{4}$	$4\frac{1}{4}$	$2°1\frac{1}{4}$	$1\frac{1}{4}$	$1\frac{3}{4}$	27^3	27^4	28^3	28^3	1.52³	A.Montini	L ∗1.40
5-25-1TgD	Just A Con Man	B.Sears	4	6^2	$6°nk$	$6°1\frac{1}{4}$	$3\frac{1}{4}$	2no	28^2	27^3	28^2	28^2	1.524	M.Silva	L 12.20
5-23-6M1	Im A Cool Breeze	Ti.Tetrick	3	$5\frac{1}{2}$	$5\frac{1}{2}$	$4°1\frac{1}{4}$	$2\frac{1}{2}$	3^3	28	27^3	28^3	28^3	1.524	J.Bobby	L 2.00
5-23-6M1	Macho Lindy	L.Stalbaum	8	2hd	$3\frac{1}{2}$	5no	6no	$4\frac{3}{4}$	27^2	27^4	291	29	1.53²	K.Asher	L 5.60
5-23-6M1	Talk About Me	Dv.Miller	9	$1°1\frac{1}{4}$	$2\frac{1}{4}$	3no	$5\frac{1}{4}$	$5\frac{1}{4}$	271	273	292	291	1.53²	F.Maceachern	L 49.80
5-14-10ChD	Jabez	R.Pierce	10	$7\frac{2}{4}$	$7^2\frac{3}{4}$	71	72	$6\frac{5}{4}$	28^4	271	284	29	1.534	P.Kleinhans	L 43.60
5-22-qM1	Chancey Hall	A.Miller	5	$9\frac{1}{4}$	91	$9°\frac{3}{4}$	$9\frac{5}{4}$	$7\frac{3}{4}$	29^3	271	28^3	29^2	1.544	A.Lorentzon	48.70
5-23-6M1	Tonight Aas	Jo.Campbell	6x	10	10°	$8°2\frac{1}{4}$	$8\frac{3}{4}$	$8\frac{1}{2}$	30	27	28	30	1.55	B.Saunders	L 42.80
5-23-6M1	‡Hope Reins Supreme	G.Brennan	7	$3°1\frac{1}{4}$	$1\frac{1}{4}$	1no	4nk	9^{18}	27^2	271	292	31	1.55	J.Hartline	L 5.80
5-16-1M1	‡Nepp Hanover	Y.Gingras	1	$8\frac{1}{4}$	$8\frac{1}{4}$	10	10	10	291	272	29	331	1.584	A.Skultety,Jr.	L 66.00

Lasix: Mystical Ryan, Just A Con Man, Im A Cool Breeze, Macho Lindy, Talk About Me, Jabez, Tonight Aas, Hope Reins Supreme, Nepp Hanover.

Off: 8:57 Time: 0:27.1, 0:54.3, 1:24.0, 1:52.3. Mutuel Pool: $344,209. Temp. 74°

MUTUELS: **Mystical Ryan** $4.80, 3.80, 2.60; **Just A Con Man** $9.60, 4.40; **Im A Cool Breeze** $2.60

EXACTA (2-4) $40.00. TRIFECTA (2-4-3) $59.50. PICK 3 (5-1-2) $23.80.

MYSTICAL RYAN made a first over bid going to three quarters, engaged the leader and applied heavy pressure, swallowed that one up turning for home and edged clear under urging. JUST A CON MAN followed third over, angled wide to take dead aim and closed with a solid kick while held at bay. IM A COOL BREEZE tracked the winner's cover while well positioned, loomed large for the stretch run, hung when it counted and was outkicked late for second. MACHO LINDY darted right to the front, yielded around the opening turn and was shuffled back to third, stayed in down the backstretch and was buried, found room up the inside and rallied with late trot. TALK ABOUT ME fired out from the outside and was parked going to the lead at the quarter, cleared, yielded past that marker, sat the pocket and weakened in the stretch. JABEZ lagged on the cones, shot up the gap as the outside flow developed, closed up the inside and passed tired ones. CHANCEY HALL was away next to last, pulled out at three quarters and beat the stragglers. TONIGHT AAS broke after the start, trailed the field while fourth over down the backside and had no shot. HOPE REINS SUPREME left, got looped heading into the first turn, drove and was parked going to the lead, cleared past the first quarter, set the fractions, faced heavy heat going to three quarters and folded. NEPP HANOVER put in a dismal effort.

b g 6 by Striking Sahbra, Eclectia by Mr Vic

Owners: 1. Frank Cirillo,Kleinburg,ON, CA, 2. Barnik Racing Stable,Schenectady,NY, 3. Julianne Bobby,McDonald,PA;Scott D Woogen,Mechanicsville,VA, 4. Christopher J Mazzone,Palm Harbor,FL, 5. A&M Floral Inc,Pierson,FL, 6. P Kleinhans Racing Inc,Flemington,NJ, 7. Acl Stuteri Ab,Paris,KY, 8. M&M Harness Racing LLC,Nanuet,NY, 9. Stephen W Demeter,Tarrytown,NY;Thomas George Aquilino,Yonkers,NY, 10. Kyle Wendy Skultety,Hightstown,NJ.

In all, I believe there were four next-out winners that either set the pace or contested the pace on May 16. A bias like that doesn't happen very often, but when it does, it's *uber*-important to recognize it and take advantage of it. For that reason, I feel that watching race replays and recap shows is worth the time invested.

TRACK BIAS

Unlike Thoroughbred racing, where track biases occur frequently, harness racing sees a true bias only once in a while. A bias exists when it becomes very clear that the track surface itself is favoring horses with speed, or horses that come from behind. It's usually pretty easy to spot. A tiring horse is able to hold on longer, or the 3-5 favorite that should go right to the lead and wire the field suddenly stops for no apparent reason. After a while it can become rather obvious, but by then the drivers have recognized it too and are already making adjustments—at least, the smart drivers are.

It could be caused by wind, cold, rain, or any number of factors, but there is no more powerful force in handicapping than a track bias. After a race or two where things aren't what they seem, the light bulb in your head has to go off. When it occurs, you must be ready to react—not only during the rest of the card, but also in the following weeks, when many of those horses will race back. You'd be surprised at the prices you can get on horses that battled against a bias.

Earlier, we looked at the Meadowlands' card of May 16, 2008, when speed horses stopped in every race. If you were on the lead that night, you had absolutely no chance. The night of February 1 was exactly the same at the Big M. It was a Friday and it poured all day. The track-maintenance crew elected not to scrape the surface, which turned deep and boggy. We don't get many deep and boggy surfaces anymore, and in the stretch of most races that night, it looked as if the horses were going through quicksand. Every race was won by a horse that was out in the flow on the outside and came sweeping past the leaders in the stretch.

All of that eventually led us to Happy Hour Bliss, a gifted mid-range claiming pacer who owned natural speed. This is what she looked like in her follow-up race.

Gray **HAPPY HOUR BLISS(L)** — ch m 6, by Blissfull Hall, La Towner by Big Towner — Steven Demeter,NY;Thomas George Aquilino,NY — 1:51.2 M1 08 23 5 1 0 $79,
8 George Brennan (150) (0-0-0-0 .000) — Tr.Jake Hartline — 1:56.3 Scr 07 31 8 15 4 $49,9
Last 6 Sts-$16,625 — 6 1:51.2 (1) — Lifetime $141,8

	2-1 08	M1	1	sly	28^{1}	57	1.26	1.54^{3}	35/45000 FM	27000	1	2 1¼	3° 1¼	2° ½	3^{1}	4 4½	29^{2}	1.55^{2}	L	4.40	BrennanG	LDesRsml 1,FinalRen ¾	left,uncvrd,bid,ti
	1-25 08	M1	1	fst	27^{2}	55^{4}	1.24^{4}	1.52^{4}	35/40000 FM	26000	6	1no	2 1½	3 1¼	2 1¼	2 ½	27^{4}	1.52^{4}	L	13.30	BrennanG	TwnyRsrvN ½,HppyHrBlss 3¼	top,pckt,ang,all
	1-11 08	M1	1	gd	27^{2}	55	1.23^{2}	1.52^{2}	35000 FM	23500	7	1°hd	2nk	1 1¼	2hd	5 2¾	29^{3}	1.53	L	9.10	BrennanG	TwnyRsrvNno,AmbrBlChpnk	loop,top,prs,gave w
$42,000	12-28 07	YR	1	fst	27	56^{1}	1.25	1.54^{4}	NW18000FM	19000	2	2 1¾	1 1¼	2nk	2 1¾	8 8¼	31^{2}	1.56^{2}	L	3.40	StrattonJ	DolcezzA ½,Nrthwstrn 3½	rtk,press,gave w
3-1	12-21 07	YR	1	fst	28^{3}	58	1.26^{4}	1.56	NW18000FM	19000	5	5 6¼	4° 3¾	2° ¾	2 ¾	2 1¼	29^{1}	1.56^{1}	L	8.80	StrattonJ	LttlMschvs 1¼,HppyHrBlss ½	unc,chall,outkick
	12-6 07	M1	1	fst	28^{1}	56^{4}	1.26^{1}	1.54^{3}	c20000 FM	17000	2	2no	1 1½	1^{2}	1^{1}	3 ½	28^{2}	1.54^{3}	L	2.40	ManziC	Debupantnk,HrmnyOksQstnk	2 mvs,press,all

Happy Hour Bliss was involved in a hot-and-heavy battle up on the pace the prior week, which was exactly where you didn't want to be. Her performance was a good one, but obviously hidden due to the circumstances. She ended up finishing fourth, beaten almost five lengths, but the past-performance line in the program didn't do justice to the effort she had put forth.

When I looked at the field she was facing on February 8, I felt we had a sure winner, even from post 8. Even more attractive was the probability that she wouldn't be the favorite. That role would go to a mare who drew post 1, was getting first-time Lasix, and had been claimed out of her last start. However, her record at the Meadowlands was 0 for 10, and I felt she was tailing off. I knew the Meadowlands regulars would end up overbetting her. There were no other strong early speedsters in the race, so Happy Hour Bliss would sail to an easy lead, if all went as expected. Here's what I wrote in my race review in the program to illustrate that point, and here's what happened.

RACE 5 REVIEW   Friday, February 8, 2008   *By David Brower*

1   **AMBER BLUE CHIP** - Adds Lasix tonight, so that probably explains her stopping last week. No problem. I still don't think she'll offer a big price.

2   **SWARDE** - Switches to claimers here and she might be an attractive prospect. All of her starts off the layoff have been good. Post relief too.

3   **TU TU TWAIN** - Chased an uncatchable winner last time, but this is also a big step back up in class. No match last time she faced these mares.

4   **L DEES ROSEMEL** - Mr. Longshot struck again, putting a perfect trip and drive on this mare for Croghan. Won't be 29-1 tonight, needs similar trip.

5   **FOX VALLEY PERDITO** - I thought she would be in a good spot last week. I was wrong, since she was flat. Needs a lot more than that to win this.

6   **ALLTHATNABAGACHIPS** - Probably in need of some class relief and she loses Yannick here. I'm willing to wait for the softer spot.

7   **SECRETRENDEZVOUS N** - Back over from Yonkers and this mare does have some history here. Should be firing out and I would consider using.

8   **HAPPY HOUR BLISS** - I know she's going to blast out for Brennan. The track bias was not to her advantage last time. It might be different tonight.

9   **JULIE'S SHADOW** - Has not come back sharp yet, so this is an impossible play from the bad post. We have to wait for renewed signs of life here.

TOP CONTENDERS 8-7-2-1

Happy Hour Bliss went right to the lead, carved out a nice, soft, rated pace, and then dashed clear for "the Minister of Speed," George Brennan, scoring an easy win in lifetime-best time (see chart, next page). If only it were that easy every time, but unfortunately, it's not. The price wasn't bad, either. I'd take $8 on a horse like that every day of the week. L Dees Rosemel had beaten Happy Hour Bliss on that biased night at odds of 29-1, but now the decision was reversed. It was an easy exacta to have (even though I didn't), and the overbet co-favorite ended up third.

FIFTH RACE: MEADOWLANDS, FEB. 8-1 Mile Pace. $35,000 Clm. Alw. Fillies & Mares. Purse $23,500.

2-1-6M1	Happy Hour Bliss	G.Brennan	7	1°1½	11½	11¼	11¼	1¾	273 283 283 274	1.523	J.Hartline	L 3.00
2-1-6M1	L Dees Rosemel	E.Goodell	4	22	21¾	2nk	2½	21¼	274 283 283 274	1.524	R.Croghan	★2.70
2-1-6M1	Amber Blue Chip	B.Sears	1	51½	5½	5½	4½	3hd	29 281 282 272	1.53	C.Oakes	L ★2.70
2-1-9M1	Swarde	A.Miller	2	41¾	4°1	3°1¼	32	41	283 282 28 28	1.53	C.DixonJr	L 6.10
2-1-12YR	Julies Shadow	D.Dube	8	8	8	7hd	62¼	59	294 274 282 271	1.531	F.Bisaccia	L 51.60
2-1-6M1	Allthatnabagachips	Ti.Tetrick	6	31½	3¾	41¼	51½	62	281 283 283 293	1.55	J.Mcdermott	L 15.40
2-1-6M1	Fox Valley Perdito	Jo.Campbell	5	71¾	7°nk	8°°	8	73	293 28 282 292	1.552	G.Wrubel	L 19.00
1-30-5M1	Tu Tu Twain	Y.Gingras	3	61½	6°1¼	6°1¼	7no	8	291 28 282 302	1.56	M.Burke	L 5.40

Scratched: Secretrendezvous N -judges.

Lasix: Happy Hour Bliss, Amber Blue Chip, Swarde, Julies Shadow, Allthatnabagachips, Fox Valley Perdito, Tu Tu Twain.

Claimed: L Dees Rosemel by JML Stable & Sholty Stable, Inc., FL. & KY..

Off: 8:22 Time: 0:27.3, 0:56.1, 1:24.4, 1:52.3. Mutuel Pool: $296,434. Temp. 38°

MUTUELS: **Happy Hour Bliss** $8.00, 4.20, 2.80; **L Dees Rosemel** $4.20, 2.40; **Amber Blue Chip** $2.60

EXACTA (8-4) $30.40. TRIFECTA (8-4-1) $42.40. PICK 3 (5-7-8) $36.90.

HAPPY HOUR BLISS left to the front near the quarter, rated out the fractions at own clip, faced mild pressure in the lane but was able to hold sway to pick up the score. L DEES ROSEMEL left to the front, yielded for a pocket, angled to the cones late but lacked real rally. AMBER BLUE CHIP was locked in a four-hole all the way, had to search for room in the lane with pace but never found a clear path. SWARDE was out uncovered past the half, challenged final turn, kept coming in the lane but finally tired in a dull effort. JULIES SHADOW sat in all the way, went up the cones in the lane and passed tired rivals. ALLTHATNABAGACHIPS left for a first turn tuck, raced from a three-hole and tired. FOX VALLEY PERDITO flushed cover past the half, gapped badly final turn and was done for the evening. TU TU TWAIN was out third over, had to go wide around the former final turn and lost any chance at that point.

ch m 6 by Blissfull Hall, La Towner by Big Towner

Claiming Prices: 1. $42,000, 2. $42,000, 3. $49,000, 4. $42,000, 5. $42,000, 6. $42,000, 7. $42,000, 8. $42,000.

Owners: 1. Stephen W Demeter,Tarrytown,NY;Thomas George Aquilino,Yonkers,NY, 2. Brian Nixon,Centerport,NY, 3. Susan M Oakes,Wilkes-Barre,PA;Chuck Pompey,Archbald,PA, 4. Clifford Paul Dixon Jr,Rutherfordton,NC, 5. Raymond J McDonough,Mahopac,NY, 6. Centaur Stable,Oak Lawn,IL;Jordon M Sklut,Chesterton,IN, 7. Robert T Moses,West Chester,PA;John Sorrentino,Ledgewood,NJ, 8. Sylvia A Burke,Fredericktown,PA;Howard A Taylor,Penn Valley,PA;Bethann Palone,Houston,PA.

3

QUALIFIERS

In Thoroughbred racing, handicappers are forced to judge a horse's current fitness level by looking at workout times. Guess what? The times don't mean a whole lot. It's all about seeing it. That's why you hear about so many private clockers, who show up each morning at any given Thoroughbred racetrack. By seeing a horse during the workout, they are able to gauge a lot more than a simple time would reveal. The same holds true for harness racing when it comes to qualifying races.

By definition, a qualifying race is a one-mile dash against the clock only, with no purse money or wagering involved. A time standard for the mile is established by the racing secretary at each track to judge a horse's competitive level. In other words, a horse must simply pace faster than 2:00 or 1:59 to be deemed "worthy" of competing in a betting race at night.

Qualifying times are broken down by age and gait, although the ages can be different at times; you might have 3-year-olds going against older, etc.

Following are the qualifying times at the Meadowlands during the spring of 2008. The list doesn't include 2-year-olds because they were not racing yet, and the qualifying times change when the summer hits. (They get lower.)

Sample Qualifying Times
Pacers
3-year-olds: 1:59
Aged: 1:58

Trotters
3-year-olds: 2:02
Aged: 2:01

It all sounds pretty simple, but watching qualifying races in person is the single most important handicapping angle I have ever known. Let me reiterate that: Watching the qualifiers is absolutely critical, and crucial to your success. Now, I know most normal people have jobs and can't show up at the track at 10:00 a.m, but with the advent of replay kiosks and such, you can still watch them. You can also purchase the only harness-racing daily newspaper, *Harness Eye*. Charts of qualifiers with commentary from the chart caller are available a day or two after the morning trials. I can't stress it enough; it's important information.

I could probably fill this book with examples of winners and losers that hinged on qualifying performances over my years in the business. (Sometimes, it's even more critical to find a favorite that did not qualify well. When you can toss a chalk horse because he was life-and-death to beat a weaker rival in a qualifier, isn't that crucial information? Doesn't that give you an edge?) Instead, I will concentrate on a few qualifiers that translated into winners, some of them at juicy prices.

On April 2, 2008, in the second race of the night at the Meadowlands, a 3-year-old gelding by the name of Blue Claw was making his seasonal debut. Many returning sophomores start their campaigns around this time of year and several of them look the same on paper. However, Blue Claw absolutely stood out in this race, and I'll tell you why.

ack **BLUE CLAW** — b g 3, by Jenna's Beach Boy, Wonderbolt by Artsplace — 1:50.1 Lx1 08 19 6 3 1 $269,757

All Star Racing Inc,Towaco,NJ — 1:57.2 Lx1 Q 07 2 0 0 1 $720

5 Yannick Gingras (150) (0-0-0-0 .000) — Tr.Mark Ford(192-17-20-23 .089) — Last 6 Sts-$720 3 1:50.1 (1) Lifetime $293,477

	3-27 08	M1	1	fst	29^{3}	58^{1}	1.27^{1}	1.54^{3}	Qua 3YO		5	$4^{6\frac{1}{2}}$	$4^{4\frac{1}{2}}$	$4^{3\frac{1}{4}}$	4^{3}	2^{hd}	26^{4}	1.54^{3}	nb GingrasY	IdleHour^{hd},BlueClaw$^{\frac{3}{4}}$	closed beautifully
	3-20 08	M1	1	fst	28^{2}	59^{4}	1.30^{1}	1.58	Qua 3YO		5	$x8^{17}$	$8^{9\frac{3}{4}}$	8^{o5}	8^{7}	8^{9}	28^{3}	1.59^{4}	nb GingrasY	HandsToYrslf,HaveANiceDay	broke
	8-30 07	Lx1	1	fst	30^{2}	59^{4}	1.29^{2}	1.57^{2}	Qua		2	$3^{4\frac{1}{2}}$	$3^{3\frac{1}{2}}$	$3^{4\frac{1}{2}}$	$4^{3\frac{1}{2}}$	$1^{1\frac{1}{2}}$	27^{1}	1.57^{2}	nb FoleyPe	BlueClaw,NdanaWhsr,Welcometz	
	8-12 07	Lx1	1	fst	27	56^{1}	1.26^{4}	1.54^{2}	KYSS 2YOCG	20000	3	3^{3}	6^{11}	$6^{4\frac{3}{4}}$	$x4^{5\frac{1}{2}}$	6^{19}	30^{2}	1.58^{1}	3.60 ShetlerDa	RacinBest,WrnngZone,BestOfTms	
3-1	8-7 07	Lx1	1	fst	29^{1}	58^{4}	1.28	1.56	Qua		1	4^{5}	$4^{6\frac{1}{2}}$	$4^{4\frac{1}{2}}$	3^{4}	$2^{3\frac{1}{2}}$	27^{4}	1.56^{3}	nb ShetlerDa	BlueRae,BlueClaw,Carefight	
	7-30 07	PcD $\frac{5}{8}$	1	fst	27^{2}	56	1.26	1.54^{3}	2YO CG	6000	3	3^{3}	$3^{4\frac{1}{4}}$	$3^{2\frac{3}{4}}$	$3^{3\frac{1}{2}}$	$3^{8\frac{3}{4}}$	29^{4}	1.56^{2}	5.70 SimonsMi	LnstrLgnd,MacBNmbl,BlueClaw	

RACE 2 REVIEW Wednesday, April 2, 2008

By David Brower

1 **BURL HANOVER** - Suffered some tough luck last time when jammed behind a wall of horses. Might be overbet off that. Still must prove it.

2 **FISSATO** - Coming off a much improved effort, but tonight's he clearly facing a better bunch. Nothing less than A-1 best will get it done here.

3 **ONEMOREYEAR** - Still must prove he's fast enough to go with these and I haven't seen it yet. A pass.

4 **INTERNATIONALSTYLE** - Showed a lot of heart in that qualifier. Met a stiff challenge and dug in to fend it off. Loses Andy here, but will flash speed.

5 **BLUE CLAW** - Once this guy got rolling, he was simply flying in that qualifier. That stood out, due to quality of that field. Let's hop on board.

6 **SHOESHINE BOY** - Still getting used to the idea of racing. Needs more experience before we can try him in a real race.

7 **DAX HANOVER** - If he didn't win last week, then he may never win! That was prime opportunity lost and I could only use underneath. Now 0-16.

8 **CHEYENNE BARRY** - Tougher trip last time. Seems like a one move type and he'll be at mercy of both pace and trip tonight. That's not easy.

TOP CONTENDERS 5-4-1-7

Blue Claw showed two qualifiers for new trainer Mark Ford. The difference between the first qualifier on March 20 and the second attempt on March 27 was astounding. In the first one, he lagged early and made a break. Whatever was wrong, Ford fixed it. Blue Claw came back in the second attempt and, after settling early, came exploding through the lane, almost catching a top colt in Idle Hour. He was under no urging from his driver, Yannick Gingras. His final quarter was 26⁴/₅ and his final time was 1:54³/₅, but as I've said before, it's not about the time—it's how they do it. Anybody that watched this qualifier couldn't wait for Blue Claw to show up in the entry box.

He was in to go a week later, and the best part was that it looked like he might not even be the favorite. The following chart doesn't do justice to how easily Blue Claw won the race. He overcame a rather difficult, uncovered, outside trip, but steamrolled past the leaders as the third choice, returning a generous $7.20. Not bad.

SECOND RACE: MEADOWLANDS, APR. 2-1 Mile Pace. Non-winners of 1 ext. pari-mutuel race lifetime. 3 Year Olds. Purse $12,500.

3-27-qM1	Blue Claw	Y.Gingras	5	$6\frac{13}{4}$	$5°\frac{1}{2}$	$2°$nk	1^1	1^1	29	28^2 28^1	27	1.52^3	M.Ford	2.60
3-27-9M1	Dax Hanover	A.Miller	7	$2°\frac{3}{4}$	$2\frac{13}{4}$	$3\frac{11}{4}$	3nk	$2\frac{11}{4}$	27^3	28^4 29^1	27^1	1.52^4	Ju.Miller	★2.20
3-27-9M1	Cheyenne Barry	Jo.Campbell	8	$7\frac{13}{4}$	$7°\frac{13}{4}$	$4°\frac{1}{2}$	$4\frac{11}{4}$	$3\frac{11}{2}$	29^2	28^1 28^1	27^1	1.53	R.Siegelman	18.40
3-20-3M1	Burl Hanover	M.Vanderkemp	1	$3\frac{31}{4}$	$3\frac{13}{4}$	$5\frac{13}{4}$	$5\frac{11}{2}$	$4\frac{1}{4}$	27^4	29 29^1	27^2	1.53^2	N.Daley	4.20
3-27-qM1	Internationalstyle	R.Pierce	4	1^1	$1\frac{11}{2}$	1^1	$2\frac{1}{2}$	$5\frac{11}{4}$	27^2	28^4 29^1	28	1.53^2	L.Toscano	2.40
3-20-3M1	Fissato	D.Dube	2	$4\frac{13}{4}$	$4\frac{3}{4}$	6^2	$6\frac{31}{4}$	$6\frac{83}{4}$	28^2	28^4 29^1	27^1	1.53^3	J.Mcdermott	L 15.20
3-27-9M1	Onemoreyear	Dv.Miller	3	$5\frac{11}{2}$	$6\frac{3}{4}$	8	$7\frac{21}{2}$	$7\frac{21}{2}$	28^4	28^3 29^2	28^3	1.55^2	J.Drolet	59.90
3-27-qM1	Shoeshine Boy	L.Stalbaum	6	8	8	$7°$nk	8	8	29^4	28^1 28^4	29^1	1.56	K.Asher	118.40

Lasix: Fissato.

Off: 7:22 Time: 0:27.2, 0:56.1, 1:25.2, 1:52.3. Mutuel Pool: $258,946. Temp. 44°
MUTUELS: **Blue Claw** $7.20, 3.40, 3.00; **Dax Hanover** $3.20, 2.80; **Cheyenne Barry** $6.20
DD (4-5) $65.60. EXACTA (5-7) $24.80. TRIFECTA (5-7-8) $79.40.

BLUE CLAW was out on the rim going to the half, moved into contention at own pace, moved to challenge early in the lane and went by easily under mild urging. DAX HANOVER left hard and finally found a pocket past the quarter, sat all the way, angled to the cones in the lane and came with mild pace for the place. CHEYENNE BARRY worked out cover from the winner, followed to the lane, lost contact halfway home and held the rest for the show. BURL HANOVER left for a pocket, gapped enough to lose position down the backside, angled wide in the lane and came with a mild late rally. INTERNATIONALSTYLE left right to the front, pocketed all comers, rated to the lane but gave way willingly once confronted. FISSATO was buried on the cones and came with some late rally. ONEMOREYEAR had nothing to offer. SHOESHINE BOY was out weakly from the back and tired.

b c 3 by Jenna's Beach Boy, Wonderbolt by Artsplace
Owners: 1. All Star Racing Inc,Towaco,NJ, 2. Harmony Oaks Rcg Stb,IL;W Wiswell,WI;Vip Internet Stb,NJ;H Glestein,PA, 3. Lessee-The Cheyenne Gang LLC,Port Washington,NY, 4. John D Fielding,Toronto,ON, CA;Adam Victor&Son Stble LLC,New York,NY, 5. Amante Standardbreds Inc,Delray Beach,FL, 6. Brian F Martin,Roseland,NJ;Louis A Freda,Pine Brook,NJ;Jeffrey P Gordon,Morris-Plains,NJ, 7. Stephen B Schneider,Roslyn Heights,NY;Marthe Drolet,Suffern,NY, 8. Kimberly A Asher,Leslie,MI.

A few weeks earlier on March 19, a similar situation arose regarding a horse that qualified in much-improved fashion for a relatively new barn.

Blue	‡LOVE AFFAIR		b m 4, by Cr Commando, Love The Wind by Rule The Wind						2:00.1 M1	08 38 3 4 2		$18,169
	Yannick Gingras (150) (0-0-0-0 .000)		Mark A Schullstrom,Colts Neck,NJ							07 11 0 1 1		$7,690
2			Tr.Randy Giglio						Last 6 Sts-$0 4 2:00.1 (1)			Lifetime
	3-13$_{08}$ M1	‡ 1 fst 29^3 59^3 1.30^2 1.59^3 Qua 3-4YO	2	1$\frac{2}{2}$1	1$1\frac{1}{2}$	1$1\frac{1}{4}$	1^2	2$\frac{1}{2}$	29^1 1.59^3	nb GingrasY	YnkFrnzy$\frac{1}{2}$,LoveAffr1$\frac{3}{4}$	led,gamely
	3-6$_{08}$ M1	‡ 1 fst 29^1 58^3 1.27^4 1.56^4 Qua	6	4x$°^3$	6x$°^9\frac{1}{2}$	x8x$°^{23}$ 8^{39} 8^{69}			38^1 2.10^3	nb MillerA	CrftyCvr2$\frac{1}{4}$,LewiesL11$\frac{1}{2}$	extended break
	2-27$_{08}$ Fhd	‡ 1 fst 29^1 59^3 1.30^1 2.01^2 Qua	4	x5x$°^{12}$	x6dis	6dis 6dis 6dis				nb SmithSt	YankeNola,DesrdGoal,Suprrimge	
	2-20$_{08}$ Fhd	‡ 1 fst 30 1.00^2 1.30^3 2.01 Qua	3	2^{10}	2^{25}	2dis 2dis 2^{47}			2.10^2	nb FinniganG	GreenDay,LoveAfair,SedctvLdy	
6-1	1-30$_{08}$ Fhd	‡ 1 gd 30^2 1.01^3 1.32^4 2.05 Qua	x1	6^{13}	5^{15}	4x^{13} 4^{33} 5dis				nb ManziCa	Bckstrtch,SevenHbts,JeterMrvl	
	1-23$_{08}$ M1	‡ 1 fst 28^4 57^2 1.28^3 1.58^4 NW2 2-4YO	15000 2x	x7^{36}	7^{41}	7^{41} 7x^{47} 8^{66}			35^1 2.12	84.60 StalbaumL	Tableau,SexyGrin	breaks

As you can see, I doubt anybody had any real love for Love Affair prior to her qualifier on March 13, but what a turnaround that was. After being moved to the barn of trainer Randy Giglio, the mare broke in her first qualifying attempt with Andy Miller aboard. Giglio tried somebody new and put Yannick Gingras up to drive, and the result was solid. Love Affair set the pace, flashing previously unseen speed before being caught by a far superior gelding in Yankee Frenzy. The time of the qualifier was only 1:59³/₅, but watching the mile made me very aware she was ready to go much faster.

Since she'd never won a race in her 17 tries, she would likely face a field that she could beat. An added bonus for her start on March 19 was that Gingras was driving her in the race from post 2, choosing Love Affair over a seemingly faster rival that he had also driven recently. That's a double bonus with the driver's-choice angle—a topic we'll explore in more detail in Chapter 5.

Love Affair went wire to wire to break her maiden, holding off the favorite by a grudging head at 4-1. She paid $10.20. That's good value.

The *Drive Time* fans on TVG had to be happy on April 11. In the evening's seventh race, I touted the chances of another mare coming off a qualifier, Postmark.

Pink	**POSTMARK(L)**					b m 4, by Mark Johnathan, Mailorder by Abercrombie							1:51.3 M1	08 11	2 1 3	$68,965
						Charles Stillings,Indianapolis,IN;Dean E Ehrgott,Indianapolis,IN							1:53.4 ID1	07 18	5 3 5	$53,636
7	David Miller (167) (0-0-0-0 .000)					Tr.Noel Daley(273-31-35-34 .114)							Last 6 Sts-$25,376	4 1:51.3 (1)		Lifetime $162,485
	4-3⁰⁸ M1	1 fst 30 59	1.27³ 1.56	Qua			1	1¹¼	1ⁿᵒ	2¹¼	2¹½	1²	28¹ 1.56 L	nb VandrkmpM	Postmark²,GntcMrcl⁵	pckt,moderate urge
	3-27⁰⁸ M1	1 fst 27⁴ 55²	1.24³ 1.53	Qua			1	7¹³	7¹⁸	7¹³	7¹⁴	7¹⁹	29³ 1.56⁴ L	nb VandrkmpM	GrandPlc¹²,CaptnGrn²	no factor
	12-6⁰⁷ Wbn ⅞	1 fst 27¹ 56⁴	1.26² 1.54³	F-NW3R5600	20580	scr sk						scr				scratched-sick
	11-29⁰⁷Wbn ⅞	1 fst 27² 55⁴	1.24¹ 1.54³	F-NW3R5000	21210	7	7¹³	7¹⁴	6⁶¼	6⁴	1¾	29¹ 1.54³ L	14.25 ShetlerDa	Postmark,BcsJesse	gap,brush,roared by
7-2	11-23⁰⁷Wbn ⅞	1 fst 26 55²	1.25 1.54	F-NW5750L6	14140	1	7¹¹	7°8¾	4°³	1nk	1¾	28² 1.54 L	∗1.85 ShetlerDa	Postmark,NigraQun	slow,cover,aim,all out
	11-15⁰⁷Wbn ⅞	1 fst 26⁴ 55¹	1.23³ 1.54	NW2 FM	19000	4	8¹³	8¹⁷	9¹⁶	6¹¹	2¹¼	27² 1.54¹ L	4.50 ZeronR	Htshtshlbl,Postmark	gap early,swept,flying

Postmark was moving into Noel Daley's barn, and he's a trainer that I don't usually bet right off the qualifier. Many times, his starters will improve in their second start off the qualifier. This situation was different, provided you saw Postmark's qualifier on April 3. It was simply outstanding. When she pounced out of the pocket that morning in rein to Mike Vanderkemp, she was like a horse possessed—so much so that Vanderkemp visibly restrained her late just to slow her down. That's the sign of a sharp horse.

Here's where it gets even better. Despite the fact that I listed her at 7-2 in the morning line and picked her right on top, Postmark blew by the field in the stretch and paid a whopping \$16.40. In addition, the pick four that night, which I gave out on the air at TVG, paid over \$900 for a \$48 investment.

I will give one more example of why watching qualifiers works. On April 16 in the eighth race, a 4-year-old bottom-level claimer named Can't Slay Me went to the gate from post 10 at odds of 5-1, exactly where I pegged him on the morning line. Can't Slay Me was coming off a qualifier where he finished second, beaten more than seven lengths.

Blue-Red **CAN'T SLAY ME(L)** — **b g 4, by Artsplace, Dragon So by Dragons Lair** — 1:52.2 M1 08 30 1 6 5 \$45,545
M. Frank;J A Fodera; A J Ferrara; S D Wienick,NY,NJ,CT — 1:54.0 M1 07 18 3 1 3 \$29,226
10 **David Miller (167) (0-0-0-0 .000)** — **Tr.Robert (Bo) Boudon** — **Last 6 Sts-\$3,000** 4 1:52.2 (1) **Lifetime** **\$82,382**

	4-10^{08}	M1	1 fst	29	56^{4}	1.25^{2}	1.52^{1}	Qua		7	$1^{1\frac{1}{4}}$	$2^{1\frac{1}{2}}$	$2^{3\frac{1}{2}}$	2^{4}	$2^{7\frac{1}{2}}$	27^{3}	1.53^{3} L	nb	MillerDv	SthwndLynx$^{7\frac{1}{2}}$,CantSlyM$^{1\frac{1}{2}}$	pocket,2nd best
	4-2^{08}	M1	1 fst	27	56	1.24^{4}	1.53^{3}	15/20000 4YO	16000	9	$5^{\circ 6\frac{3}{4}}$	$7^{\circ 7}$	$7^{\circ 7\frac{1}{4}}$	$6x^{4\frac{1}{2}}$	$x4x^{4\frac{3}{4}}$	28^{2}	1.54^{3} L	20.60	MillerDv	EscapPss^{nk},ColHndLk$^{4\frac{1}{4}}$	dq,p.9,trip,pace,broke
	3-27^{08}	M1	1 fst	28^{3}	57^{3}	1.26^{2}	1.55^{1}	Qua		7	2^{3}	$2^{2\frac{1}{2}}$	$3^{2\frac{1}{4}}$	4^{6}	4^{4}	29^{1}	1.56 L	nb	BrennanG	SprnglkArtst$^{2\frac{1}{4}}$,LmbPwrshtA$^{\frac{3}{4}}$	locked box,blocked
\$24,375	3-8^{08}	YR	1 gd	28	57^{3}	1.28^{2}	1.57^{4}	SagamoreHill	12500	7	7^{11}	7^{12}	7^{26}	7^{33}	7^{37}	31^{3}	2.05^{1} L	13.30	BouchardS	BobsAlib$^{1\frac{1}{2}}$,StrungOt$^{5\frac{3}{4}}$	left,took back,rough
5-1	3-1^{08}	Fhd	1 fst	27^{1}	56^{2}	1.26^{4}	1.56^{4}	NW5000	4500	5	$2^{\circ 1}$	$3^{\circ 1\frac{3}{4}}$	$4^{\circ 2\frac{1}{4}}$	$6^{7\frac{1}{4}}$	6^{13}	32^{1}	1.59^{2} L	5.00	GingrasYa	WayOfLif,JazbBrwn	parked out
	2-24^{08}	M1 (A)	1 fst	27	55^{2}	1.24^{2}	1.51^{4}	STrndstFnl-D	72100	3	2^{2}	$2^{\circ 1\frac{1}{2}}$	$4^{2\frac{1}{2}}$	$7^{4\frac{3}{4}}$	9^{12}	29^{2}	1.54^{1} L	50.00	MillerA	BobsAlib^{nk},IsacNwtn$^{2\frac{1}{2}}$	yld,pocket,tired

FIFTEENTH QUALIFIER: MEADOWLANDS, APR. 10-1 Mile Pace.

3-27-qM1	Southwind Lynx	Ti.Tetrick	1	$3^{\circ 8}$	$1^{1\frac{1}{2}}$	$1^{3\frac{1}{2}}$	1^{4}	$1^{7\frac{1}{2}}$	29^{1}	27^{3}	28^{3}	26^{4}	1.52^{1}	G.Teague,Jr.	nb
4-2-8M1	Cant Slay Me	Dv.Miller	7	$1^{1\frac{1}{4}}$	$2^{1\frac{1}{2}}$	$2^{1\frac{1}{4}}$	$2^{1\frac{1}{2}}$	$2^{1\frac{1}{2}}$	29	28	29	27^{3}	1.53^{3}	R.Boudon	L nb
3-8-11YR	Jovial Joker N	Jo.Campbell	2	2no	3^{8}	3^{8}	3^{8}	3^{10}	29^{1}	28^{1}	29	27^{3}	1.54	E.Adam	L nb
8-19-Lx1	Lucky Point Blank	A.Miller	5	$6^{2\frac{1}{2}}$	$4^{\circ 1\frac{1}{4}}$	$4^{1\frac{1}{4}}$	$4^{1\frac{1}{2}}$	$4^{\frac{1}{2}}$	31^{2}	27^{3}	29	28	1.56	Ju.Miller	L nb
2-2-8M1	My Fella	D.Dube	3	$4^{1\frac{1}{2}}$	5^{2}	5^{1}	5^{1}	5no	30^{4}	28^{2}	29	27^{4}	1.56	N.Varty	nb
4-3-qM1	Jates Jake	Y.Gingras	4	$5^{1\frac{1}{2}}$	6^{4}	$6^{\circ 4\frac{1}{2}}$	6^{6}	6^{10}	31^{1}	28^{2}	28^{4}	27^{3}	1.56	J.Mcdermott	L nb
12-17-qM1	Camelot Hall	G.Brennan	x6	7	7	7	7	7	32	28^{2}	28^{4}	29	1.58^{1}	M.Harder	nb

Scratched: Ideal Lover, Big Production.
Lasix: Cant Slay Me, Jovial Joker N, Lucky Point Blank, Jates Jake.

Time: 0:29.0, 0:56.4, 1:25.2, 1:52.1. Temp. 55°

SOUTHWIND LYNX showed a bit of early speed, overtaken early before brushing to the front, opening up easily while on the lead, never asked by Tim Tetrick. CANT SLAY ME left for the early lead, relegated to the pocket going onto the backstretch, finishing strongly despite an overshadowed performance. JOVIAL JOKER N sat the pocket in the early going before the winner brushed to the front, pacing alertly throughout. LUCKY POINT BLANK brushed to the front of the second flight going into the far turn, finishing evenly. MY FELLA was the leader of the second flight, overtaken going into the far turn but finishing evenly. JATES JAKE raced from the second flight, making a mild bid at the head of the stretch, finishing evenly. CAMELOT HALL was off stride before the start, spotting the gate twelve lengths, and was last throughout.

b h 4 by Real Artist, Luxury Class by Jate Lobell

Owners: 1. K&R Racing Llc,Houston,DE;Teague Inc,Harrington,DE, 2. M Frank,Fair Lawn,NJ;J A Fodera,Staten Isl,NY;A J Ferrara,Norwalk,CT;S D Wienick,Carmel,NY, 3. Summersby Stable,Del Mar,CA, 4. Perfect World Enterprises,Old Westbury Ny., 5. Gest Millenium 2000 Inc,Trois-Rivieres,PQ, CA;Les Ecuries Sarah,Laval,PQ, CA, 6. John Paul Mc Dermott,Lyndhurst Nj., 7. D.B.Scharf,S.Arnold,J.Silva & Sampson St. Stb..

As you can see from the comment of the chart caller, Can't Slay Me was completely on his own—in fact, under a stout hold late in the mile. Finishing well ahead of him was Southwind Lynx, winner of the \$1 million Meadowlands Pace and the Art Rooney Pace at Yonkers the year before. This was a high-caliber qualifier, and watching Can't Slay Me was the key. It's not easy to like one out of post 10, but if the horse showed the same speed that he did in the qualifier, he would be okay. Here's what happened.

EIGHTH RACE: MEADOWLANDS, APR. 16-1 Mile Pace. $15,000/$20,000 Clm. Alw. Hcp. Post positions drawn to base price. 4 Year Olds. Purse $16,000.

4-10-qM1	Cant Slay Me	Dv.Miller 10	2^{o1}	$11\frac{1}{2}$	$11\frac{1}{2}$	$12\frac{1}{4}$	$11\frac{1}{2}$	$27\ 27^1\ 29\ 29^1$	1.52^2	R.Boudon	L 5.50
4-9-4M1	Rock N Bliss	D.Dube 8	10	10°	$9^{oo}\frac{3}{4}$	7hd	2nk	$29^2\ 26^4\ 28^1\ 28^1$	1.52^3	S.Didomenico	L 29.50
4-9-4M1	Tune Me Out	Jo.Campbell 3	$8^{o}1\frac{1}{2}$	7^1	$8\frac{1}{2}$	$8\frac{3}{4}$	$3\frac{1}{2}$	$28^4\ 27\ 28^2\ 28^3$	1.52^4	V.Fusco,Jr.	*1.90
4-2-8M1	Clooney Drummond	Ti.Tetrick 9	$5^2\frac{1}{2}$	$6^1\frac{3}{4}$	5^{oo}nk	3nk	4^1	$28\ 27^2\ 28^3\ 28^4$	1.52^4	Ka.Williams	L 24.80
4-4-4M1	Cc Make A Buck	E.Goodell 7	$3^1\frac{3}{4}$	$3^1\frac{3}{4}$	4^1	$4\frac{3}{4}$	5nk	$27^1\ 27^3\ 29\ 29^1$	1.53	R.Croghan	L 12.30
4-2-8M1	Escape Pass	B.Sears 2	4^2	$4\frac{1}{2}$	$6\frac{3}{4}$	6no	6^2	$27^3\ 27^3\ 28^4\ 29$	1.53	C.Fusco	L 3.30
4-9-4M1	Sparkles Dreamboat	C.Manzi 1	7hd	$9\frac{3}{4}$	10	10	7no	$28^4\ 27^2\ 28^1\ 29$	1.53^2	J.Mcdermott	L 99.30
4-5-8Fhd	Jeremy	A.Miller 6	$9^{o}1\frac{1}{2}$	$8^{o}\frac{1}{2}$	$7^{oo}\frac{1}{4}$	$5\frac{3}{4}$	$8^3\frac{3}{4}$	$29^1\ 26^4\ 28^1\ 29^1$	1.53^2	A.Sacco	23.50
4-2-8M1	Party For Two	Y.Gingras 4	1nk	$2^1\frac{1}{2}$	2^1	2nk	9^8	$27\ 27^2\ 29\ 30^4$	1.54^1	J.Czermann,Jr.	L 12.30
4-2-8M1	Lightning Desire	G.Brennan 5	6^2	5^{o1}	3^onk	9hd	10	$28^2\ 26^4\ 28^2\ 32^1$	1.55^4	J.Rubin	3.70

Lasix: Cant Slay Me, Rock N Bliss, Clooney Drummond, Cc Make A Buck, Escape Pass, Sparkles Dreamboat, Party For Two.
Claimed: Tune Me Out by Albina Montini, Acton, Ont..

Off: 9:25 Time: 0:27.0, 0:54.1, 1:23.1, 1:52.2. Mutuel Pool: $178,317. Temp. 60°
MUTUELS: **Cant Slay Me** $13.00, 7.20, 3.60; **Rock N Bliss** $26.80, 7.60; **Tune Me Out** $2.60
EXACTA (10-8) $280.60. TRIFECTA (10-8-3) $469.70.

CANT SLAY ME was used to the front, rated out the action, faced pressure final turn, sprinted away in the lane and was never in doubt to the wire. ROCK N BLISS was out from the back with excess cover, followed wide third over final turn, took aim from the clouds in the lane and came with good pace for the place. TUNE ME OUT was out early waiting for a flow but tucked in a five hole, split rivals in the lane and came with good late energy to get up for the show dough. CLOONEY DRUMMOND left for position, came out in a dull flow final turn, swung wide for the drive and closed with even pace. CC MAKE A BUCK tried to leave but took a seat in a pocket, was shuffled back down the backside, angled in the lane but never menaced. ESCAPE PASS saved ground all the way, faced traffic issues in the lane and never got it started. SPARKLES DREAMBOAT was off very slow, sat buried at the back and basted the rest. JEREMY was out every step from the back, wound up third over in the dull flow, followed wide final turn but lacked rally. PARTY FOR TWO left to the front, yielded for a pocket, sat in and faded away in the lane. LIGHTNING DESIRE was out very weakly uncovered and clogged the rim.

b h 4 by Artsplace, Dragon So by Dragons Lair
Claiming Prices: 1. $24,375, 2. $18,750, 3. $18,750, 4. $22,375, 5. $18,750, 6. $18,750, 7. $18,750, 8. $18,750, 9. $18,750, 10. $18,750.
Owners: 1. M Frank,Fair Lawn,NJ;J A Fodera,Staten Isl,NY;A J Ferrara,Norwalk,CT;S D Wienick,Carmel,NY, 2. Daniel Dube,Millstone,NJ, 3. Tamara B Williams,Parksley,VA;James T Lunn Jr,Onley,VA, 4. Sbk Stables,E Rutherford,NJ;Anthony J Ruggeri,Mamaroneck,NY, 5. Gordon C Rains,Bloomfield Hills,MI;Steve M Main,Byron,MI, 6. Soft Kiss Racing Stable LLC,Secaucus,NJ, 7. Arthur W Brewer II,Hartly,DE, 8. Kenneth D Iulo,Passaic,NJ, 9. Frederick H & Anita C Fialkow,Wellington,FL, 10. Lightning Stable,Manalapan,NJ.

Since most people don't have the time to show up and watch the qualifiers themselves, my best advice is to get to the track early with a list of ones that you want to review. If you do that ahead of time, you won't be caught flat-footed when another Postmark romps and pays $16. Believe me, you don't want to miss out on them, because they are few and far between.

If you're watching in your living room on TVG or HRTV, or on your computer, pull up my analysis from the Meadowlands' website: www.meadowlandsracetrack.com. It's available a few days in advance when you navigate through "Handicapping" to "Race Reviews & Picks." Otherwise, purchase *Harness Eye* and read the chart caller's comments. Watching qualifiers will make you money, provided you're patient and do the homework.

4

BARN CHANGES

As we saw in the previous chapter, my favorite betting angle is paying close attention to qualifying races. My second-favorite method in trying to find a winner is the ol' barn-change angle. I like to call it the Barn-Change Bonanza. It can come up in many different ways—through a claim, a private or auction purchase, or an owner's transfer of horses from one trainer to another. For many years, barn changes were hard to identify because most track programs didn't list the trainer of record in the past performances. Now, they do, so everybody can see it.

Barn changes are often successful because the horse enters a new environment. Different equipment might be used. A horse that has been stabled at a racetrack may move to a farm setting where he gets more paddock and outside time. Sometimes, even a new groom will wake a horse up. Several trainers out there are superb at getting the most out of their new acquisitions, so pay attention and get to know the ones who do it well.

Trainer Rick Bilach worked the barn-change angle to perfection on March 15, 2008, with veteran pacer Armbro Acquire.

Yellow	**ARMBRO ACQUIRE(L)**										**b g 8, by Rustler Hanover, Fiddletoons by Artsplace**										**1:51.4 ChD 5/8**		**08 41 10 4 4**	**$147,76**
											Mildred B. Ventriglio,Manalapan,NJ										**1:50.0 M1**		**07 25 6 3 1**	**$126,80**
6	**Eric Goodell (165) (0-0-0-0 .000)**										**Tr.Richard Bilach**								**Last 6 Sts-$6,520**		**4 1:49.2 (1)**		**Lifetime**	**$824,77**
	3-8$_{08}$	M1	1	gd	27	55^{2}	1.24^{3}	1.54^{1}	40000	26000	8	8^{10}	8°^{6¾}	8°°^{6}	6^{3½}	6^{6}	29^{3}	1.55^{2}	L	7.10 MillerA	YankeLnc^{no},SlppryPhl^{2¼}		followed wide,no po	
	3-1$_{08}$	M1	1	fst	27^{1}	55^{2}	1.23^{4}	1.51^{3}	50/60000	33000	3	6^{8¾}	4°^{3½}	3°^{1¾}	3^{2¼}	6^{7¼}	28^{4}	1.53	L	8.50 GingrasY	CrrsChrctr^{1¾},AllHall^{1¼}		uncovered,no po	
	2-23$_{08}$	M1	1	fst	26^{3}	54^{3}	1.23^{1}	1.50^{1}	50/60000	33000	2	5^{4¼}	4°^{2½}	3°^{1}	3^{¾}	3^{4¾}	27^{4}	1.51^{1}	L	21.90 GoodellE	OtOnABndr^{2},StckMrktWz^{2¾}		cover,even	
$40,000	2-16$_{08}$	M1	1	fst	27	55^{1}	1.24	1.52	50/55000	32000	1	7^{7¾}	7^{5½}	9^{5¼}	9^{4½}	7^{3½}	27^{3}	1.52^{3}	L	24.80 GingrasY	AllHal^{lnk},DynmtExprss^{1}		buried,no factc	
10-1	2-9$_{08}$	M1	1	fst	27^{1}	54^{4}	1.23^{1}	1.50^{3}	50/60000	33000	4	8^{7½}	7^{4}	7^{3¾}	6^{4½}	8^{9}	28^{2}	1.52^{2}	L	21.40 DubeD	OtOnABndr^{1¼},SoulChsr^{2¾}		slipped out fnl,littl	
	2-2$_{08}$	M1	1	fst	27	54	1.22^{3}	1.52^{1}	c50/55000	32000	1	4^{2¾}	4°^{2¾}	3°^{1½}	1^{1¼}	4^{1½}	29^{3}	1.52^{2}	L	3.20 DubeD	MdlndMdlA^{hd},JllbySprtA^{1½}		3 wide,led,flattene	

This 8-year-old gelding was claimed for $50,000 in February by Delaware-based trainer Mike Hall. After several unsuccessful starts for the same tag, Hall dropped the gelding in for $40,000 and ended up with another off-the-board result. That's when the barn change occurred, and he was sent to Bilach. At the time, Bilach had trained eight winners at the Meadowlands meet from just 23 starters.

Bilach changed several pieces of equipment, including the overcheck bit, while also removing both headpoles. He changed the horse's bridle from blind to open, removed a Murphy blind, and lengthened his hopples by one full inch: in short, a complete job of rerigging. Bilach also put up Eric Goodell, who was just beginning to establish himself as a great longshot driver. The field held no monsters, just average claimers with mostly inconsistent records. In other words, this was the perfect spot for a big wake-up call for Armbro Acquire, who owned 23 lifetime wins. Here's what happened.

ELEVENTH RACE: MEADOWLANDS, MAR. 15-1 Mile Pace. $40,000 Clm. Alw. Purse $26,000.

3-8-9M1	Armbro Acquire	E.Goodell	5	3°^{2¼}	1^{1½}	1^{1}	1^{½}	1^{½}	28^{3}	27^{2}	29	27^{1}	1.52^{1}	R.Bilach	L	4.10
3-8-8M1	Michelles Gemstone	B.Sears	2	5^{1½}	4°^{nk}	2°^{1}	2^{1}	2^{nk}	29^{2}	27^{2}	28^{2}	27	1.52^{1}	M.Silva	L	*3.00
3-8-8M1	Itsjustabeginning	Ti.Tetrick	3	6°^{1¼}	6°^{½}	4°^{1}	3^{nk}	3^{½}	29^{3}	27^{2}	28^{2}	27	1.52^{2}	C.Fusco	L	3.50
3-8-1M1	Kennans Josh	D.Dube	6	2^{½}	3^{1}	5^{½}	5^{hd}	4^{1}	28^{2}	28^{1}	29	26^{4}	1.52^{2}	M.Kesmodel	L	10.60
3-7-4M1	Sony Hanover	G.Brennan	8	7°^{¾}	8°^{1¼}	6°^{1¾}	6^{4}	5no	30	27^{1}	28^{3}	26^{4}	1.52^{3}	S.Rollins		4.50
3-8-9M1	Incredible Art	Y.Gingras	7	1^{1½}	2^{1½}	3^{nk}	4^{¾}	6^{4¾}	28^{1}	28	29^{1}	27^{1}	1.52^{3}	M.Burke		9.50
3-6-qM1	Activator	Dv.Miller	4	8^{½}	7^{½}	9	8^{hd}	7^{1}	30	27^{1}	29^{1}	27^{1}	1.53^{3}	E.Miller	L	33.70
3-8-1M1	T Gs Majority	Jo.Campbell	9	9°	9°	8°^{½}	9	8^{3¼}	30^{1}	27^{1}	28^{4}	27^{3}	1.53^{4}	B.Saunders	L	26.70
3-8-9M1	Northern Edge	C.Manzi	1	4^{1¾}	5^{1}	7^{¾}	7^{nk}	9	29	27^{4}	29^{1}	28^{2}	1.54^{2}	Mi.Gorshe	L	7.80

Scratched: Big Production -sick.
Lasix: Armbro Acquire, Michelles Gemstone, Itsjustabeginning, Kennans Josh, Activator, T Gs Majority, Northern Edge.
Claimed: Itsjustabeginning by Soft Kiss Racing Stable LLC, Secaucus, N.J.; Kennans Josh by Jeff Gillis, Ont..

Off: 10:37 Time: 0:28.1, 0:56.0, 1:25.0, 1:52.1. Mutuel Pool: $271,009. Temp. 50°
MUTUELS: **Armbro Acquire** $10.20, 4.60, 3.40; **Michelles Gemstone** $6.00, 3.80; **Itsjustabeginning** $3.00
EXACTA (6-3) $45.80. TRIFECTA (6-3-4) $119.10. PICK 3 (6-8-6) $173.70.

ARMBRO ACQUIRE left and settled to the three hole, pulled to the half, brushed to the lead, set a good clip, met pressure the last quarter and held well. MICHELLES GEMSTONE pulled uncovered passing the half, came to the winner, pressed, had aim but was held at bay. ITSJUSTABEGINNING was second over to good cover and closed steadily. KENNANS JOSH left to the early pocket, got shuffled when the winner brushed, sat in, had willing pace but was in traffic through the lane. SONY HANOVER was parked, gained third over cover, came wide into the stretch but had no kick. INCREDIBLE ART was on the lead turn one, yielded to the winner, sat pocket and weakened in the lane. ACTIVATOR had no rally. T GS MAJORITY was parked and fourth over with little to offer. NORTHERN EDGE tired.
b g 8 by Rustler Hanover, Fiddletoons by Artsplace
Claiming Prices: 1. $40,000, 2. $40,000, 3. $40,000, 4. $40,000, 5. $40,000, 6. $40,000, 7. $40,000, 8. $40,000, 9. $40,000.
Owners: 1. Mildred B Ventriglio,Manalapan,NJ, 2. Jeffrey S Snyder,New York,NY, 3. Howard S Jacobs,W Orange,NJ;Brian & Ira Ross Wallach,Closter,NJ;Ronald Gold,Norwood,NJ, 4. Larry Baron,Horsham,PA, 5. Threes A Charm Stb LLC,West Orange,NJ, 6. S Burke,Frdrcktwn,PA;Weaver Bruscemi,Cnsbrg,PA;L Karr,Rndlph,NJ;H Taylor,Pn Vly,PA, 7. Joseph J Petrera,Harrison,NY, 8. George A & Gerald W Jaeger,Malverne,NY;Karl Jaeger,Princeton Junction,NJ, 9. Clifford N Grundy,Howell,MI;Melvin G Fink,Bloomfield Hills,MI.

Now, the Armbro Acquires of the world don't come along every night, but when they do, you must be ready to pounce. The $10.20 mutuel was more than fair value, and as the season progressed, prices on Rick Bilach barn changes plummeted.

Before we get into claims, let's look at one more example of a barn change that paid major dividends for an owner, but not necessarily at the windows.

Late in the season at the Meadowlands, with top 3-year-old trotters preparing for the Hambletonian, I stumbled upon a barn change for Pine After Pine with a backstory that still makes me want to cry.

Yellow	**PINE AFTER PINE**	br c 3, by Muscles Yankee, Pine Nugget by Pine Chip	1:55.1 M1	08 8 2 2 1 $156,554
6		Norman Smiley,Boca Raton,FL;Gerald Smiley,PQ,CA;T L P Stable,NJ	1:58.3 Sp1 Q	07 2 0 2 0 $15,175
	Ron Pierce (160) (0-0-0-0 .000)	Tr.Jonas Czernyson(53-6-10-3 .113)	Last 6 Sts-$15,800	3 1:55.1 (1)	Lifetime $171,729

	7-3^{08} M1	1 fst 29^1 59	1.28^1 1.57	Qua 3YO		7	4$°3\frac{1}{4}$	44	4$°1\frac{1}{4}$	42$\frac{1}{4}$	31$\frac{3}{4}$	29 1.57^2	nb CampbellJo	VkngDfndr^1,SrtsHnvr$\frac{3}{4}$	prkd,tuck,cover,even
	6-25^{08} M1	1 fst 27^3 57^4	1.27^3 1.56^2	NW1 3YO	12500	3	5x7$\frac{1}{4}$x10^{13}	10$°°8$	76	56$\frac{1}{4}$	28^2 1.57^3	*1.20 PierceR	BdySrfnghd,MccMdnss$\frac{3}{4}$	big recovery,wd,fltnd
	6-12^{08} M1	1 fst 30^1 59^4	1.29 1.58^1	Qua 3YO	9	10^{15}	9^{17}	89$\frac{1}{2}$	86	54$\frac{3}{4}$	28^2 1.59^1	nb PierceR	SpamSpad$\frac{3}{4}$,YnkyCnwy^2	late,beat weakest
	8-14^{07} Sp1	1 fst 27^3 55^2	1.24^4 1.53^4	Review	56000	4	6$°7\frac{3}{4}$	67$\frac{1}{2}$	6$°6\frac{1}{4}$	52$\frac{1}{4}$	2$\frac{1}{2}$	27^4 1.53^4	3.40 MillerA	MuscleMas,PinAftrPn,OverRuled	
7-2	8-4^{07} Sp1	1 fst 32 1.01^1	1.30 1.58^3	Qua	1	2	2$°$	13	17$\frac{1}{2}$	129	28^3 1.58^3	nb MillerE	PinAftrPn,DreamWavs,	
	7-11^{07} Hw1	1 fst 31 1.00^3	1.30^1 2.01^3	Qua	2	2^3	25	2^{10}	2^8	2nk	29^2 2.01^3	nb HollandBr	GreatGtwy,PinAftrPn,SweetLcfr	

Take nothing away from former trainer Erv Miller, who is one of the sport's top conditioners; I think this was more a case of bad luck for him than anything else. He broke Pine After Pine as a 2-year-old, and the colt's final start as a freshman was a great one. He finished a fast-closing second to Muscle Mass in the Review Stakes at the Illinois State Fair in August. The time of 1:53^4/$_5$ set a world record for 2-year-old trotters (which has since been broken).

With that kind of talent, Pine After Pine was turned out to mature with sights set on the Hambo the following August.

The bad-beat backstory begins with some colleagues and I, who were "fortunate" enough to witness Pine After Pine go a schooling mile behind the gate one morning after qualifiers. We saw a strong training performance, and after some investigation, we found out who the horse was. (We asked Ron Pierce who trained him.) When Pine After Pine was in to go in a maiden race on June 25, 2008, my colleagues and I were also in . . .

all-in, and you see the result. Pine After Pine was brushing to the lead and made an unfortunate break.

The colt's owners immediately transferred him to another top trotting trainer, Jonas Czernyson. Needless to say, he jogged on July 9, romping away by more than three lengths in 1:55$^1/_5$ and paying the princely sum of \$3.60. Three weeks later, Pine After Pine raced in the \$1.5 million Hambletonian on national television. He was no match for the great Deweycheatumnhowe, but the barn change worked for everybody but me, my friends, and Erv Miller. We spotted a good one, but were not able to capitalize. Sometimes, those things happen.

Barn changes are frequently the result of claims, but for me, the toughest part of handicapping harness racing is trying to figure out the claiming races. They present a mystifying mix of new barns, price hikes and drops, and driver changes. In other words, they're usually too hard to decipher.

On April 3, 2008, I saw a good opportunity to hop on the bandwagon of a freshly claimed horse named AJ's Send Money.

Gray	**‡AJ'S SEND MONEY(L)**	**b g 5, by Wilson Wyoming, Swift Connection by Swiss Connection**	**1:57.2 M1**	**08 30 8 3 2**	**\$98,290**
8	**George Brennan (150) (0-0-0-0 .000)**	**Mary Ellen Abbot,Circleville,NY**	**1:57.1 PM1**	**07 28 7 3 3**	**\$21,035**
		Tr.Basil Aldrich,Jr.(7-0-0-1 .000) **Last 6 Sts-\$9,600**	**3 1:56.3 (1)**	**Lifetime**	**\$173,065**

	3-26$_{08}$	M1	‡	1	fst	28^3	57^1	1.27	1.56	c15000	12000	10	$4^{5\frac{1}{4}}$	$4^{5\frac{1}{4}}$	$4^{\circ 2}$	$2^{1\frac{3}{4}}$	$2^{1\frac{3}{4}}$	29	1.56^2	L	3.30 SearsB	SndngOtAnSs$^{1\frac{3}{4}}$,AjsSndMny$^{\frac{3}{4}}$	tuck,wnnr's cvr,2d bst
	3-13$_{08}$	M1	‡	1	fst	29	58^3	1.28^2	1.56^2	Qua		4	$5^{9\frac{1}{4}}$	5^{10}	$6^{\circ 8\frac{1}{4}}$	5^8	4^9	28^1	1.58^1	L	nb SearsB	PumpedAndGldn,BgZWisdom	evenly
	2-21$_{08}$	M1	‡	1	fst	29^1	58^3	1.29^3	1.59^3	Qua		x1x	9^{38}	9^{43}	9^{46}	9^{32}	9^{73}			L	nb DubeD	ItaDeVie$^{\frac{1}{2}}$,ImageBll$^{1\frac{1}{4}}$	extended early break
\$20,000	2-1$_{08}$	Fhd	‡	1	sly	29^2	1.00^3	1.32^1	2.05	Opt15000	5400	7	$7^{9\frac{3}{4}}$	$7^{9\frac{3}{4}}$	6^{13}	7^{18}	7^{33}	36^4	2.11^3	L	37.00 PantalanoJ	YnkeeSlm,VictrBch	quit badly
3-1	1-25$_{08}$	YR	‡	1	fst	29	59^2	1.28^4	1.59	NW12000	15000	8											scratched-sick
	1-16$_{08}$	M1	‡	1	fst	27^4	56^2	1.26^4	1.55^2	20/25000	18000	8	2^2	$2^{1\frac{3}{4}}$	4^3	6^{13}	6^{26}	33^1	2.00^3	L	5.60 DubeD	AtmnVctry$^{5\frac{3}{4}}$,LocalGrl$^{\frac{1}{2}}$	p.5,tuck,sat,quit

In his last start, the gelding was claimed by one of the sharp young trainers in the business, Jake Hartline. Hartline was astute enough to claim AJ's Send Money right out of a nondescript qualifier where he finished fourth, beaten nine lengths. Looking at the horse's prior races, there wasn't much good going on, so this was a risky kind of claim. AJ's Send Money raced very well from post 10 the night he was claimed by Hartline and his gang of owners, however, and they promptly jumped him up in price from \$15,000 to the \$20,000 level, which is a sign of positive intent. All systems appeared to say go, and that's exactly what AJ's Send Money did. He made multiple moves for the lead with George Brennan aboard and won handily, his first tally of the year at the price of $6.80.

Again, I just want to reiterate that claiming races make up the weakest part of my handicapping arsenal and I approach them with extreme caution. However, there are several trainers who are adept at this game. The following list recognizes a few that enjoyed great success over the 2008 meet at the Meadowlands. When you see these names, take a closer look.

Rick Bilach
Mickey Burke
Ross Croghan
Carmine Fusco
Jake Hartline
Mark Kesmodel
Anthony Montini
Scott Rollins
Ken Rucker
Mark Silva
Nat Varty

5

DRIVER'S CHOICES
AND DRIVER CHANGES

When a day's entries are drawn by the racing office, they put out what is called an overnight sheet. It is a simple list of race conditions, the horses entered, the post positions, and the drivers who were named by trainers. I pay extra attention to situations where a driver is named on more than one horse in a race.

For example, as the top driver in the sport right now, Brian Sears is a wanted man, and is often listed on several horses in any given race. It then becomes his job to make a choice on whom to drive. That's like letting Brian Sears do the handicapping for you. Who would pass up that opportunity if given the chance? It's not foolproof, but it often gives a lot of insight. You can check out the overnights for any parimutuel track or fair in the United States by going to the United States Trotting Association website (www.ustrotting.com) and looking at "Entries/Results."

A perfect example of driver's choice came on May 30, 2008, with Final Curtain.

Black **FINAL CURTAIN(L)** — **b c 3, by Pro Bono Best, Lola by Artsplace**
Bulletproof Enterprises,Boca Raton,Fl

5 **Brian Sears (145) (0-0-0-0 .000)** — **Tr.Kevin McDermott** — **Last 6 Sts-$22,750**

1:48.2 M1	**08 31 11 6 2**		**$177,450**
1:57.0 M1 Q	**07 1 0 0 0**		**-**
3 1:48.2 (1)		**Lifetime**	**$177,450**

	5-24$_{08}$	M1	1	fst	27^{3}	55^{1}	1.23^{2}	1.50^{4}	NW3 2-4YO	22000	10	$6^{8\frac{1}{2}}$	$6^{\circ 7}$	$5^{\circ 2\frac{3}{4}}$	$6^{2\frac{3}{4}}$	$7^{6\frac{1}{4}}$	28	1.52 L	4.50 SearsB	ShrThDlght$^{2\frac{1}{2}}$,RealTogh^{nk}	gap on rim,mildly
	5-15$_{08}$	M1	1	fst	26^{4}	55^{1}	1.23	1.50^{3}	NW2 2-4YO	15000	8	$1^{1\frac{1}{2}}$	$1^{1\frac{1}{2}}$	$1^{1\frac{3}{4}}$	$1^{1\frac{3}{4}}$	1^{2}	27^{3}	1.50^{3} L	2.30 SearsB	FinlCrtn^{2},ArtistCf$^{3\frac{3}{4}}$	on own to wire
	4-24$_{08}$	M1	1	fst	28^{3}	57^{3}	1.25^{1}	1.51^{4}	NW2 2-4YO	15000	8										scratched-sick
	4-17$_{08}$	M1	1	fst	27^{4}	54^{4}	1.23^{2}	1.51^{3}	NW2 2-4YO	15000	3	$1^{1\frac{1}{2}}$	$2^{1\frac{1}{2}}$	$2^{\circ 1}$	2^{1}	$1^{\frac{1}{2}}$	28	1.51^{3} L	★.80 SearsB	FinlCrtn$^{\frac{1}{2}}$,ThRclsOn^{1}	top,pckt,attk,driving
7-2	4-10$_{08}$	M1	1	fst	27^{1}	55^{2}	1.22^{4}	1.50^{3}	NW2 2-4YO	15000	6	9^{11}	$9^{6\frac{1}{4}}$	$9^{5\frac{1}{2}}$	$9^{4\frac{1}{4}}$	$6^{3\frac{3}{4}}$	27^{3}	1.51^{2} L	54.90 StalbaumL	AllamericanMajor,RedStrCatch	no room
	3-27$_{08}$	M1	1	fst	28^{2}	57	1.26	1.53^{4}	NW2 2-4YO	15000	6										scratched-sick

Yellow **PLACEITONLUCKYDAN(L)** — **br g 4, by Camotion, Armbro Voluminous by Abercrombie**
Engel Stb & Rucker Stb,IL;Panhellenic Stb Corp,NY;Sheffield

6 **Tim Tetrick (160) (0-0-0-0 .000)** — **Tr.Ken Rucker(462-64-57-79 .139)** — **Last 6 Sts-$8,975**

1:51.1 M1	**08 18 4 2 4**		**$46,203**
1:53.1 BP1	**07 21 3 7 0**		**$23,943**
4 1:51.1 (1)		**Lifetime**	**$84,270**

	5-21$_{08}$	M1	1	fst	27^{1}	55	1.23^{1}	1.51^{4}	NW5000	11000	4	$6^{7\frac{3}{4}}$	$6^{\circ 6}$	$6^{\circ\circ 2\frac{3}{4}}$	2no	$1^{2\frac{1}{2}}$	28	1.51^{4} L	★.60 SearsB	Plctnlckydn$^{2\frac{1}{2}}$,HpptyHpN^{1}	3d ov,fllw wd,going awy
	5-9$_{08}$	M1	1	sly	27^{4}	57^{1}	1.24^{1}	1.52	NW3 2-4YO	22000	10	10^{13}	10^{9}	$7^{9\frac{3}{4}}$	$8^{9\frac{1}{2}}$	7^{12}	28^{1}	1.54^{2} L	14.40 SearsB	SgndHnvr$^{1\frac{1}{4}}$,RedHtYnk^{1}	no rally
	5-3$_{08}$	BP1	1	fst	27^{4}	55^{4}	1.24^{2}	1.52^{1}	NW4/NW5	6700	9	$4^{4\frac{1}{2}}$	$4^{4\frac{1}{4}}$	$6^{3\frac{1}{2}}$	$5^{4\frac{1}{2}}$	$2^{\frac{3}{4}}$	27^{2}	1.52^{2} L	15.10 OostingMi	EdonRdExp,Plactnlck,AllZip	
	4-23$_{08}$	BP1	1	fst	30	59^{3}	1.28^{1}	1.55^{4}	Qua		7	$2^{\circ 1}$	$2^{1\frac{1}{2}}$	$2^{3\frac{1}{2}}$	2^{3}	$2^{4\frac{3}{4}}$	28	1.56^{4} L	nb StaffordPa	CornrBltz,Plactnlck,YouRock	
9-2	12-29$_{07}$	BP1	1	fst	28^{4}	57^{3}	1.26^{2}	1.54^{2}	NW5500	7200	4	$5^{6\frac{1}{4}}$	$6^{6\frac{1}{4}}$	$7^{\circ 5\frac{3}{4}}$	8^{13}	8^{15}	29^{4}	1.57^{2} L	2.10 OostingMi	Loslpsnks,JoPsBnchM,TheLngGdb	
	12-22$_{07}$	BP1	1	gd	28^{3}	56^{4}	1.25^{2}	1.55	NW5500	7200	9	9^{16}	9^{11}	9^{8}	$7^{9\frac{1}{4}}$	6^{4}	28^{4}	1.55^{4} L	★2.20 OostingMi	HeavnTchd,CarmlDmpl,JoPsBnchM	

When the overnight sheet came out, Sears was listed on both of the above horses in the fourth race at the Meadowlands. Final Curtain was coming off a seventh-place finish from post 10 for this condition, and Placeitonluckydan was entering off a romping win in lifetime-best time at odds of 3-5 for one of the leading trainers at the meet. Who should Sears have chosen?

FOURTH RACE: MEADOWLANDS, MAY 30-1 Mile Pace. Non-winners of 3 ext. pari-mutuel races or $50,000 lifetime. 4 Year Olds & Under. Purse $22,000.

5-24-12M1	Final Curtain	B.Sears	5	$1^{1\frac{1}{2}}$	$1^{1\frac{3}{4}}$	$1^{1\frac{1}{4}}$	$1^{1\frac{1}{2}}$	$1^{2\frac{1}{4}}$	26^{2}	27^{3}	27^{3}	26^{4}	1.48^{2}	K.Mcdermott	L ★1.30
5-24-12M1	Red Hot Yankee	Dv.Miller	4	2^{3}	2^{2}	2^{2}	$2^{2\frac{1}{2}}$	$2^{4\frac{1}{2}}$	26^{3}	27^{4}	27^{2}	27	1.48^{4}	M.Capone	L 6.80
5-24-4M1	The Flim Flam Pan	R.Pierce	2	$3^{4\frac{1}{4}}$	3^{2}	$3^{1\frac{1}{4}}$	3^{2}	$3^{1\frac{1}{2}}$	27^{1}	27^{3}	27^{2}	27^{3}	1.49^{4}	E.Cruise	8.20
5-21-6M1	Placeitonluckydan	Ti.Tetrick	6	$5^{2\frac{1}{4}}$	5^{2}	$5^{\circ 1\frac{1}{2}}$	$4^{\frac{3}{4}}$	$4^{3\frac{1}{2}}$	28^{3}	26^{4}	27^{2}	27^{1}	1.50	K.Rucker	L 11.90
5-24-12M1	Vapor In The Wind	A.Miller	1	4^{2}	$4^{1\frac{1}{2}}$	$4^{\circ 1\frac{1}{2}}$	5^{2}	$5^{2\frac{1}{4}}$	28^{1}	27	27^{1}	28^{2}	1.50^{4}	E.Miller	2.90
5-24-1M1	Cowboy Hanover	R.Plano	7	9^{2}	$8^{\circ\frac{1}{2}}$	$8^{1\frac{3}{4}}$	$8^{\frac{3}{4}}$	$6^{\frac{1}{2}}$	29^{3}	26^{3}	27^{1}	27^{4}	1.51^{1}	R.Plano	L 54.10
5-24-1M1	Western Trademark	Y.Gingras	10	10	10	$9^{\frac{3}{4}}$	$9^{2\frac{1}{4}}$	$7^{1\frac{1}{2}}$	30	26^{3}	27^{1}	27^{2}	1.51^{1}	K.O'donnell	60.70
5-18-7TgD	Red Star Catch	G.Brennan	8	$7^{1\frac{1}{2}}$	$7^{\circ 1\frac{1}{4}}$	$6^{\circ no}$	$7^{2\frac{1}{4}}$	$8^{6\frac{1}{2}}$	29^{1}	26^{3}	27^{1}	28^{3}	1.51^{3}	M.Harder	8.80
5-24-1M1	Grab Your Keys	Jo.Campbell	9	$8^{\circ hd}$	$9^{\circ 2\frac{1}{4}}$	10°	10	9^{13}	29^{3}	26^{3}	27^{4}	28^{4}	1.52^{4}	T.Gower	38.50
5-24-1M1	Shoot First	C.Manzi	3	$6^{1\frac{1}{2}}$	6^{nk}	$7^{1\frac{3}{4}}$	6^{xno}	10	29	26^{4}	27^{1}	32^{2}	1.55^{2}	D.Niccum	L 21.40

Lasix: Final Curtain, Red Hot Yankee, Placeitonluckydan, Cowboy Hanover, Shoot First.

Off: 8:11 Time: 0:26.2, 0:54.0, 1:21.3, 1:48.2. Mutuel Pool: $326,588. Temp. 74°

MUTUELS: **Final Curtain** $4.60, 3.00, 2.80; **Red Hot Yankee** $5.40, 2.80; **The Flim Flam Pan** $4.20

EXACTA (5-4) $21.20. TRIFECTA (5-4-2) $60.30. 10 CENT SUPER (5-4-2-6) $34.73. PICK 3 (10-1-5) $93.80.

FINAL CURTAIN was hustled right to the front, carved out very strong splits while unchallenged throughout, kicked out the plugs turning for home and received only one tap of the whip by Sears who was just a passenger, sprinted clear with a final quarter of 26.4 and deserved to take a bow after this dazzling mile. RED HOT YANKEE was sent to the top, yielded to the winner, sat the pocket trip throughout, had no excuses and nothing to be ashamed of while finishing second in a 1:48. 2 winning mile. THE FLIM FLAM PAN sat a three hole trip and held the rest at bay while no match to the top two. PLACEITONLUCKYDAN followed second over behind poor cover and beat the weak in the lane. VAPOR IN THE WIND made a slow first over move going to three quarters, stalled and faded. COWBOY HANOVER lagged behind the gate, got stuck fourth over at the half, tucked on the rail and tired. WESTERN TRADEMARK trailed the field and did not have a prayer. RED STAR CATCH raced third over and was empty. GRAB YOUR KEYS was parked out at the back behind cover briefly at the half before dropping back sharply. SHOOT FIRST was off the gate, sat while dull on the pylons and broke in the stretch.

b c 3 by Pro Bono Best, Lola by Artsplace

Owners: 1. Bulletproof Enterprises,Boca Raton,FL, 2. No Mercy Racing Stables,Syracuse,NY;Michael D Butler,Auburn,NY, 3. Robert F Wincowski,Clifton Park,NY, 4. Engel Stb & Rucker Stb,IL;Panhellenic Stb Corp,NY;Sheffield Stb,PA, 5. Tanah Merah Farms LLC,Springfield,IL, 6. Maryann Plano,Sacramento,CA;Dave H Haness,Sacramento,CA;Kimberly M Haness,Citrus Hgts,CA, 7. Diamond Creek Farm Llc,Paris,Ky, 8. Robert M Murphy,Surrey,BC, CA, 9. Laura Anne Raimondo,New Egypt,NJ;Sam W Demchak,Beachwood,NJ, 10. Daniel J Altmeyer,Washington,PA;Jack B Piatt II,Washington,PA;Richard B Kelson,New York,NY.

Well, he opted for Final Curtain, and that was all I needed to know. I made Final Curtain the top choice and he freaked to an amazing win, timed in 1:48⅖. The payoff wasn't great ($4.60), but the effort certainly was, and Sears had made the right choice.

On March 12, I sniffed out a driver's choice that turned me on to L A Girl in the ninth race. Yannick Gingras could have opted to go another way in this event, but he chose this mare after an encouraging start on March 5, which was his first time aboard the 4-year-old. I noted both the choice, and the improved form, in my program comment.

lue **L A GIRL(L)** — **br m 4, by Pacific Fella, Alba Fina by Mckinzie Almahurst** — 1:55.2 M1 08 40 5 8 2 $55,757
Frank Scamporino,Jr.,Monroe Twp.,NJ — 1:53.4 M1 07 38 8 5 4 $37,100
2 **Yannick Gingras (150) (0-0-0-0 .000)** — **Tr.Frank Scamporino,Jr.** — **Last 6 Sts-$5,562** 3 1:53.4 (1) **Lifetime $105,527**

	$3\text{-}5_{08}$	M1	1	fst	27^{3}	57^{2}	1.26^{2}	1.54^{3}	15000 FM	12000	7	2^{1}	$3^{2\frac{1}{4}}$	$4^{2\frac{3}{4}}$	$5^{2\frac{3}{4}}$	$2^{1\frac{3}{4}}$	28	1.55	L	10.70	GingrasY	$Jssllmxp^{1\frac{3}{4}}$,$LAGirl^{\frac{3}{4}}$	pckt,3 hole,ang,mild
	$2\text{-}27_{08}$	M1	1	fst	26^{4}	57^{4}	1.27^{4}	1.55^{4}	15000 FM	12000	9	10^{13}	$10^{\circ 8}$	$10^{\circ 6\frac{1}{4}}$	$9^{4\frac{3}{4}}$	$6^{2\frac{3}{4}}$	27^{2}	1.56^{2}	L	12.00	SearsB	$Jeeterbg^{nk}$,$BlCrkAng^{nk}$	out,little
	$2\text{-}13_{08}$	M1	1	sly	28^{2}	57^{1}	1.27	1.55^{4}	NW6500FM	13000	2	$4^{\circ 1\frac{3}{4}}$	1^{nk}	$2^{1\frac{1}{2}}$	$5^{1\frac{1}{2}}$	$6^{8\frac{1}{2}}$	30^{1}	1.57^{2}	L	9.20	PierceR	$Pntthcrwnrd^{\frac{3}{4}}$,$WstrnSwtrt^{3}$	brush,pressed,gave way
21,000	$2\text{-}6_{08}$	M1	1	gd	28^{2}	57^{2}	1.26^{1}	1.55^{1}	15000 FM	12000	6	$3^{2\frac{1}{2}}$	$4^{2\frac{1}{4}}$	5^{3}	$6^{2\frac{1}{4}}$	7^{4}	29^{1}	1.56	L	4.20	PierceR	$Marley^{nk}$,$RuthieJn^{\frac{1}{2}}$	tuck,sat,no kick
9-2	$1\text{-}18_{08}$	YR	1	fst	28^{3}	59	1.28^{1}	1.57^{1}	Opt15000M	9500	8	$8^{9\frac{3}{4}}$	$8^{8\frac{3}{4}}$	$8^{6\frac{3}{4}}$	$7^{4\frac{1}{4}}$	7^{6}	28^{4}	1.58^{2}	L	6.50	StrattonJ	$KrhpDmnd^{\frac{1}{2}}$,$DnclnThWnd^{\frac{3}{4}}$	left,took back,no shot
	$1\text{-}11_{08}$	YR	1	gd	29^{3}	59^{4}	1.27^{3}	1.57^{2}	15/20000 FM	10250	4	$5^{5\frac{1}{2}}$	$2^{\circ 1}$	$1^{\circ hd}$	2^{2}	$2^{\frac{1}{2}}$	29^{4}	1.57^{2}	L	8.80	StrattonJ	$LucilleA^{\frac{1}{2}}$,$LAGirl^{\frac{1}{2}}$	chl,blew turn 4,cm bck

RACE 9 REVIEW Wednesday, March 12, 2008

By David Brower

1 RUTHIE JANE - It might be time to give her a break from racing on the lead. Tired in last several starts. Let's see if she can sit and rally. Maybe.

2 L A GIRL - Rapidly rounding back into form and I could make a strong case for success here. This is how she did it last year. Ready now. Very usable.

3 KALLIE'S LADY - Coming off a pretty gutsy try. Grinded a long way and wasn't exactly giving way late. Loses Dube, but still has a chance at price.

4 TUSSY MUSSY - One of these nights, she might get lucky. Needs a few things to set up for her, like hot pace and live cover. It's not out of question.

5 AMY'S DREAMBOAT - Took ALL the tote action last time and did not pay off. The trip was difficult, but barn is on a roll right now. Cannot be ignored.

6 JEETERBUG - She won at 9-2 and then won at 6-1. What price tonight? I suspect a lot lower, but she is razor sharp and she will be gunning out here.

7 ALLAMERICAN HAPPY - Tough trip have cost her so far. I feel she's primed now, with a few mile track starts under her belt. Possible upsetter.

8 ROSAGATHA - A variety of excuses here. Tonight, it will be the post. She'll probably leave and it won't be easy to get by #6 early going. It's your call.

9 PARK FREE - One of the two outside longshots. Not a lot to like here.

10 JOVEALE - How's she going to win from post 10? Don't worry, she's not.

TOP CONTENDERS 2-6-5-7

L A Girl won handily, given a perfect trip by Gingras, and the price was great. She returned $10.80 and the cold exacta I selected in the program came back an astounding $48.20 with the favorite finishing second.

The angle of driver's choice pays its biggest dividends—albeit in reverse—when the choice doesn't seem to add up or make sense. If something looks funny, it usually is. Keep in mind that drivers make choices for the long haul. They try to remain loyal to the trainers they do the most business with, but they will also choose carefully when dealing with a horse that might have a future in later stakes or series races. They do not want to lose the drive behind a good horse. That is paramount in their minds. If it costs them a winner once in a while, that's the price they are willing to pay in the short run.

DRIVER CHANGES

In addition to keeping a close eye on driver's choice, I also like to watch for specific driver changes. There is no doubt that some of today's best-known drivers are very, very good at getting increased effort the first time they hop in the bike behind a horse. Also, you need to look for the reason behind a driver change. Is the trainer just looking for someone different? Did last week's driver get fired? Was the trainer prepping a horse over a few starts before naming one of the top drivers? All of these situations happen from time to time and must be taken into account. You don't want to miss the boat on a $20 winner being handled by Brian Sears for the first time.

Most trainers have go-to guys in certain instances, and it helps to mentally keep track when those situations present themselves. For example, George Brennan is nicknamed the Minister of Speed because of his uncanny knack for making a horse go faster. He can wake up a horse behind the gate. He can keep them going on the lead and sometimes he just amazes me.

Another gentleman who was always incredible at getting maximum effort out of a horse the first time he was aboard was Howard Parker, who still drives on the Pocono Downs and Tioga Downs circuit. I can't tell you how many times I would watch him win with a longshot and then peer at my program past-performance lines in disbelief. He is that good.

Following are some key trainer/driver combinations to watch for:

Ken Rucker—Dave Miller
Mark Harder—George Brennan
Rick Bilach—Dan Dube
Carmine Fusco—Tim Tetrick

Other driver names that come to mind in the first-time scenario at the Meadowlands are Ron Pierce, Yannick Gingras, Tim Tetrick, and Andy Miller. Whenever they sit behind a horse for the first time, they almost always seem to get something extra, and we all know it's that little extra that often wins photo finishes.

A perfect example of this in action came on April 11, 2008, with Focus for trainer Jim Raymer. Raymer is a tremendous trainer of trotters and wins a lot of races all over the East Coast just about the whole year long. He's equally adept with young and old horses, male or female. Now, with that said, Raymer often elects to drive a lot of his own horses, and while I don't want to insult Mr. Raymer, I feel that his strengths lie in the training aspect of the game. Take a look at the past performances of Focus going into the April 11 race.

Blue **2** **‡FOCUS(L)** — 6-1
Tim Tetrick (160) (0-0-0-0 .000)
br g 5, by S Js Photo, Beverly Crusher by Balanced Image
Trillium Racing Stable,New Holland,PA
Tr.Jim Raymer(64-10-11-12 .156) **Last 6 Sts-$22,265**

1:53.2 M1	08	23	5 2 4	$91,164	
1:55.4 PcD 5/8	07	16	2 1 1	$15,150	
5 1:53.2 (1)				Lifetime	$155,152

3-28 08	M1	‡ 1	fst	27^{2}	57^{1}	1.26^{3}	1.55	NW25000	37500	5	$4^{\circ 4}\frac{1}{4}$	$2^{\circ 1}$	2°nk	3nk	$3^{2}\frac{1}{4}$	28^{4}	1.55^{2} L	26.20	RaymerJ	SirrsDrm$1\frac{3}{4}$,RalPssbl$\frac{1}{2}$	uncovered,game try
3-14 08	M1	‡ 1	fst	27^{4}	55^{4}	1.24^{3}	1.53^{3}	NW25000	37500	4	$5^{4}\frac{1}{2}$	7^{6}	10^{8}	$9^{7}\frac{3}{4}$	5^{4}	28^{1}	1.54^{2} L	16.90	RaymerJ	JstACnMnnk,SwanImag$1\frac{1}{2}$	bad shuffle,trot
3-7 08	M1	‡ 1	sly	28^{3}	57^{2}	1.26^{2}	1.55	NW12500	26000	3	$2^{1}\frac{1}{4}$	$1\frac{3}{4}$	$1^{1}\frac{3}{4}$	$1^{3}\frac{1}{2}$	$1^{6}\frac{1}{2}$	28^{3}	1.55 L	18.10	RaymerJ	Focus$6\frac{1}{2}$,Dsprthswf1	pocket,top,romped
2-14 08	M1	‡ 1	fst	28^{2}	57^{2}	1.26^{4}	1.56	20/25000	18000	1	$3^{3}\frac{1}{2}$	2°nk	2°nk	$3^{1}\frac{1}{2}$	4^{4}	30	1.56^{4} L	10.20	RaymerJ	ClsEncntr$1\frac{1}{4}$,DrknCrwn$2\frac{1}{4}$	hard challenge,denied
1-25 08	M1	‡ 1	fst	28	57	1.26^{1}	1.55^{3}	NW12500	29000	1	$5^{7}\frac{3}{4}$	$5^{\circ 6}$	$5^{\circ 5}$	6^{7}	$5^{8}\frac{3}{4}$	30^{1}	1.57^{2} L	18.30	RaymerJ	ImAHtShthd,SlimDown$7\frac{1}{4}$	gap on rim,clogged
1-10 08	M1	‡ 1	fst	29	58^{4}	1.28^{1}	1.56^{4}	Qua		8	9^{11}	$8^{\circ 9}\frac{1}{2}$	$8^{\circ\circ 6}\frac{1}{4}$	$7^{6}\frac{3}{4}$	3^{5}	28^{2}	1.57^{4} L	nb	RaymerJ	MedVac3,BjsChink2	lag early,good late

The 5-year-old gelding was competing at a pretty high conditioned level with Raymer doing the driving. His last start was a particularly good one, especially with the tough trip he endured. When a horse has a trip like that and digs in to hold a board spot at odds of 26-1, that catches my eye. Focus was racing himself back into shape after a short layoff from November to January. Raymer had driven his gelding in his first five starts of the year, even winning one at odds of 18-1 on March 7 against a lesser conditioned field.

For this race, Raymer put up Tim Tetrick, and Tetrick is a master of getting primo speed out of a horse. He had driven Focus a few times during the prior year, but this was his first assignment behind the gelding in 2008. This was no easy spot, either! Focus was up against several rivals who were clearly in sharp form, but he enjoyed a significant inside-post advantage.

After an early move to the lead, Focus re-rallied in the stretch, squeezing through at the pylons to win by a head as the 3-2 favorite. His winning time for the mile was 1:53^{2}/$_{5}$, which bested his lifetime mark by almost two full seconds. The only problem was the price, $5, as the astute fans were all over it.

If you have a favorite driver, or one that you feel can "wake up" a horse that is currently in less than ideal form, don't ever be afraid to bet when the price is right. It's one of the few ways to come up with a live longshot, and that's the reason we're all in the game of harness handicapping. In the next chapter, contributing author Derick Giwner will illustrate another example of a simple driver change that produced some big results at Yonkers Raceway.

6

YONKERS RACEWAY

The Meadowlands isn't the only harness racetrack in the world, so in order to give a broader perspective on handicapping the Standardbreds, I felt we needed to look at a few of the others that generate decent-size handle and have a strong fan base.

"The Old Hilltop," Yonkers Raceway in Yonkers, New York, has a great history in the sport and played host to the glory days of harness racing— that era in the 1950s, 60s, and 70s when 20,000-plus fans routinely packed the grandstand on any given night. Some of the greatest Hall of Famers called Yonkers home. We all remember Stanley Dancer, Carmine Abbatiello, Buddy Gilmour, and Billy Haughton. Every once in a while, I'm still quizzed about the old Racing from Yonkers *(and* Racing from Roosevelt*) broadcasts that used to air in the New York area. Remember those shows, with Stan Bergstein, Spencer Ross, and sometimes Dave Johnson? I do. I grew up with them, and sometimes my dad and I would head into New York City to an OTB and plunk down a couple of wagers so we could go home and watch those programs at night.*

For a look at Yonkers, I solicited the help of born-and-bred New Yorker Derick Giwner. He is the editor of Harness Eye, *the only daily publication in the sport, and has been a loyal supporter of the trotter for as long as I've known him. Derick also likes to dabble in the amateur-driving aspect of the business, so he knows what to look for.*

By Derick Giwner

It is hard to be an expert in all aspects of handicapping. There are many angles, thoughts, and systems that can be used, but it is always best to focus on one or two areas. My specialty is half-mile tracks.

I have always been a less-is-more type of guy. I feel the same way about harness tracks. The half-mile oval is cozier. It allows you to view the entire race without a pair of binoculars. The sound of drivers chirping to their horses and whips striking the bike shaft at the head of the stretch can easily be heard by fans at the finish line.

Finally, let us not forget that the races are more predictable.

"Predictable" does not mean that only favorites win or that the races are easily fixed. It means that a reasonable handicapper can look at the past performances (hopefully in *Harness Eye*) and decipher how the race will shape up with some accuracy.

With the amount of movement that normally takes place over five-eighths or mile tracks, it is impossible to figure out whether your speed horse will make it to the top of the stretch with the lead or wind up shuffled to the back of the pack.

On a half-mile track these handicapping problems disappear. Horses simply do not line up on the rim at the quarter pole and play musical chairs on the lead. There is a sense of consistency on a half-mile track. You can read the program and feel confident that the race will shape up the way it reads.

Tracks such as Yonkers, Monticello, Northfield, and Freehold, to name a few of the more popular half-mile venues, require something that is basically useless on bigger ovals—trip handicapping.

If you could tell me how the horses will line up coming by the three-eighths pole at one of the tracks listed above, I would wager that I could correctly select the winner at a 75 percent clip or better.

The best way to look at trip handicapping on a half-mile track is to place each trip into one of several groups and then rank them all. A typical eight-horse field can yield eight possible trips. Those trips can be separated into four categories:

DREAM TRIPS

There are three dream trips on any half-mile track: on the lead, in the pocket, and second-over behind cover. Any sharp horse sitting one of those trips as the field enters the stretch has a much greater chance of winning than the rest of the field.

DECENT TRIPS

Following the top three trips in rank is the third-over journey, followed by a three-hole trip. Each of these trips comes in second-best to the dream trips because a horse must close more ground in the stretch to win from this spot. Sitting third-over is more advantageous than the three-hole at almost every half-mile track (except maybe Yonkers) because that horse has the option of moving wide for clearance. The trips are a bit more even at Yonkers Raceway, where the long stretch gives the horse sitting along the pylons a bit more opportunity to make up ground.

TOUGH-BUT-POSSIBLE TRIPS

Ranked sixth on the trip scale is the uncovered or first-over path. You can make a serious case for ranking this trip as high as fourth, because a sharp horse is very capable of winning this way. But winning uncovered requires a horse to produce an above-average effort, while an average effort can result in a win from the three-hole or third-over.

ONCE-IN-A-BLUE-MOON TRIPS

The final spots are fourth-over and any horse that is last (and second-to-last in a nine-horse field) on the rail. If fourth-over is described as an impossible spot, sitting last on the rail is the equivalent of trying to travel 60 miles in 30 minutes; it can be done, but as the road signs say, "Conditions Permitting."

Knowing which trips are best is one thing; figuring out which horse will obtain each trip is another animal altogether. To determine where each horse will settle in the pack, you will need to make an educated guess as to which horses will show early speed, which will be content to stay along the inside and conserve their speed for later in the mile, and which may not have early speed but are sharp enough to make an aggressive uncovered move.

Start off by circling every horse on your program that is likely to show early speed. Next, draw a square around any horse that is in dull form and seems likely to save its energy for the stretch. Finally, draw a triangle around any horse that might be likely to make an aggressive uncovered move.

The key is to figure out which of the early-speed horses will actually get to the front and which will have to settle along the rail or wind up parked on the outside the entire mile. Any race can be picked apart to serve as an example. Let's look at a race from December 15, 2008, at Monticello Raceway.

Race 9 was a $4,000 claiming event for fillies and mares. These cheaper races serve as some of the best examples because it can be difficult to know which horses are likely to "wake up" on any given day or night.

The program (as illustrated) is marked with three horses circled (numbers 3, 6, and 7), three squared (numbers 1, 2, and 8), and two with triangles (numbers 4 and 5).

MONTICELLO MONDAY, DECEMBER 15, 2008

9

PACE — **F&M $4000 CLAIMING/ALLOWANCES** — **PICK THREE RACES 9 - 11**
ONE MILE — **EXACTA & TRIFECTA WAGERING**
WARM-UP PURPLE
PURSE $2,400

Red **1** **GIVEN ME WINGS** — **b m 4, by Cole Muffler, Shes An Angel by Troublemaker** — 1:58.3 MR 08 18 2 1 3 $7,404
Georgia L Mosher,Middletown,NY — 2:04.0 Stg 07 6 1 0 1 $2,596
Jordan D. Stratton (160) (1725-357-250-225 .207) — **Tr.Ross Cohen(159-34-14-29 .214)** — **Last 6 Sts-$2,480** 4 1:58.3 Q Lifetime $10,000

	12-15^{08}MR	1 fst	30	1.01^{3}	1.30^{3}	1.59^{3}	4000 FM	2400	1	3^{3}	$4^{4\frac{1}{4}}$	$5^{7\frac{3}{4}}$	5^{12}	5^{13}	30	2.02^{1}	2.50 StrattonJo	RubyC,Clasylvry,MonltTori	
	12-4^{08} YR	1 fst	28^{4}	1.01	1.29^{4}	2.00	4000 FM	4000	6	$6^{6\frac{3}{4}}$	$6^{6\frac{1}{2}}$	6^{5}	$7^{5\frac{1}{2}}$	7^{14}	32	2.02^{4}	27.50 StrattonJ	StrmnJrdn^{nk},NShrtctzN^{1}	no rally
	11-20^{08}YR	1 fst	27^{4}	58	1.27^{3}	1.58^{2}	4000 FM	4000	3	$5^{6\frac{1}{4}}$	$6^{5\frac{1}{4}}$	$7^{6\frac{3}{4}}$	$6^{6\frac{1}{4}}$	5^{6}	30^{3}	1.59^{3}	5.10 BartlettJ	SldWthAKss$\frac{3}{4}$,StrmnJrdn$\frac{3}{4}$	boxed,ang,no rally
$5,800	11-6^{08} YR	1 gd	29	59^{3}	1.28^{2}	1.59^{2}	4000 FM	4000	5	$6^{6\frac{1}{2}}$	$5^{\circ 3\frac{3}{4}}$	$3^{\circ 3\frac{1}{2}}$	$3^{2\frac{3}{4}}$	$3^{1\frac{1}{2}}$	30^{3}	1.59^{3}	4.90 StrattonJ	ShsTrndy^{1},TrymnwBlgrss$\frac{1}{2}$	lost cover,late gain
7-2	10-30^{08}YR	1 fst	29	59^{4}	1.29^{1}	1.59	4000 FM	4000	3	$4^{5\frac{3}{4}}$	$5^{4\frac{3}{4}}$	$5^{4\frac{1}{4}}$	5^{4}	$4^{4\frac{3}{4}}$	30	2.00	8.30 GregoryJ	CammyBth^{1},TrymnwBlgrss$^{1\frac{1}{4}}$	saved,outkicked
	10-23^{08}YR	1 fst	29^{2}	1.00	1.29^{2}	1.59^{3}	4000 FM	4000	4	$4^{4\frac{1}{2}}$	$5^{4\frac{3}{4}}$	6^{4}	$5^{2\frac{3}{4}}$	$2^{2\frac{1}{4}}$	29^{4}	2.00	25.25 GregoryJ	CammyBth$^{2\frac{1}{4}}$,GvnMWngs$\frac{1}{2}$	sat,saved,ins,flew
	10-16^{08}YR	1 fst	29	59^{4}	1.28^{4}	1.58	4000 FM	4000	2	3^{3}	$3^{2\frac{3}{4}}$	4^{4}	$4^{5\frac{1}{2}}$	$3^{7\frac{1}{4}}$	29^{4}	1.59^{2}	28.25 GregoryJ	ButtonRd$^{2\frac{1}{4}}$,TrymnwBlgrss^{5}	sat,up 3rd

CAMAN(L)

James Piontek (170) (25-1-3-2 .040)

b m 10, by Camluck, Translide by Landslide
William J Piontek,Greenfield Park,NY;Donald A Appel,Thompson
Tr.James Piontek(18-1-4-4 .056) Last 6 Sts-$2,853

1:59.2 MR 08 16 2 1 4 $5,228
1:57.0 MR 07 37 2 6 3 $10,325
3 1:56.3 5/8 Lifetime $172,638

12-1508MR	1	fst	30	1.013	1.303	1.593	4000 FM	2400	2	44½	65½	710	717	719	304	2.032 L	22.00	PiontekJ	RubyC,Clasylvry,MonltTori
12-808 MR	1	fst	283	584	1.284	1.591	4000 FM	2400	3	46¼	47¼	510	616	619	321	2.03 L	3.50	MertonMi	ColChrctr,ArtsInves,BvrCrkSze
11-2408MR	1	fst	302	1.012	1.31	2.001	4000 FM	2700	3	33¼	33¼	55¼	47¼	48	294	2.014 L	*1.60	MertonMi	JfrysGirl,ColChrctr,CamlaClsc
11-1708MR	1	fst	291	593	1.293	1.591	FM5000CLOP	3300	1	11¾	11½	11½	11½	2¾	294	1.592 L	2.00	DobsonBy	Spendthmn,Caman,GreystnCr
11-1008MR	1	fst	293	1.00	1.302	1.593	NW200ps	2400	1	1no	21½	14½	18½	114	291	1.593 L	*1.05	MertonMi	Caman,Flyltalia,OdsAriel
11-308 MR	1	fst	291	1.001	1.303	1.594	4000 FM	2700	2	21½	21½	21½	32	31½	291	2.00 L	3.50	MertonMi	WestrnSmn,MonltTori,Caman
10-2708MR	1	fst	301	1.013	1.32	2.02	4000 FM	2400	7	67¾	67	6°3¼	55½	31½	293	2.021 L	60.00	MertonMi	RivrChnce,ItsDecsnT,Caman

MOONLIT TORI(L)

Michael Merton (150) (1177-153-165-176 .130)

b m 6, by Rustler Hanover, Armbro Pulse by Artsplace
Woody Hoblitzell,Destin,FL;Linda L Bushu,Miramar Beach,FL
Tr.Maureen Aldrich(163-24-16-17 .147) Last 6 Sts-$2,829

1:57.2 MR 08 38 6 7 9 $15,038
1:58.3 FID 07 34 5 2 3 $13,367
3 1:56.1 5/8 Lifetime $91,787

12-2108MR	1	sly	30	1.02	1.321	2.03	4000 FM	2400	2	33½	43½	2°1½	35¼	2dh2¾	311	2.033 L	6.00	MertonMi	TrstFndng,MonltTori dh
12-1508MR	1	fst	30	1.013	1.303	1.593	4000 FM	2400	3	1¼	21¾	46¼	49½	310	294	2.013 L	9.00	MertonMi	RubyC,Clasylvry,MonltTori
12-808 MR	1	fst	30	1.011	1.311	2.01	4000 FM	2400	4	34¼	34¼	4°5	35¾	35¼	294	2.02 L	4.50	AldrichBrJr	JuliasGrl,KatysFnle,MonltTori
11-2408MR	1	fst	29	593	1.294	2.002	4000 FM	2700	6	57½	5°7	4°3¾	34¾	44¾	304	2.012 L	4.00	AldrichBrJr	JuliasGrl,KatysFnle,ChrismrsJ
11-1008MR	1	fst	284	59	1.294	1.591	4000 FM	2700	7	78	6°6	6°3¾	79¼	59½	302	2.01 L	27.00	DobsonBy	CamlaClsc,InDireNed,BjsMyrtle
11-308 MR	1	fst	291	1.001	1.303	1.594	4000 FM	2700	5	11½	11½	11½	1½	2½	291	1.594 L	*1.80	AldrichBrJr	WestrnSmn,MonltTori,Caman
10-2708MR	1	fst	293	1.00	1.301	1.594	4000 FM	2700	1	33	3°1¾	2°¼	21	1hd	293	1.594 L	1.60	StrattonJo	MonltTori,DremArndJ,MySwetFnn

CLASSY IVORY(L)

Bruce Aldrich,Jr. (155) (1540-259-248-205 .168)

b m 4, by Ameripan Gigolo, Pancetotherhythm by The Panderosa
Cannon Bone Express Inc,Las Vegas,NV
Tr.April Aldrich(640-135-116-84 .211) Last 6 Sts-$2,031

2:01.0 MR 08 28 2 7 0 $10,346
2:00.1 MR 07 26 2 6 6 $15,122
3 2:00.1 Lifetime $35,316

12-1508MR	1	fst	30	1.013	1.303	1.593	4000 FM	2400	4	55½	3°3¼	3°3½	28	28½	30	2.011 L	33.00	AldrichBrJr	RubyC,Clasylvry,MonltTori
12-108 MR	1	gd	293	1.003	1.313	2.042	NW200ps	2400	3	33¼	3°1¾	2°1	22	12½	323	2.042 L	3.35	AldrichBrJr	Clasylvry,PltnmDrms,OldyBeGod
11-1708MR	1	fst	294	1.001	1.30	1.592	4000 FM	2700	5	611	78½	7°°6	710	48	294	2.01 L	16.00	BeckwithMa	KzBezz,OnFtsylsl,ColChrctr
11-1008MR	1	fst	29	1.00	1.303	2.022	4000 FM	2700	3	45	65¾	6°°3¾	54¾	57	322	2.034 L	4.50	AldrichBrJr	OnFtsylsl,Underthcv,LilCmsCrt
10-2708MR	1	fst	293	1.00	1.301	1.594	4000 FM	2700	4	56½	4°3¼	4°2	32½	43¼	294	2.002 L	14.00	AldrichBrJr	MonltTori,DremArndJ,MySwetFnn
10-2008MR	1	fst	292	1.00	1.293	1.594	4000 FM	2700	6	79	3°3½	3°5	716	be8dis		L	6.00	AldrichBrJr	RivrChnce,CamlaClsc,NasaBlBty
10-1408MR	1	fst	282	572	1.263	1.58	NW250ps	3300	3	55½	4°4¾	3°7¾	37¾	45¾	31	1.591 L	14.00	AldrichBrJr	MyAntMrgt,CnnSandra,KtrnaMare

RUBY C(L)

Billy Dobson (155) (308-62-43-35 .201)

b m 6, by Here's A Quarter, Rasberry Swirl by Abercrombie
Gregory C Gardner,Sheridan,MI
Tr.Todd Marciano(305-56-52-40 .184) Last 6 Sts-$2,881

1:59.0 MR 08 30 8 3 5 $12,384
2:00.4 Jac 07 17 2 4 2 $3,715
6 1:59.0 Lifetime $31,249

12-1508MR	1	fst	30	1.013	1.303	1.593	4000 FM	2400	5	67½	5°5¼	1°°3	18	18½	29	1.593 L	*1.00	DobsonBy	RubyC,Clasylvry,MonltTori
12-108 MR	1	gd	303	1.02	1.312	2.011	4000 FM	2700	5	57¼	5°6¼	4°°4¼	44½	54	294	2.02 L	4.50	DobsonBy	ButonRoad,ItsDecsnT,DwsAbby
11-1708MR	1	fst	291	592	1.292	1.59	4000 FM	2700	5	55¾	5°5½	2°1	1¾	1¾	292	1.59 L	3.15	DobsonBy	RubyC,TrstFndng,DoninaHnv
10-3108Nor	1	fst	281	583	1.284	1.593	4000 FM	1700	7	810	6°3¾	3°2	41¾	54	311	2.002 L	8.60	CasagrndaJ	CarliDey,GrantaHnv,JimsLtlWn
10-2408Nor	1	sly	284	593	1.294	2.012	NW1000FM	1500	6	56½	4°3	13	14	12¾	313	2.012 L	*.90	CasagrndaJ	RubyC,GetchSmFr,URFrntstc
10-1008Nor	1	fst	281	572	1.273	1.584	4000 FM	1700	7	713	7°7¼	54½	32	21½	303	1.59 L	9.90	CasagrndaJ	sucsbrjoy,RubyC,ClaLlyGal
10-308 Nor	1	fst	291	1.002	1.301	2.00	4000 FM	1700	6	57½	55½	2°1	2hd	43	301	2.003 L	6.70	LakeDa	Bradeen,Timwtsfrn,CandyLand

ITS DECISION TIME(L)

Gregory Merton (120) (870-159-140-113 .183)

b m 8, by Stand Forever, Directors Decision by Silent Majority
El Lobo LLC,Merrick,NY
Tr.Steven Moore(496-42-43-55 .085) Last 6 Sts-$3,573

1:57.3 Fhd 08 34 6 6 5 $19,269
1:56.0 Fhd 07 20 5 4 2 $18,877
4 1:55.0 5/8 Lifetime $125,355

12-1508MR	1	fst	30	1.013	1.303	1.593	4000 FM	2400	6	2°¼	1¾	23	39	412	304	2.02 L	4.00	MertonG	RubyC,Clasylvry,MonltTori
12-108 MR	1	gd	303	1.02	1.312	2.011	4000 FM	2700	3	22½	21¾	32¾	23	21½	292	2.012 L	8.00	HollandBr	ButonRoad,ItsDecsnT,DwsAbby
11-1708MR	1	fst	291	1.002	1.304	2.021	4000 FM	2700	6	33¼	33¼	43	45	33¼	312	2.024 L	12.00	DiBndttoK	JuliasGrl,BjsMyrtle,ItsDecsnT
11-308 MR	1	fst	284	584	1.292	2.00	4000 FM	2700	1	21½	21½	21½	22¾	12½	302	2.00 L	*.75	StrattonJo	ItsDecsnT,RivrChnce,IntmteHal
10-2708MR	1	fst	301	1.013	1.32	2.02	4000 FM	2400	6	21½	21¾	31¼	22¾	2hd	294	2.02 L	4.00	StrattonJo	RivrChnce,ItsDecsnT,Caman
10-1408MR	1	fst	291	592	1.282	1.581	4000 FM	2700	7	44¼	45½	43¾	34¼	46¼	301	1.592 L	12.00	DiBndttoK	DremArndJ,RivrChnce,PolarQuen
10-608 MR	1	fst	282	592	1.291	2.01	4000 FM	3400	4	44¾	2°1½	2°1½	2¾	3½	313	2.01 L	4.00	DiBndttoK	IntmteHal,DremArndJ,ItsDecsnT

HEART OF TRUST(L)

William Parker,Jr. (165) (1446-205-206-189 142)

b m 4, by Cole Muffler, Abacus Abby by Bret Hanover
Chris A Drongosky,Amherst,NY
Tr.Alexander Giuliani(4-0-1-1 .000) Last 6 Sts-$3,365

1:58.2 Btv 08 38 9 6 6 $21,935
1:53.4 BP1 07 33 4 5 2 $17,893
3 1:53.4 (1) Lifetime $41,433

11-2908Btv	1	gd	29	591	1.292	1.59	FM5000CLOP	4200	6	68	5°3¼	3°°2¼	42½	68¾	31	2.004 L	10.30	BoringTr	HotHpHpnn,MsLonely,CNGrey
11-2208Btv	1	gd	284	593	1.311	2.02	4000 FM	3000	5	11½	11	11	11	33	312	2.023 L	*1.05	BoringTr	Miscardle,Incidentl,HrtOfTrst
11-708 Btv	1	fst	282	1.001	1.301	1.593	4000 FM	3100	5	2°1	22	22	22	22	292	2.00 L	*.40	MorrillJiJr	MisGrveTo,HrtOfTrst,Mardi
10-1708Btv	1	fst	293	1.002	1.311	2.012	FM5000CLOP	4000	6	66	6°4¼	5°2¾	31¼	3½	293	2.012 L	9.40	DeLongJo	Blurdglng,HotHpHpnn,HrtOfTrst
10-1008Btv	1	fst	281	584	1.284	1.583	5000clFM	4000	4	55	74	7°4¼	73¾	56	301	1.594 L	8.10	AgostiT	EbonyIsle,KotonKndi,HrcneKlsy
10-308 Btv	1	fst	281	593	1.293	2.003	4000 FM	3100	6	66	5°2¾	4°3¼	42¼	1nk	302	2.003 L	1.90	AgostiT	HrtOfTrst,HrcneKlsy,CcsSmalFr
9-1908 Btv	1	fst	283	59	1.301	2.00	4000clFM	3000	5	7°6¾	8°5½	6°°2¾	51¾	31½	292	2.001 L	4.60	AgostiT	LizzBizz,Mardi,HrtOfTrst

SISTER SEZ

Kyle DiBenedetto (140) (1280-146-209-193 .114)

b m 6, by Dream Away, Another Pretty by Cam Fella
Brenda A Ohol,Lockport,NY
Tr.Brenda Ohol(83-9-12-12 .108) Last 6 Sts-$1,500

1:59.2 BR 08 18 3 1 1 $6,183
2:00.0 BR 07 32 2 0 2 $6,381
4 1:58.4 Lifetime $22,250

12-508 Btv	1	gd	303	1.02	1.322	2.022	Qua		3	34	45	47	49	312	31	2.044	nb	BoringTr	RedBullet,VendtaHal,SisterSez
11-708 Btv	1	fst	291	1.00	1.302	2.011	4000 FM	3000	8	810	85½	88¾	816	827	342	2.063	59.75	DeLongJo	SasyCasie,Blurdglng,Lafawnduh
10-2708MR	1	fst	301	1.013	1.32	2.02	4000 FM	2400	2	33	43½	53	66¼	611	313	2.041	16.00	AldrichBrJr	RivrChnce,ItsDecsnT,Caman
10-1508Btv	1	fst	301	1.023	1.324	2.022	Qua		5	44	54	57½	48	310	301	2.042	nb	AgostiT	AllDeuce,Dreamnbiu,SisterSez
10-1008Btv	1	fst	291	591	1.291	1.593	4000clFM	3000	5	65½	5°4½	88¼	814	828	342	2.051	36.25	BoringTr	Sumaturo,LadyComic,BandtsPas
10-308 Btv	1	fst	29	1.003	1.30	2.001	4000 FM	3100	1	22	22	22	34	78½	312	2.014	5.10	BoringTr	MisGrveTo,Mardi,SasyCasie
9-1908 Btv	1	fst	283	59	1.301	2.00	4000clFM	3000	6	87	74½	85	88¼	818	322	2.033	44.00	BoringTr	LizzBizz,Mardi,HrtOfTrst

PARK C.	PETE I.	STEVE M.	CONSENSUS
Ruby C	Caman	Heart Of Trust	Its Decision Time
Its Decision Time	Its Decision Time	Its Decision Time	Caman
Given Me Wings	Moonlit Tori	Moonlit Tori	Ruby C

.ECTIONS: 2-1-5

Given Me Wings has a square around her because she has only left the pylons once in her last five starts and has shown suspect form. Could she take a chance uncovered? Yes. But last week's 32-second final quarter says NO loud and clear.

Caman is in a similar situation. She paced home in a weak $32^{1}/_5$ seconds last week and has not seen the rim in over a month. There is virtually no chance that driver Jim Piontek will pull her with a forceful move.

Moonlit Tori is not your typical early-speed horse, but she did attempt to leave the previous two times she drew post 5 or better and she faces no real speed to her inside. It makes complete sense that she might leave.

Classy Ivory and **Ruby C** are clearly not going to leave, but the fact that they have been guided first-over many times in the last few weeks suggests that either of them could be on the move yet again in this event.

Its Decision Time looks like the most likely leaver in the field of eight. The 8-year-old mare has displayed at least some early speed in each of her previous five starts.

Heart Of Trust is the wild card of the field. She left strong in two of her last three starts, but those races were at a different track, with a different driver, and from better posts. She gets a circle because she could leave, but you must imagine one scenario in which she tries to leave and another where she settles in at the back of the pack.

Sister Sez has been sluggish lately and is clearly going to travel around the track in last.

On paper there are two likely situations that could develop. Moonlit Tori, Its Decision Time, and Heart Of Trust could all leave, likely leaving Heart Of Trust parked on the outside or taking a tuck along the rail. The other, possibly more likely scenario, has only Moonlit Tori and Its Decision Time flashing early zip and those two coming away first and second with the field lining up in post order behind them.

Now that we have a picture of how the field will set up at the three-eighths pole, we can start to figure out how the race will unwind. We already decided that Classy Ivory and Ruby C were likely to make aggressive moves. Since Classy Ivory has the better post position, she is looking at an uncovered trip with Ruby C following in the perfect second-over spot. Heart Of Trust seems most likely to follow third-over since Given Me Wings and Caman are stuck along the pylons in the three- and four-hole and Sister Sez is a throwout.

So, by the trip-handicapping logic stated above, Its Decision Time (on the lead), Moonlit Tori (in the pocket), and Ruby C (second-over) have the best chances of winning the race.

Now that we have decided which three horses boast the best chance of succeeding, we can make an informed judgment as to which horse is sharp enough to take home the winner's share of the purse.

I am not going to sit here and tell you that horses do not win from third-over or other positions during the race. It is simply a fact that a greater number of winners will win from the dream-trip positions.

While trip handicapping is probably the most important factor when deciphering a half-mile race, there are certainly other issues that require attention. Let's take a look at a few additional factors.

Handicapping races can be difficult and it can be easy. The majority of the time it takes a lot of hard work and research to consistently come out in the black. But sometimes the racing gods throw you a bone. You are presented with an angle that is so obvious, a price that is so juicy . . . and yet somehow everyone else is asleep at the wheel.

Picture it. Yonkers Raceway, September 18, 2008. You are standing on the apron outside the famed hilltop oval studying the program for the seventh race. It is for nonwinners of $5,000/$12,500 claiming (nonwinners of $5,000 in the last six starts or $12,500 claiming with allowances). The bookends (numbers 1 and 8) are complete throwouts, so you have to decide between horses 2 through 7. The favorite (AB Ruff Stuff) appears legitimate enough coming off a neck victory in the same class, but a closer look reveals a three-week layoff. The close second choice (Miss Thrill) has a double angle going for her—class drop and driver change. She also has some negatives going against her. She has no wins or seconds in 14 starts and is winless (0 for 18) over the last three years at Yonkers.

Rather than run down each horse, let's get to the point at hand—obvious plays and angles. Twin B Sassy is double-dropping in class from the nonwinners of $8,000/$20,000 claiming level. That alone at the healthy 9-1 mutuel should be enough to draw some interest. She also shows a winning performance line in nonwinners of $6,000 at Yonkers in July. But, there is still more to go on. "Sassy" is picking up Stephane Bouchard, who has driven her to five victories over the previous year. Some may avoid Twin B Sassy, citing that she is "off form," but she was also racing against much better from bad posts (6, 6, 8, and 7) in each of her last four starts. Her last three starts from good posts (5 or better) resulted in one third-place finish; getting shuffled out of the race by a tired leader; and a victory in nonwinners of $6,000. To go back a bit farther—and not everyone has this liberty without spending plenty of bucks on Pathway (the United States Trotting Association's database)—she had won four of her last six starts in the nonwinners of $6,000/$15,000 claiming level for this barn.

What makes Twin B Sassy such an interesting case study is the fact that she had so many angles in her favor and still went off at 9-1—although maybe I'm prejudiced, because I owned her at the time. Undoubtedly the odds were due to her 1-for-27 record for the year. But one has to consider that her performance was built almost entirely while racing up in class, or in a barn that was not having success with her. There are so many lessons to be learned from Twin B Sassy that perhaps we should list them.

1. Driver changes can be a major key regardless of the switch.
2. A drop in class will almost always produce at least some improvement.
3. Not all horses perform well for all barns.
4. A horse's record must be viewed in the context of the class in which it has been racing.
5. Knowing the backstory (more than the 8 to10 lines available in the program) is invaluable.

As the chart plainly displays, Twin B Sassy waited patiently behind cover and motored past the leaders in the stretch to win easily. Interestingly enough, another double-dropper, Twice The Pleasure, finished second at 7-1.

SEVENTH RACE: YONKERS, SEP. 18-1 Mile Pace. Non-winners of $5,000 in last 6 starts. Winners over $30,000 in 2008 not eligible. A.E.: Opt. $12,500 Clm. Alw. A.E.: 3 & 4 Year Olds that are non-winners of $18,000 lifetime. Fillies & Mares. Purse $10,000.

3-11-8YR	Twin B Sassy	S.Bouchard 7	$7^2\frac{1}{4}$	$7^{o2}\frac{1}{2}$	$5^{o1}\frac{1}{2}$	3^1	1^1	30^1	29^4	29	28^3	1.57³	D.Laterza	L 9.20
3-11-8YR	Twice The Pleasure	S.Vallee 2	$2\frac{1}{2}$	$2\frac{1}{4}$	2^{nk}	2no	$2\frac{1}{2}$	28^4	30^1	29^3	29^1	1.57⁴	A.Vallee	L 7.10
3-28-8YR	Ab Ruff Stuff	J.Bartlett 3	$4^1\frac{1}{4}$	$3^{o1}\frac{3}{4}$	4no	5^3	$3^3\frac{1}{4}$	29^2	30	29^3	28^4	1.57⁴	M.Medeiros	*1.40
3-10-9ChD	Missthrill	J.Gregory 6	$1^{o1}\frac{1}{2}$	$1^1\frac{1}{2}$	$1^1\frac{1}{4}$	$1^1\frac{1}{4}$	4^{nk}	28^3	30^1	29^3	30^1	1.58³	F.Caleca	L 1.85
3-4-1YR	Mojo Mama	G.Merton 5	$6^1\frac{1}{4}$	6no	6^3	$6^2\frac{1}{2}$	$5^3\frac{1}{2}$	30	30	29^1	29^2	1.58³	R.Merton,Jr.	27.50
3-11-9YR	Miss Chris	P.Berry 4	$5^1\frac{1}{4}$	$5^{o1}\frac{1}{4}$	$3^{o1}\frac{1}{2}$	$4^1\frac{1}{4}$	$6^1\frac{3}{4}$	29^3	30^1	28^4	30^3	1.59¹	B.Aldrich,Jr.	L 5.70
3-1-6Rk1	Molly Angel	M.Forte 8	8	8	8°	7^8	7^{17}	30^3	30	29^1	29^4	1.59³	M.Infante	71.50
3-4-5ChD	Bonnie Bennett	M.Beckwith 1	$3^1\frac{1}{4}$	4no	7no	8	8	29^1	30^3	30	33^1	2.03	C.Marino	L 23.90

Lasix: Twin B Sassy, Twice The Pleasure, Missthrill, Miss Chris, Bonnie Bennett.

Off: 9:25 Time: 0:28.3, 0:58.4, 1:28.2, 1:57.3. Temp. 66°

MUTUELS: **Twin B Sassy** $20.40, 12.60, 4.80; **Twice The Pleasure** $8.80, 4.40; **Ab Ruff Stuff** $2.30

EXACTA (7-2) $107.50. TRIPLE (7-2-3) $340.00. SUPERFECTA (7-2-3-6) $1,033.00.

PICK 3 (4-7-7) $211.00.

TWIN B SASSY was out second over turn two, followed to the final turn, swung wide, swept into the lane, exploded home. TWICE THE PLEASURE was fast to the top, yielded, sat pocket and closed well as the winner cruised home. AB RUFF STUFF pulled to the half, tucked in front of a gapper, sat in, closed mildly. MISSTHRILL was on the lead to the quarter, set a good clip and gave way turning home. MOJO MAMA chased third over with little. MISS CHRIS came uncovered with mild pace but was done in the final turn. MOLLY ANGEL had no rally. BONNIE BENNETT gave way badly.

b m 5 by Bettor's Delight, Stryper by Artsplace

Claiming Prices: 1. , 2. , 3. $15,000, 4. , 5. , 6. $18,125, 7. , 8. .

Owners: 1. All Business LLC,Levittown,NY, 2. Shaun F Vallee,Jackson,NJ, 3. Robert W Sumner,Windsor,CT;Anthony C Scussel,Enfield,CT;Anthony C Annunziato Jr,Dix Hi,NY, 4. John F Lyddy,Yonkers,NY, 5. Danbry Racing Inc,Allentown,NJ, 6. Mary Ellen Abbot,Circleville,NY, 7. Praim Harrinauth,Jersey City,NJ, 8. Daniel L & Michael Markowitz,Mountain Lakes,NJ;Vincent Fusco Jr,Manalapan,NJ.

The Twin B Sassy situation is a perfect example of the differences between handicapping and wagering on a half-mile track versus a larger oval. If the same eight-horse field that went behind the gate at Yonkers had raced at the Meadowlands instead, there is little doubt that the odds would have been different. While no one wants to start from the outside at any track, the 8 hole at Yonkers wins at half the rate that the 10 hole wins at the Meadowlands (6.9 percent to 3.3 percent, in 2008), and the 7 hole is not that much better.

I touched on the driver-change angle in the Twin B Sassy example above, but from time to time an obvious driver change jumps off the page and yet is ignored by the betting public. October 30, 2008, at Yonkers Raceway presented such an example.

Trainer Ron Abbott elected to use catch-driver Greg Grismore on his 5-year-old pacing mare Koko In Paris when she competed in a nonwinners of $2,000 event that night. She was not the sharpest horse in the race, but let's face it, Abbott does not win many races as a driver, and that makes her form hard to judge.

Sometimes you have to use a bit of blind faith and hope that the new driver can lift a horse to new heights. A good rule of thumb is that a positive driver change can add one to two seconds to a horse's final time.

Faith is easier to exhibit when the horse you are backing goes off at 17-1, as did Koko In Paris on that night. I would always demand a good price on the driver-change angle if the horse is not already displaying a clear pattern of good form.

As it turns out, Grismore did lift Koko In Paris to new heights. In fact he improved her recent final times by nearly two seconds and won the race (despite a first-over trip) in 1:57 2/5.

FOURTH RACE: YONKERS, OCT. 30-1 Mile Pace. Non-winners of $2,000 in last 6 starts. Winners over $17,500 in 2008 not eligible. AE: Opt. $5,000 Clm. Alw. Fillies & Mares. Purse $5,000.

10-17-2Fhd	Koko In Paris	G.Grismore 6	$6^{1\frac{1}{2}}$	$4^{\circ\frac{3}{4}}$	$2^{\circ1\frac{1}{4}}$	$2^{1\frac{1}{4}}$	$1^{\frac{1}{2}}$	29^{2}	30	28^{4}	29^{1}	1.57^{2}	R.Abbott	L 17.70
10-23-1YR	Polly S Turr	J.Stratton 4	$1^{\circ1\frac{1}{4}}$	$1^{1\frac{1}{4}}$	1^{nk}	1^{nk}	$2^{\frac{1}{2}}$	28^{1}	30^{3}	29^{2}	29^{1}	1.57^{2}	D.Stratton	L *1.55
10-23-6Fhd	Ellen Hanover	P.Berry 2	$2^{1\frac{1}{4}}$	$2^{1\frac{1}{4}}$	3^{nk}	3^{1}	$3^{1\frac{3}{4}}$	28^{2}	30^{3}	29^{2}	29^{1}	1.57^{3}	J.Czermann,Jr.	L 3.20
10-23-1YR	Button Road	J.Bartlett 7	$7^{1\frac{1}{2}}$	$6^{\circ\frac{3}{4}}$	$4^{\circ1\frac{1}{4}}$	$4^{\frac{1}{2}}$	4^{nk}	29^{4}	29^{4}	29	29^{2}	1.58	H.Rohr	L 3.20
10-2-1YR	Late Rose	J.Baggitt,Jr. 5	$4^{1\frac{1}{2}}$	$5^{\frac{1}{2}}$	7^{2}	$7^{1\frac{3}{4}}$	$5^{1\frac{1}{2}}$	29	30^{3}	29^{3}	28^{4}	1.58	Ri.Jones	L 8.10
10-20-10MR	Switch Lanes Mac	S.Bouchard 8	8	8°	$6^{\circ1\frac{1}{2}}$	$6^{\frac{1}{2}}$	6^{nk}	30	29^{4}	29	29^{2}	1.58^{1}	D.Laterza	L 47.75
10-23-1YR	Charge Off	J.Gregory 1	$3^{1\frac{1}{4}}$	$3^{\frac{1}{2}}$	5^{nk}	5^{1}	7^{2}	28^{3}	30^{3}	29^{3}	29^{3}	1.58^{2}	B.Aldrich,Jr.	17.20
10-16-1YR	Wishwell Dreamgirl	M.Forte 3	$5^{1\frac{1}{4}}$	$7^{\frac{1}{2}}$	8	8	8	29^{1}	30^{3}	29^{4}	29^{1}	1.58^{4}	R.Cohen	7.50

Lasix: Koko In Paris, Polly S Turr, Ellen Hanover, Button Road, Late Rose, Switch Lanes Mac.

Off: 8:33 Time: 0:28.1, 0:58.4, 1:28.1, 1:57.2. Temp. 44°

MUTUELS: **Koko In Paris** $37.40, 17.20, 14.80; **Polly S Turr** $3.70, 3.20; **Ellen Hanover** $3.80

EXACTA (6-4) $132.00. TRIPLE (6-4-2) $678.00. PICK 3 (6-8-6) $1,142.00.

KOKO IN PARIS pulled uncovered to the half, rallied to the leader, challenged in the final turn, kept coming in the lane despite a bad bobble nearing the wire, righted and was all out. POLLY S TURR grabbed the top off turn one, set the pace under the winner's pressure, could not stall the bid but held the rest. ELLEN HANOVER took the top turn one, yielded, sat pocket with aim on the leader but could not dent her margin when needed. BUTTON ROAD had the winner's cover second over, failed to step it up. LATE ROSE tucked off turn one, sat in and closed evenly. SWITCH LANES MAC raced third over and faltered. CHARGE OFF sat three-holed and tired. WISHWELL DREAMGIRL had no rally.

b m 5 by Dream Away, Koko Lobell by Slapstick

Claiming Prices: 1. , 2. $6,000, 3. , 4. $7,250, 5. $6,000, 6. $7,250, 7. $6,000, 8. $7,250.

Owners: 1. David A Nielsen,Pittstown,NJ, 2. Pacer Enterprises, Inc,Sarasota,FL, 3. Frederick H & Anita C Fialkow,Wellington,FL, 4. Marc J Reynolds,Hermon,ME, 5. Troy Stables,Columbus,NJ, 6. Dennis A Laterza,Huntington,NY, 7. Abc Melissa Stables,Monticello,NY, 8. Ronald L Cohen,Woodmere,NY.

Sometimes history repeats itself, and that is what makes Koko In Paris an interesting example for this book.

Fast-forward six weeks to December 11 at Yonkers. Koko In Paris was back, this time in a nonwinners of $4,000 race. She had displayed her usual nonexistent form in two attempts versus better with Abbott in the sulky. But tonight she was facing a dull group and Grismore was back in the bike.

Her final time was an uninspiring 2:00 4/5 as she crossed the wire on a rainy night—that is, unless you bet her at nearly 8-1. That's right, six weeks apart, Koko In Paris got the same positive driver change and won with the public somehow still in the dark.

Situations like the Koko In Paris driver changes or the Twin B Sassy class-dropper angle occur all the time. Too often, handicappers spend seconds trying to decipher a race instead of minutes. Take your time to figure out how each race will unfold. Look over the races for horses dropping in class, for driver changes, for trainer changes, and anything else that could alter the performance of each horse.

7

NORTHFIELD PARK

Nowhere in North America do they have more fervent harness-racing fans than in the state of Ohio. In the introduction to this book, I talked about the Little Brown Jug, which is held in Delaware, Ohio, on the third Thursday of September, and how important that event is to harness racing. Fifty thousand people show up at the fairgrounds for Jug Day, and they all love their harness horses.

Northfield Park, "the Home of the Flying Turns," is about 15 minutes from downtown Cleveland and has been racing since 1957. Even though Ohio is not one of the states that allows slot machines at its racetracks, Northfield Park continues to offer a great product and some very bettable races.

At Northfield, the racing action itself is usually hot and heavy for a half-mile track. It's more like auto racing, because there is always movement at every point in a race. Northfield also boasts having been the birthplace for some great careers. Dave Miller is an Ohio native and raced at Northfield for many years. Greg Grismore plied his craft there and has now fit in nicely at Yonkers Raceway on the East Coast. Even the great Walter Case battled his way to driving titles over Northfield's famed strip. Currently, a young driver named Matt Kakaley seems to have a great career ahead of him.

To give you a clue on what happens around those flying turns, contributing author Keith Gisser steps in. "The Giss" serves as the publicity director for the track, on-air handicapper, and has produced a book of his own, illustrating the great history of Northfield Park.

By Keith Gisser

When I was asked to put together a chapter on handicapping Northfield Park, I was afraid I would repeat a lot of what has already been written about half-mile tracks—how the twice-arounds favor inside posts and horses with good gate speed. But the more I thought about it, the more I realized that Northfield is not like a lot of half-milers. So, let's take a look at some of the keys that make Northfield a track that still gets a great deal of play (with decent-size pools to wager into) and still provides good value.

DRIVER ANGLES

Over the years, Northfield's driver colony has always been regarded as being very aggressive, and that goes back to the mid-1970s and the likes of Hall of Famer Lew Williams, Mel Turcotte, and Don Irvine Jr. Williams was one of the drivers to make the quarter move, and through-out the years, the drivers there have been known for that style. In the past 10 to 12 years, every driving champ at Northfield—Jim Pantaleano, Ray Fisher Jr., Dave Hawk, Ken Holliday, Walter Case Jr., Brett Miller, Greg Grismore, and Aaron Merriman—has been highly aggressive. And while that serves them well in negating the disadvantage of an outside post, it also creates a problem. Half-mile driving requires more decision-making than driving on a five-eighths-mile or large track (seven-eighths of a mile and one mile are not much different in my eyes). And, an aggressive driver is more likely to make glaring mistakes than a patient one. That opens up a lot of opportunities for the patient drivers. I don't mean that as a knock, just as a handicapping angle.

If you look at the current full-time driving colony at "the Home of the Flying Turns," I would consider Aaron Merriman, Josh Kash, and J. D. Wengerd to be very aggressive drivers. Seasonal participants Andy Shetler and Elliott Deaton also fall into that category. Matt Kakaley, Ryan Stahl, Wyatt Irvine, and Kurt Sugg are more patient. This "driver-style" angle is often overlooked when assessing a horse's chances at Northfield Park.

The lateral, or "fresh set of hands," driver change is an angle that tends to be ignored at many tracks, but that is very important to consider, especially at Northfield. If a horse has been racing poorly for a regular driver (my definition of "regular" is the same driver for four or more starts) and he gets a change to a driver with similar stats, he will often improve his form in the first start, even if the new driver's numbers are slightly lower than the previous driver's. Similarly, it seems that Northfield horses that have been racing poorly for aggressive drivers often do better with a switch to a patient driver, even if that driver's stats are not quite as good. The reverse is also often true.

So, do not automatically dismiss a speed horse that has a bad post at Northfield. If he gets an aggressive driver, that horse may fire out, get the top, and then get covered up on the retake for a perfect two-hole trip. And don't automatically pitch a horse because of what may appear on the surface to be a negative driver change.

POST POSITION

Another reason outside horses can have success leaving aggressively at Northfield is the structure of the track itself. Although the turns are not as highly banked as they once were, the banking allows outside horses to maintain their speed better than outside horses on a flatter track could.

So, the conventional wisdom is that the inside posts are the best on a half-mile track, and while post 1 is traditionally the most successful, both for wins and on-the-board finishes at Northfield, the generalization can be a dangerous one. Most handicappers do not separate the win and on-the-board ratios, but I think it is important, depending on what type of bettor you are. If you bet a lot of exactas and trifectas, win percentage may not be as important as on-the-board percentage. I am primarily a win bettor, so that stat is more important to me.

In 2009, as of mid-March, posts 1 and 2 at Northfield had nearly equal win percentages, with post positions 3 and 4 just behind, and all four scoring at between 15.2 and 16.8 percent. That may bear out the inside-is-best theory, but over the past five years, posts 4 and 5 just behind the rail have actually been the most effective posts for winners. It will be interesting to see if this bias returns to the historical situation, or if we are seeing a change in post-position dynamics.

As we look at on-the-board percentages, posts 4 and 5 are both ahead of post 3, while post 9 (the second tier or trailer) is just behind post 3, despite being well behind the inside five posts in win-and-place stats. The 9 horse, of course, has an inside-post draw, meaning he does not need to do much work to be forward early and he does not need to do much work from there to be third on a trifecta ticket. I rarely leave the 9 horse off one of my rare trifecta plays at Northfield, simply because even an inferior animal with a superior (in this case, easy) trip can help to cash a ticket.

The bottom line is that stats are provided. Analyze them. Regardless of what methodology you use, the information is there for you. But sometimes all handicappers get far too concerned with the numbers. They are only as good as what we do with them.

PURSES, CLASS, AND CONDITIONS

As of March 2009, Northfield's purses had dropped over the last six months, but the racing remained pretty competitive. The horsemen there work exceptionally hard to be successful, but the change in purses also changed some of the classes, and while horsemen are notorious for not being able to read condition sheets, it is critical that handicappers learn how to read them—especially when exceptions are made to get horses into races.

The normal condition sheet at Northfield is easy to read. Conditions work up from nonwinners of $600 over the last five starts (the absolute bottom) to nonwinners of $200, $250, $300, $350, and $400 per start. Each of these classes generally allows an also-eligible condition of nonwinners "the same amount per start in the last five," with an earnings cap (for example, NW$1,000L5 who are nonwinners of $15,000 in 2008-09 would be an also-eligible condition with NW$200PS). We have a maiden claimer ($5,000 tag), a nonwinners-of-two or $6,000 conditioned/claimer ($7,500 tag), and a NW3 or $15,000 ($10,000 tag). Conditioned claimers get full allowances. We often race NW2, but NW4, 6, 8, or 10 PM (parimutuel races, as opposed to nonwagering events at fairs) are usually combined with conditioned races. We offer a $3,000 claimer (often divided by winner over or under $1,000 last five), and then $4,000, $5,000, $6,000, $7,000, and $8,000 claimers, always unrestricted. We also have an open class.

It is an unfortunate commentary on the state of racing in Ohio, where there are no subsidized purses from expanded wagering, that Northfield has had to raise the conditioned/claiming tags from $4,000, $6,000, and $8,000 just to protect our horsemen from out-of-state poachers. They are the same horses racing for the same purses, but do not be confused when you handicap. It is also a shame that we can no longer fill $10,000 or $15,000 claimers, but until the bureaucrats in Columbus bring the Buckeye State into the 21st century, that is unlikely to change.

The most important to thing to remember when betting claimers is that maiden claimers are maiden claimers, whatever the tag. Similarly, minimum claimers are minimum claimers nearly everywhere. The maiden claimers at the Meadows carry an $8,000 tag, yet they have not proven to be any better than Northfield's maiden claimers with the $5,000 tag. Similarly, $5,000 claimers at the Meadows, $4,000 claimers from Balmoral/Maywood, and $7,500 claimers from Dover are not dropping in class when they race in $3,000 claimers at Northfield. If they have not been competitive in the bottom claiming class at the previous track, they will probably not be competitive at Northfield, either. It is a fact that is often ignored, and an angle I have often been able to exploit.

On paper, it would appear that a $3,000 claimer with a $2,000 purse is a lower-class race than a NW$250PS with a $2,400 purse. It would also seem that a $4,000 claimer, which is often combined with the NW$250PS race due to its $2,400 purse, would be equal to the conditioned event. At Northfield, nothing could be farther from the truth.

Here is the truth, at least the truth according to Northfield Park.

Claimers are generally sharper than the conditioned horses racing for equivalent purses. In other words, $3,000 claimers are generally going to be in better form and more likely to win than NW$200PS horses, even though they may race in the same race (due to our horse population, we often have to combine the claimers and conditioners).

As horses move up the ladder, the difference decreases, and by the time we get to the NW$400PS and $8,000 claimers, we have to look closely at also-eligible conditions to determine which race is tougher. That is because with multiple divisions of NW$400PS, there can be a big difference in the caliber of horses. Check the also-eligible conditions. We may see NW$4,000L5 in one split, drawing outside, while in another we may see NW$3,000L5, drawing in with the NW$400 per start. Obviously, the first example features tougher horses, but it may not be reflected in the charted line. Check the results on the Internet or in the backs of programs and keep them for reference, if you do not have Web access. Be very careful when a race is opened up for a nonwinner of a certain amount of money lifetime. This horse usually is way over the earnings cap, but may not quite be ready to race against the open pacers. He probably won't be a value, but probably will overlay the field.

Opening up classes to fill fields is a controversial topic with horsemen at some tracks, but at Northfield it is pretty common, and often necessary. One of the best angles at the track is to identify which horses are eligible due to a change in the condition of a race (for instance, making it nonwinners of $260 per start instead of $250 per start) or by noticing a change in the earnings cap. These are horses that would not be eligible otherwise, and that usually makes them good plays, assuming a good draw and driver. In the spring, when horses (and smart horsemen) can use either current-year or combined earnings, it can be a bit tougher to figure out, but if you take the time, you can often find some good values.

Personally, I find this to be most valuable when an earnings cap is increased—in other words, the horse has won his way out of the condition, but is allowed back in because of an increase in the earnings cap. It is regularly seen with nonwinners of two and the $10,000 conditioned/claimer at this track. When a per-start cap is raised, it is just as likely to allow a horse in bad form to drop down as to keep a sharp horse in class. So, again, read the past performances; it should be pretty simple to figure out.

Due to its relatively hard track surface, Northfield is not a colt-training mecca. We sometimes have problems filling races for inexperienced horses. One class that we often see opened up in winter and early spring, before the young horses are racing in large numbers, is nonwinners of a race lifetime, which may become nonwinners of a race in the previous year (or calendar year). This can be a tricky class, one of the hardest to handicap. On one hand, young horses have the license to step up and are racing against horses that are in miserable form; on the other, older, experienced horses still usually beat young horses. This is one class that must really be looked at on a case-by-case basis. If you have a couple of youngsters who have done good work, play them. But don't just assume that the younger horses are automatically better.

When classes are combined (as compared to being opened up to fill the field), the horses eligible to the lower class are typically assigned inside, while those eligible to the higher class draw for outside positions. The horse that draws farthest inside of the higher-class entrants gains a big advantage and often is an overlay. Also, as you handicap, remember that the higher-class competitors who have been in the class for a while are actually getting class relief, while a horse that won its way out the previous week gets a break by only facing a partial group of tougher horses.

A very important angle, especially during Northfield's five-day-a-week racing schedule (typically January, February, November, and December each year), is the eligible-at-time-of-entry angle. Few tracks have this situation on a regular basis, but it is prevalent at the Route 8 oval. During the five-day season, mare races are typically used on Tuesdays and Fridays, with Friday races drawn on Tuesday morning and Tuesday races drawn Friday morning. So, a horse could be in to go Tuesday night and be re-entered in the same class on Friday. The horse can win the Tuesday race, meaning she is no longer eligible to the class, but she is permitted to race as "eligible at time of entry." It often happens when a horse is dropping in class, since the trainer wants to take advantage of the softer competition. "ETE" horses, especially at low levels like NW$600L5 and NW$200PS, are almost must-plays. One note: As always, read the past performances. Sometimes, a horse can drop out of a condition—for instance, $3,000 claimers winners over $1,000 last five—and we still must denote that horse as eligible at time of entry, so do not wager blindly.

A FINAL NOTE

One last minor, but very important, factor in wagering at Northfield Park is the "drag." This is the interval between the listed post time and the moment the race actually goes off. While management has taken a great deal of grief for the policy of delaying off times by several minutes, the facts are simple. People are natural procrastinators, and we do not want anyone to get shut out. The vast majority of money wagered on any race is wagered at the last minute, whether on-track or at a remote location, so by creating an appearance of urgency, handle is increased. In the long run, this helps everyone—gamblers, who get bigger pools to wager into; horsemen, who see the purse pool maintained, if not increased; and yes, the track operators, who also make a few extra bucks.

So hopefully you have picked up a few angles that will help you specifically with Northfield Park wagering and handicapping. Many of them have some significance at other tracks. Some don't, but regardless, being aware of them should help. Now, go cash!

SPOTTING STRENGTH:
KEY RACES AND SHIPPERS

KEY RACES

When you follow a particular track closely and watch the races just about every night, you get a feel for each of the conditions that are raced. One of my favorite angles is to find key races that will likely produce next-out winners. Sometimes you watch a race and just know that it was strong. It happens all the time. Either the race was extraordinarily fast, or there were some higher-quality horses in it that were dropping in class. Not every $15,000 claimer is created equal, and the same can be said for just about every class level. It's especially important in races for younger horses, like nonwinners of two or three. The gulf between those levels is large, and learning to recognize which races were strong, and which ones were not, is paramount to one's success.

The key then is to follow up on the horses that come out of key races. Many times they are overlooked, because their performance in that key race was incorrectly deemed sub-par. When you can find a horse that faced a key good field one week, and then meets an average field in a subsequent race, you are on the right track to finding winners.

My first example of such an instance happened at the Meadowlands on April 9, 2008, in the sixth race with Burl Hanover.

Blue **BURL HANOVER** — b g 3, by Dragon Again, Bet Me Hanover by Matts Scooter — 1:53.0 ChD 5/8 — 08 25 4 2 4 $46,84

Brian S Gordon,NJ;Stephen Gordon,NY;4 West Group LLC,NJ — 1:59.3 Lx1 Q — 07 3 0 0 0

2 David Miller (167) (0-0-0-0 .000) — Tr.Noel Daley — Last 6 Sts-$1,625 — 3 1:53.0 5/8 — Lifetime $46,84

	4-2$_{08}$	M1	1	fst	27^2	56^1	1.25^2	1.52^3	NW1 3YO	12500	1	$3^{1\frac{3}{4}}$	$3^{3\frac{1}{4}}$	5^3	5^3	$4^{3\frac{3}{4}}$	27^2	1.53^2	4.20	VandrkmpM	BlueClaw^1,DaxHanvr$^{1\frac{1}{4}}$	3 hole,ang,mild lat
	3-20$_{08}$	M1	1	fst	28	58	1.29^4	1.57^1	NW1 3YO	12500	7	$2^{\circ 1\frac{1}{2}}$	$2^{1\frac{1}{2}}$	$4^{1\frac{1}{2}}$	6^1	5^2	27^3	1.57^3	10.10	VandrkmpM	FunFiest$^{1\frac{1}{4}}$,Fissato^{nk}	top,pkt,traff,pac
	3-6$_{08}$	M1	1	fst	29^1	57^1	1.27^3	1.55^1	Qua		3	$6^{6\frac{3}{4}}$	$6^{8\frac{1}{4}}$	$7^{4\frac{1}{4}}$	$6^{6\frac{1}{2}}$	$4^{6\frac{1}{4}}$	28	1.56^2	nb	VandrkmpM	AllDRspct$^{2\frac{1}{2}}$,MysnDylnN$^{\frac{3}{4}}$	gapped on cones,even
	2-28$_{08}$	M1	1	fst	28^2	59^3	1.29^2	1.57^2	Qua 3YO		2	$4^{5\frac{1}{2}}$	5^6	$5^{3\frac{3}{4}}$	$7^{9\frac{1}{2}}$	4^8	28^4	1.59	nb	VandrkmpM	FarTooLd$^{4\frac{3}{4}}$,ALttlCrzy^3	shuff,found seam lat
7-2	9-17$_{07}$	Lx1	1	fst	28^4	56^3	1.25	1.52^4	SIMpsON 2C	12400	8	$8^{8\frac{3}{4}}$	8^{11}	$8^{5\frac{3}{4}}$	7^6	7^{12}	29	1.55^1	124.30	JohnsonBr	ItsThtTme,MCA,Unopposed	
	9-10$_{07}$	Lx1	1	fst	28	56^3	1.25^2	1.53^3	2YOCG EC	6000	10	$1^{\circ hd}$	$2^{1\frac{1}{2}}$	$6^{5\frac{1}{4}}$	$7^{3\frac{1}{2}}$	9^{12}	29^3	1.56	7.30	JohnsonBr	LivngltUp,GodesJstn,OneFlsMv	

At first glance, Burl Hanover didn't look any better than the other nine maidens he was facing that night, but with a little deeper analysis, I can give you four solid reasons why he was a great bet.

First, there was the driver-change angle. Mike Vanderkemp is an assistant to trainer Noel Daley and also does a lot of driving. He had driven Burl Hanover in his first two starts off the layoff. One race showed speed and one showed a rail ride with an apparent even finish. In reality, however, both those efforts were much stronger than they appeared.

Dave Miller was named to drive on April 9, and that was an immediate sign of positive intent.

Another factor in the colt's favor was the barn's tendency to race their horses back into shape. Daley's horses almost always improve with a start or two under their belt.

Third, if you watched Burl Hanover on March 20, you'd know that he was completely blocked through the stretch and appeared to be overloaded with pace. Now, unless you take your own notes, or purchased a *Harness Eye* with chart comments, you probably wouldn't know that.

Last, the race that Burl Hanover came out of on April 2 was an extremely high-quality race for a maiden event. The winner, Blue Claw, was coming out of a sensational qualifier that I mentioned in Chapter 3. The field Burl Hanover faced on April 9 didn't have quite the same power, so this was definitely a key play with a chance at some decent betting value.

In the end, Burl Hanover attacked uncovered under Dave Miller and drew away to his maiden-breaking win, but the return was only $5.80, so we didn't get rich on that one. With a little imagination, though, you could have easily hit an exacta, a trifecta, or keyed Burl Hanover in the first leg of the nightly guaranteed pick four.

Another example of a horse coming out of a key race was Im Warning U in the first on May 9.

In her prior start on April 25, Im Warning U found the winner's circle with a giant rally for Tim Tetrick at odds of almost 5-1. In that win, she overcame a difficult post (8) and beat a mare by the name of Parkontheroad by a nose. Parkontheroad followed up this effort with a sensational win the week after in lifetime-best time; therefore, we have another key race.

d	**IM WARNING U**									**br m 5, by As Promised, Tsunami Warning by Scruffy Hanover**									**1:50.3 M1**		**08 31 5 5 5**	**$120,352**
										Steve W. Calhoun,Chatham,ON,CA									**1:53.4 NP 5/8**		**07 21 2 5 4**	**$86,288**
	Tim Tetrick (160) (0-0-0-0 .000)									**Tr.Casie Coleman**								**Last 6 Sts-$25,336**	**5 1:50.3 (1)**		**Lifetime**	**$252,008**
	$4\text{-}25_{08}$	M1	1	fst	28^{2}	55^{3}	1.24^{1}	1.51^{3}	Opt50000M	29500	8	$7^{9\frac{1}{2}}$	$7^{\circ 7\frac{1}{2}}$	$6^{\circ\circ 3\frac{1}{4}}$	$4^{1\frac{1}{2}}$	1no	26^{4}	1.51^{3}	4.80 TetrickTi	$ImWrnngU^{no}$,$Prknthrd^{3}$		3rd over,wide,just up
	$4\text{-}18_{08}$	M1	1	fst	27^{4}	55	1.24	1.51^{3}	Opt50000M	29500	5	7^{10}	$7^{\circ 9\frac{1}{2}}$	$7^{\circ 4\frac{3}{4}}$	$6^{2\frac{3}{4}}$	$3^{3\frac{1}{4}}$	27^{1}	1.52^{1}	10.70 TetrickTi	$Postmark^{1\frac{1}{4}}$,$PenBbbls^{2}$		dull cover,angled,mild
	$4\text{-}11_{08}$	Wbn $\frac{7}{8}$	1	fst	26^{1}	55^{4}	1.24^{4}	1.52^{4}	NW10000FM	16660	7	4	4	6°	6^{3}	$3^{2\frac{1}{2}}$		1.53^{1}	5.30 McDonaldMa	MnhtnKln,Tricky		tuck,3rd over,game
000	$4\text{-}4_{08}$	Wbn $\frac{7}{8}$	1	fst	26^{3}	55^{2}	1.24^{1}	1.53	F-NW11500L	16830	3	$3^{3\frac{1}{2}}$	$3^{3\frac{1}{2}}$	$4^{3\frac{1}{4}}$	$4^{2\frac{1}{4}}$	2^{nk}	28^{1}	1.53	6.90 McDonaldMa	LadyDM,ImWrnngU		tucked,aim,game try
1	$3\text{-}28_{08}$	FlD	1	fst	30^{1}	1.00^{4}	1.29^{1}	1.57^{4}	F-NA600psC	10486	5	$5^{5\frac{1}{2}}$	5^{5}	$5^{\circ\circ 4}$	5^{4}	4^{3}	28^{2}	1.58^{2}	2.40 CoulterR	FastDesre,JosPchPie,Wanhcklgi		
	$3\text{-}14_{08}$	Wbn $\frac{7}{8}$	1	fst	26^{2}	54^{4}	1.23^{2}	1.52^{3}	F-NW12000L	18180	scr	sk				scr						scratched-sick

Im Warning U received a week off and showed up with post 1 on May 9, so not only was she coming out of a key race, but she was also getting post relief. Needless to say, this was a very attractive proposition and the mare responded with a victory that night, returning a healthy $6.60 to her backers. It's not always that easy, but with some due diligence, you can come up with winners like this.

My last example of a key race will deal with Omen Hanover from July 4, and if you were paying attention to some of her previous races, there were ample signs that she was soon to visit the winner's circle.

rple	**OMEN HANOVER(L)**									**b m 4, by Western Hanover, Ooh's 'n Aah's by Albert Albert**									**1:51.0 M1**		**08 41 8 11 5**	**$217,865**
										Kdm Stables Corp,Farmingdale,NY									**1:52.2 PcD 5/8**		**07 20 5 3 2**	**$108,402**
9	**Yannick Gingras (150) (0-0-0-0 .000)**									**Tr.Eric Abbatiello(25-2-2-4 .080)**								**Last 6 Sts-$16,515**	**4 1:51.0 (1)**		**Lifetime**	**$393,499**
	$6\text{-}27_{08}$	M1	1	fst	26^{2}	53^{4}	1.22^{1}	1.51	NW16000FM	29500	7	$3^{\circ 2\frac{1}{4}}$	$1^{1\frac{1}{4}}$	1^{nk}	$1^{1\frac{3}{4}}$	$4^{1\frac{1}{2}}$	29	1.51^{1} L	6.80 GingrasY	$MarthMxn^{\frac{3}{4}}$,$Nrthwstrn^{\frac{1}{2}}$		used hard,duel,game
	$6\text{-}20_{08}$	M1	1	fst	27	54^{3}	1.22^{3}	1.50	NW15000FM	29500	4	$2^{\frac{1}{2}}$	$3^{2\frac{3}{4}}$	$6^{4\frac{3}{4}}$	$7^{5\frac{1}{2}}$	$2^{3\frac{1}{4}}$	27	1.50^{3} L	33.30 GingrasY	$MarthMxn^{3\frac{1}{4}}$,$OmenHnvr^{nk}$		top,shffld,split,pace
	$6\text{-}13_{08}$	YR	1	fst	28^{1}	57	1.26	1.55^{1}	Prf Hcp FM	22000	7	$3^{1\frac{1}{4}}$	$4^{2\frac{1}{2}}$	$4^{2\frac{1}{2}}$	$3^{2\frac{1}{2}}$	$3^{\frac{1}{2}}$	28^{4}	1.55^{1} L	2.45 AbbtielloE	$LttlMschvs^{no}$,$OrGrlsChncN^{\frac{1}{2}}$		tuck,shuffled,gd rally
	$6\text{-}7_{08}$	YR	1	fst	27	56^{3}	1.24^{3}	1.53^{3}	Open Hcp FM	30000	6	$6^{8\frac{1}{4}}$	$5^{\circ\circ 3}$	$5^{\circ 4\frac{3}{4}}$	$5^{5\frac{3}{4}}$	$5^{5\frac{1}{4}}$	29	1.54^{3} L	12.80 AbbtielloE	$Benear^{1\frac{3}{4}}$,$MssGlvntrA^{1\frac{3}{4}}$		bothrd,wide,cvr,wknd
3-1	$5\text{-}30_{08}$	YR	1	fst	27^{3}	57^{4}	1.26^{3}	1.55^{4}	Prf Hcp FM	22000	7	$5^{5\frac{3}{4}}$	$6^{\circ 4\frac{1}{2}}$	$6^{\circ 3\frac{1}{4}}$	$5^{1\frac{1}{2}}$	$3^{\frac{1}{2}}$	28^{3}	1.55^{4} L	3.50 AbbtielloE	$LauraLnN^{no}$,$BrckyrdTrbl^{\frac{1}{2}}$		3rd over,good rally
	$5\text{-}12_{08}$	ChD $\frac{5}{8}$	1	sly	27^{3}	56^{2}	1.25	1.54^{4}	NW27500L6F	30000	2	4^{2}	$2^{\circ 1}$	$1^{\circ\frac{1}{2}}$	$2^{\frac{1}{4}}$	8^{4}	30^{3}	1.55^{3} L	11.30 AbbatielloEr	DrmsArGr,DntBlmHr		1st over,faded

The mid-range conditioned level of pacing mares at the Meadowlands is always a difficult race to handicap, so you need every edge to pick a winner. Omen Hanover's last two starts came against a raging machine known as Martha Maxine, who was in the midst of a sterling winning streak. Omen Hanover's race on June 27 was an absolute sparkler, even though she finished fourth. Look at the internal fractions and you see some amazingly fast times. Omen Hanover was used very hard to secure the lead in that race and then succumbed to Martha Maxine's incredible rally. Omen Hanover didn't exactly stop that night, either, losing by only a length and a half—an incredible try, considering the circumstances.

Now, the problem with wanting to bet on Omen Hanover this night was the bad post. She drew the 9 hole, so trying to anticipate what driver Yannick Gingras would do was guesswork. I hoped he would blast her out, since speed was her best weapon, and that's exactly what he did. Gingras utilized two early moves to get the lead and then the mare battled off heavy pressure from Marnie Hall, a millionaire, to score at better than 6-1.

This story has an even better kicker, but the moral of Part 1 is that just watching races and learning to recognize when you've seen a good one can pay off in the long run. No, not all of these horses will win, but enough of them will succeed that you can turn a profit. Sometimes, you can even use the key-race theory the other way. By recognizing a weak race when you see it, you can often play against horses in their next start. I've bet against many a favorite that I felt was exiting a weak race.

SHIPPERS

Every once in a while, the "gods of racing" smile on you and give you a chance to make a score. Independence Day 2008 gave me that opportunity, where everything just fell into place.

As at most racetracks, the last two races at the Meadowlands comprise the late daily double, and it just so happened that on July 4, the first half of the double was Omen Hanover, who returned a hefty $14.20 despite being my top pick in the program. The second half of the double saw me liking Legal Muscles, another mid-range longshot from an outside post. The clincher was that Legal Muscles was 0 for 16 on the year going into the night. That helped the price, as did his last start, a break at Harrah's Chester.

Gray **LEGAL MUSCLES(L)** — b g 7, by Muscles Yankee, Ms Last Chance by Armbro Goal — 1:57.4 M1 — 08 26 1 4 5 $40,370
Frank & Lisa Matassa,Plainview,NY — 1:56.3 TgD 5/8 — 07 31 2 3 3 $39,240
8 Daniel Dube (150) (0-0-0-0 .000) — Tr.Ron Coyne,Jr. — Last 6 Sts-$12,070 — 8 1:56.0 (1) — Lifetime $216,639

	6-26$_{08}$	ChD $\frac{5}{8}$	1 fst	27^{3}	56^{2}	1.25^{4}	1.54^{4}	25000	16000	7	$x8x^{15}$	7^{16}	7^{16}	7^{17}	6^{20}	29^{4}	1.58^{4} L	8.50	DubeDa	Ptndthpn,ClytnDlny	broke 1st turn
	6-13$_{08}$	M1	1 fst	28	56^{3}	1.25^{4}	1.55^{3}	20/25000	18000	7	$3^{3\frac{1}{2}}$	$4^{3\frac{1}{4}}$	7^{4}	6^{3}	$2^{1\frac{3}{4}}$	29^{2}	1.56 L	15.00	DubeD	HZEasy$^{1\frac{3}{4}}$,LglMsclsnk	tck,shff,shk free,rally
	6-5$_{08}$	ChD $\frac{5}{8}$	1 fst	28	57^{4}	1.27^{1}	1.57	25000	16000	8	1^{1}	$2^{\frac{1}{4}}$	$4^{1\frac{1}{4}}$	$6^{3\frac{1}{4}}$	4^{6}	30^{4}	1.58^{1} L	14.80	DubeDa	PrdseLnN,JustALad	pocket,shuffled
25,000	5-28$_{08}$	ChD $\frac{5}{8}$	1 fst	28^{1}	58^{2}	1.26^{4}	1.55	NW17500L6	24000	2	5^{4}	$4^{\circ 2\frac{1}{2}}$	$4^{\circ 2\frac{1}{4}}$	4^{3}	6^{13}	30^{2}	1.57^{3} L	27.30	GoodellEr	Ripped,ShortSty	1st over,empty
8-1	5-19$_{08}$	ChD $\frac{5}{8}$	1 fst	28^{3}	58^{3}	1.27^{1}	1.56^{2}	NW9500L6cd	17000	2	$2^{\frac{1}{2}}$	1^{1}	1^{1}	$1^{\frac{1}{4}}$	$2^{1\frac{3}{4}}$	29^{3}	1.56^{4} L	6.20	GoodellEr	MsclTSpr,LglMscls	led,prssrd,all-out
	5-5$_{08}$	ChD $\frac{5}{8}$	1 fst	27^{1}	57	1.25	1.53^{1}	NW9500L6cd	17000	5	7^{10}	7^{8}	$5^{\circ 4}$	4^{4}	3^{15}	30^{2}	1.56^{1} L	12.40	BrennanGe	WldfreJl,MsclTSpr	uncov,out-trotted

It isn't always easy to gauge a horse that's shipping in from another track, especially when they ship to the Meadowlands, but this situation was different. Legal Muscles had been a regular campaigner at the Big M for most of the past two seasons and trainer Ron Coyne was pretty sharp about finding good spots for his gelding.

As you can see from his race on June 13, Legal Muscles was sitting on a big one. The second-place finish behind HZ Easy was a solid mile, with speed flashed at both ends. The shuffle that he suffered during the middle half probably cost him any chance at the upset, but he definitely landed on my "watch list" for a superior performance. Coyne shipped Legal Muscles back to Chester, only to have him make an uncharacteristic break. He came right back to the Meadowlands and caught a rather suspect field, so I felt this was the time to bet, and I thought the price would be right after showing the Chester break. As it turned out, I was right on both counts.

Despite my morning line of only 8-1, the fans sent Legal Muscles off at better than 10-1. The gelding responded as I'd hoped with the expected big mile, bursting past the field to pay a whopping $22.80. Now, you would think that a double of 6-1 in the first half and 10-1 in the back end would be a lucrative payoff, but it returned just $78.40. This was a holiday weeknight, however, so the pools just weren't as large as they normally would be. Also, the late-double pool is usually one of the smallest pools for any gimmick at the Big M.

The very next night, however, there was another opportunity to cash with a shipper. This time the horse was coming down from Canada and moving back into the stable of trainer Karen Williams.

Red **FOX VALLEY TRIBAL** — **br g 5, by Sportsmaster, Yankee Blue by Incredible Finale** — 1:50.0 M1 — 08 40 6 5 7 $170,97
Sbk Stables,E Rutherford,NJ;VIP Internet Stable LLC,Piscataway,NJ — 1:50.4 PcD 5/8 — 07 14 4 3 1 $87,94
1 **David Miller (167) (0-0-0-0 .000)** — **Tr.Karen Williams** — **Last 6 Sts-$14,958** 3 1:49.0 (1) — **Lifetime** $773,99

	6-29 08	RdC $\frac{5}{8}$	1	fst	26^{4}	54^{4}	1.22^{1}	1.50^{4}	D-DES SMIT	183150	1	1	2	3	7^{10}	7^{14}		1.53^{3}	34.00	StPierreDe	SilntSwng,WstrnShre,EagleLuck	
	6-14 08	Mhk $\frac{7}{8}$	1	fst	26	54^{1}	1.22^{4}	1.51^{3}	NW20000L6C	26460	9	1^{2}	$1^{1\frac{3}{4}}$	1^{1}	$2^{\frac{1}{2}}$	$7^{7\frac{1}{4}}$	30^{1}	1.53	6.10	MoiseyevJa	SkddlHnv,EscpThWn	rush top,rated,qu
	6-7 08	Mhk $\frac{7}{8}$	1	fst	27^{1}	55	1.23	1.51^{2}	NW21000L6C	26460	4	$2^{1\frac{3}{4}}$	$1^{1\frac{3}{4}}$	$1^{\frac{1}{2}}$	$1^{\frac{1}{4}}$	$2^{\frac{1}{2}}$	28^{2}	1.51^{2}	2.95	MoiseyevJa	HyprnHnv,FxvTribl	retook,prssd,caug
	5-31 08	Mhk $\frac{7}{8}$	1	fst	27^{1}	55^{1}	1.23^{2}	1.51^{3}	NW27500L6C	29290	8	$1^{1\frac{1}{4}}$	$3^{3\frac{1}{2}}$	$6^{4\frac{1}{2}}$	$5^{3\frac{1}{4}}$	$4^{1\frac{3}{4}}$	27^{4}	1.52	33.65	StPierreDe	Activatr,OneMreTm	blast,yld,shuff,ral
9-2	5-23 08	Lon	1	fst	26^{3}	55^{4}	1.23^{4}	1.53	Molson	25250	4	$1^{\circ 1\frac{1}{2}}$	$1^{1\frac{3}{4}}$	$3^{2\frac{3}{4}}$	4^{6}	6^{12}	31	1.55^{2}	7.50	StPierreDe	Zooka,SilntSwng,RareJewel	
	5-18 08	HM $\frac{7}{8}$	1	fst	25^{4}	54	1.22^{3}	1.52^{1}	WO40000L	12000	4	1^{1}	1^{2}	1^{3}	1^{5}	1^{2}	29^{3}	1.52^{1}	★.05	StPierreDe	FxvTribal,DylChance,PowerPark	

Fox Valley Tribal had been sent north of the border with the goal of making an impact in some serious stakes races, such as the Molson Pace at Western Fair Raceway, and then the Des Smith at Rideau Carlton. Unfortunately for his connections, he got his head handed to him in both, tiring badly.

Williams had her gelding put on a truck and sent right back to her home base at the Meadowlands. The first race he fit the conditions for was six days later in a nonwinners of $16,500 in the last six starts. Fox Valley Tribal had earned $14,958 in his last six, so he fit perfectly. As an added bonus, the gelding drew the rail and picked up Dave Miller. The race favorite was Exterminator, who got stuck with post 10 while hiking way up in class. Nothing derails a hot streak quicker than post 10 at the Meadowlands, especially on a giant class jump.

Since this was a pretty steep drop in class for Fox Valley Tribal, I wasn't sure about what his odds would be. I started him as the 9-2 third choice in the morning line and he ended up going off at 5-1. A little juice, as we say, since he responded to Miller's aggressive driving and got lucky to squeeze through inside and pay $12.40. He won by more than two lengths over Exterminator, who endured a tough trip from post 10.

Sometimes, handicappers who play primarily one track tend to overlook shippers, even those with a good chance. Pay attention. It all depends on which track they're coming from and what the situation is. It helps for a horse to have experience over a strip, especially the Meadowlands. The two examples above fit the profile perfectly. They had experience over the surface and they both had some back class. In the case of Fox Valley Tribal, the start on July 5 was probably the weakest field he'd faced in over a month. To make it even more attractive, you were getting a great post, a strong driver change, and some tremendous value at 5-1. Those are the ones you don't want to miss out on.

9

TOTE-BOARD ACTION
AND VALUE

THE TOTE BOARD

One of the things we highlight on TVG during our Friday-night *Drive Time* show is the action on the tote board. More often than not, it tells a tale. When a horse takes a lot more money than it should, especially early in the wagering, it's an incredible sign of positive intent. Now, these horses don't always win, but they usually deliver quality efforts. The old phrase "money talks" is a true one. People bet their money for a reason.

Actually, it could be for any number of reasons. People get tips. Trainers like their horse that night. A driver could be on a roll that evening, so people are parlaying the action. Positive word of mouth can have its downside, though. Sometimes I've heard about a horse training well that week, only to watch him open up at 3-5 on the tote board, and that is disheartening. Taking a bad price or getting less than fair value is never a good thing, and will find you heading to the ATM more times than not.

I try to watch the early action for two reasons. First, I like to check that my morning line is somewhat in order, because if it isn't, I want to know why. Second, if I'm going to bet the race, I just want to see if anything out of the ordinary is happening. There was one race in 2008 that had me scratching my head, but wound up validating the theory of tote-board action. Take a look at Da Boy's past performances heading into the first race on July 12.

Blue-Red **DA BOY(L)** — b h 5, by Jennas Beach Boy, Da Lady by Life Sign — 1:51.0 M1 — 08 27 4 2 3 $27,87

Mack Racing Stables LLC,Bartlett,IL — 1:51.3 BP1 — 07 30 5 2 4 $33,44

10 Ron Pierce (160) (0-0-0-0 .000) — Tr.Ken Rucker — Last 6 Sts-$4,400 5 1:51.0 (1) — Lifetime $117,99

	$6\text{-}27_{08}$	M1	1	fst	26^{4}	54^{1}	1.22^{3}	1.51^{3}	25000	18000	9											scratched-sic
	$6\text{-}15_{08}$	M1 (A)	1	fst	28	56^{2}	1.25	1.52^{2}	NW5000	11000	5	$1^{1\frac{3}{4}}$	$2^{1\frac{1}{2}}$	$3^{1\frac{1}{2}}$	$4^{1\frac{1}{4}}$	$4^{1\frac{1}{4}}$	27^{2}	1.52^{3} L	2.90	AllenB	LoveShrk$\frac{3}{4}$,JcckTrbN$\frac{1}{2}$	top,yld,pckt,outkck
	$5\text{-}31_{08}$	BP1	1	fst	28^{1}	55^{3}	1.23^{4}	1.51^{2}	NW2500	4800	8	$3^{2\frac{1}{4}}$	3^{3}	$4^{2\frac{3}{4}}$	$3^{1\frac{1}{4}}$	$1^{1\frac{1}{2}}$	27	1.51^{2} L	9.60	WarrenTo	DaBoy,Falcatraz,EnoughHnv	
	$5\text{-}24_{08}$	BP1	1	fst	27^{3}	56^{1}	1.24^{2}	1.51^{4}	NW2500	4800	2	2^{2}	$2^{1\frac{1}{2}}$	2^{3}	$2^{2\frac{1}{2}}$	$3^{2\frac{3}{4}}$	27^{2}	1.52^{2} L	7.30	WarrenTo	WiniesMak,GrandFrdm,DaBoy	
12-1	$5\text{-}17_{08}$	BP1	1	fst	27^{3}	56	1.24^{3}	1.51^{4}	NW5500	6800	10	10^{17}	$10^{\circ 10}$	$10^{\circ 9}$	10^{13}	10^{10}	27^{2}	1.53^{4} L	12.90	AndersonR	RelMenArt,NintynHwk,DstnctClr	
	$5\text{-}3_{08}$	BP1	1	fst	28^{1}	55^{1}	1.22^{4}	1.51^{3}	NW5500	6800	7	9^{10}	9^{10}	$9^{9\frac{3}{4}}$	8^{11}	$4^{1\frac{3}{4}}$	27^{1}	1.52 L	8.80	AndersonR	TatlrsTpG,ThePnfctr,DstnctClr	

When I put the morning line on this race and got to Da Boy, I didn't see a whole lot to like and I reflected that in my 12-1 price. Da Boy hadn't raced in about a month, including a sick scratch, and was coming off a disappointing, even effort at odds of nearly 3-1 with Brian Allen aboard. He now had post 10 in a first race on a Saturday night in the summer, which means a blazing kind of race. In the summer, those daylight races are always quick.

So, imagine my surprise when I got to the track, peered out at the tote board about an hour before the race, and saw Da Boy sitting up there at 2-1 with a lot of money in the pool. As stated before, there could be several reasons for that kind of action, but it was definitely worth looking into.

First, the connections were Ron Pierce and trainer Ken Rucker. Rucker was currently second in the trainers' standings, just three behind the leader, and his barn was going well. Pierce has had a knack in the past of overcoming post 10, often at a price.

Regardless, when I reviewed Da Boy's chances in the context of the overall race and how I figured it would shape up, I still couldn't like him, or bet on Da Boy at the ridiculous price.

Here's what happened:

FIRST RACE: MEADOWLANDS, JUL. 12-1 Mile Pace. Non-winners of $6,500 in last 6 starts. Winners over $30,000 in 2008 ineligible. Purse $13,000.

15-6M1	Da Boy	R.Pierce	10	5$1\frac{1}{2}$	3°$\frac{3}{4}$	2°1	1$1\frac{1}{2}$	1nk	283	271	274	272	1.51	K.Rucker	L 3.40
21-12M1	Armbro Cayenne	B.Sears	1	6$2\frac{1}{4}$	5°$\frac{1}{2}$	4°$\frac{3}{4}$	2nk	26$\frac{1}{4}$	284	272	274	27	1.51	T.Case	L •2.30
28-7M1	Herzon	Dv.Miller	6	4$1\frac{1}{4}$	6$1\frac{1}{4}$	7$\frac{3}{4}$	84	3hd	282	274	281	274	1.521	S.Rollins	L 11.10
3-qM1	Your Best Bet	Jo.Campbell	2	22	21	3$\frac{1}{2}$	4$\frac{3}{4}$	41	273	28	281	282	1.521	B.Saunders	L 4.50
5-12M1	Eyes On Kassa	Y.Gingras	9	1°$1\frac{1}{4}$	1$1\frac{1}{2}$	1$\frac{1}{2}$	3$1\frac{1}{4}$	5$1\frac{1}{4}$	272	28	281	284	1.522	J.Czermann,Jr.	L 8.30
28-8M1	Love Shark	L.Plano	7	10	8°nk	8°2$\frac{1}{4}$	7hd	6$1\frac{1}{2}$	302	263	273	281	1.524	R.Plano	L 7.40
28-8M1	Fibber Magee A	A.Miller	3	3$1\frac{1}{2}$	4$\frac{3}{4}$	5$\frac{1}{2}$	6nk	7$\frac{1}{2}$	28	28	281	284	1.53	E.Cruise	L 57.50
1-6PcD	U Bettor Watch Out	M.Lachance	4	7$1\frac{1}{2}$	7°2$\frac{3}{4}$	6°$\frac{3}{4}$	5$\frac{3}{4}$	8$9\frac{1}{4}$	292	271	273	29	1.531	S.Cruise	27.40
26-qM1	Ideal Lover	P.MacDonell	5	9$1\frac{3}{4}$	10°	9$2\frac{1}{4}$	9$6\frac{1}{4}$	9$6\frac{1}{4}$	301	271	273	30	1.55	A.Glide	L 73.00
18-2ChD	Double Your Moves	D.Dube	8	8$2\frac{1}{4}$	9$1\frac{1}{4}$	10	10	10	293	273	281	304	1.561	R.Bilach	7.00

Basix: Da Boy, Armbro Cayenne, Herzon, Your Best Bet, Eyes On Kassa, Love Shark, Fibber Magee A, Ideal Lover.

Off: 7:02 Time: 0:27.2, 0:55.2, 1:23.3, 1:51.0. Mutuel Pool: $187,245. Temp. 84°

MUTUELS: **Da Boy** $8.80, 4.80, 4.00; **Armbro Cayenne** $3.60, 2.60; **Herzon** $4.80

EXACTA (10-1) $33.20. TRIFECTA (10-1-6) $113.80.

DA BOY was put into play early tucking fifth from the ten post around turn one, pulled uncovered going to the half, grinded up to engage the leader, applied steady pressure, wore that one down to take over and was dead game to hold off the late surge of ARMBRO CAYENNE at the wire. The latter set it up second over behind the winner's cover, loomed large while well positioned, took dead aim through the stretch with no excuse and came up a neck short. HERZON left and tucked fourth, stayed in and got buried, split rivals turning for home and rallied with late pace. YOUR BEST BET yielded around turn one, sat the pocket as the leader got tested and had no pop. EYES ON KASSA fired out to the front, cleared just past the first quarter, set the pace, faced a first over challenge from a determined rival and gave way. LOVE SHARK trailed the field, got stuck behind excess cover and beat the weak. FIBBER MAGEE A raced in the three hole, sat in and faded. U BETTOR WATCH OUT was away slow, followed third over and tired. IDEAL LOVER sat next to last and had nothing. DOUBLE YOUR MOVES made no moves and was empty.

h 5 by Jennas Beach Boy, Da Lady by Life Sign

Owners: 1. Richard A Schilling,Saint John,IN;David L Jabaay,Crete,IL;Ted Schilling,St John,IN, 2. Vip Internet Stb LLC,Piscataway,NJ;S Korn,Monmouth Bch,NJ;A Dunayer,Springfield,NJ, 3. Scott A Dillon,Anson,ME, 4. George A & Gerald W Jaeger,Malverne,NY;Karl Jaeger,Princeton Junction,NJ, 5. Frederick H & Anita C Fialkow,Wellington,FL, 6. Maryann Plano, Sacramento, CA, 7. Jesmeral Stable,Woodridge,NJ, 8. Stephanie D Cruise,Woodridge,NJ, 9. Jack Vitale,Manalapan,NJ;Anna M Glide,Freehold,NJ, 10. Boy Oh Boy Stable Too,Manalapan,NJ.

Da Boy promptly floated out of the gate, got parked the entire mile, and still surged late to win in a lifetime-best time of 1:51. His odds drifted up to 3-1, but were still far below my "off" morning line.

The point is that when a horse takes far more betting action than he should, there is often a reason. When it seems to make no sense, then start to look deeper and try and figure out what is going on. Sometimes, it will save you a lot of money, or maybe even make you a lot of money. If you've taken a thorough second look and still can't make a case for the horse, at least you'll know that you did your work—and that will pay off in the long run.

VALUE AND OVERLAYS

In a couple of chapters, I will discuss why you don't want short-priced favorites when betting 2-year-olds. I should expand that to say you must always look for value in every situation. When I say "value," I mean the proper price adjusted to the horse's true chance of winning. Since I do the morning line, I have an easy feel for what a horse's proper odds should be. How many times have you looked at the tote board and said to yourself, "Why is this horse 6-5? He should be 3-1." That's a perfect example of when not to play, or to play something else.

On the other hand, you've also looked out at that tote board and said, "How can this horse be 10-1? He should be 7-2." When you get that feeling, it's time to bet. The more value you perceive, the more you should bet. Now, they won't all win, I promise you that, but enough of them will win to make it a profitable angle.

Here are two examples of such ridiculous good value—one from 2009, and one from a Hambletonian elimination from the summer of 2008.

First, take a gander at Sportsfancy's lines from March 6, 2009. She showed up in leg one of the Overbid series after a tough trip in the Cape and Cutter series final two weeks prior. In that final, she went off at only 5-1 against a prohibitive favorite in Martha Maxine.

Yellow	SPORTSFANCY(L)					b m 5, by Sportsmaster, Finish Firstfancy by Life Sign										1:49.4 M1	09 8 3 0 1	$68,87
						Larry Baron,Horsham,PA										1:51.1 ChD 5/8	08 18 8 2 0	$140,42
6	Brian Sears (145) (636-92-84-89 .145)					Tr.Josh Green(21-7-0-2 .333)								Last 6 Sts-$49,875		5 1:49.4 (1)		Lifetime $692,77
	2-20⁰⁹ M1	1 fst 27 55²	1.24 1.50⁴	Cape&CtFnl-D	87500 9	5°4¾ 1°1¼ 2hd	3¹½	57½	28¹ 1.52¹ L	5.60 SearsB	MarthMxn³¼,ChncyLdy²	used to lead,prss,ti
	2-13⁰⁹ M1	1 fst 27² 56²	1.25¹ 1.52	Cape&Cutter	40000 5	7⁷½ 7°6¼ 6°3¼	6²	1¾	26¹ 1.52 L	2.70 SearsB	Sprtsfncy¾,IdelWthrhd	3rd over,aim,drivin
PP 6	2-6⁰⁹ M1	1 fst 28 56²	1.23⁴ 1.51¹	Cape&Cutter	40000 2	43¾ 2°nk 2°nk	4¹	6⁴	28¹ 1.52 L	7.10 SearsB	EnhncThNght1½,GoOnBbno	attacked,repelle
	2-3⁰⁹ DD⅝	1 sly 27² 57¹	1.25² 1.54	Open Hcp FM	26000 scr	jg		scr				scratched-judge
6-1	1-27⁰⁹ DD⅝	1 gd 26⁴ 55⁴	1.24¹ 1.52²	Open Hcp FM	27000 8	6⁷ 6°4 5°3¼	3½	1¹¾	27³ 1.52² AL *1.50 GoodellEr		Sprtsfncy,LcksOfLve,ApcheDame	
	1-17⁰⁹ M1	1 fst 28 56	1.23³ 1.51	Inv FM	35000 9	9¹¹ 9⁸¾ 9°8¾ 8¹¹		6⁹¾	27³ 1.53 L	7.30 SearsB	ChncyLdy1,IdelWthr6¼	last over,no sho

Now, the problem here is that she had to face Martha Maxine again, so at the very least you had to respect that. I will even admit that I didn't have the guts to pick Sportsfancy on top in this spot, but I did select her for second behind Martha Maxine.

Since March 6 was a Friday, I was live on TVG for the race. As Gary Seibel and I were discussing it, I kept hammering home the point of the odds on Sportsfancy. She continued to drift up and went off at 13-1. I used both Martha Maxine and Sportsfancy in my on-air pick four, but kept telling the viewers that this was a remarkable overlay.

IXTH RACE: MEADOWLANDS, MAR. 6-1 Mile Pace. The Overbid. 1st Leg. Free For All Mares. Purse $50,000.

Date	Horse	Driver	PP										Time	Odds
20-5M1	Sportsfancy	B.Sears 6	$5\frac{1}{4}$	$5°1\frac{1}{4}$	$4°1$	$3\frac{3}{4}$	$11\frac{1}{4}$	28^2 27^2 26^4 27^1	1.49^4	Js.Green	L 13.80
20-5M1	Martha Maxine	A.Miller 2	$4\frac{1}{3}$	$3°\frac{1}{2}$	$2°1\frac{1}{4}$	1no	$22\frac{1}{4}$	28 27^2 27 27^3	1.50	E.Miller	*.50
27-5M1	Ideal Nectarine	Dv.Miller 4	$3°1\frac{1}{2}$	$4\frac{1}{2}$	5nk	$6\frac{1}{2}$	3nk	27^4 27^4 27^1 27^3	1.50^2	K.Rucker	L 19.00
26-q4M1	Darlins Delight	Y.Gingras 8	$8\frac{1}{2}$	$8\frac{1}{4}$	$8°1\frac{1}{2}$	$7\frac{3}{4}$	4nk	29^1 27^2 26^3 27^2	1.50^3	Jf.Stafford	4.50
27-6M1	Mind Boggling	E.Goodell 5	$6\frac{1}{2}$	$6°1$	$6°1$	5hd	5nk	28^3 27^2 27 27^3	1.50^3	R.Croghan	23.40
20-5M1	Ideal Weather	R.Pierce 1	$2\frac{1}{2}$	2^1	$3\frac{1}{2}$	4^1	6no	27^2 27^4 27^2 28	1.50^3	R.Burke	e9.60
20-5M1	Chancey Lady	D.Dube 3	$1\frac{1}{2}$	$11\frac{1}{4}$	$1\frac{3}{4}$	2^1	$7\frac{3}{4}$	27^1 27^4 27^1 28^2	1.50^3	M.Kesmodel	8.80
20-5M1	Go On Bb	Ti.Tetrick 9	9	9	9	9	$8\frac{1}{2}$	29^3 27^2 26^2 27^2	1.50^4	R.Burke	L e9.60
20-5M1	Cuz She Can	G.Brennan 7	$7\frac{1}{2}$	7^2	7nk	8nk	9	29 27^1 27 27^3	1.50^4	M.Harder	32.80

asix: Sportsfancy, Ideal Nectarine, Go On Bb.

e-Ideal Weather & Go On Bb - Burke trained entry.

Off: 8:47 Time: 0:27.1, 0:55.0, 1:22.1, 1:49.4. Mutuel Pool: $281,625. Temp. 47°

MUTUELS: **Sportsfancy** $29.60, 8.00, 5.40; **Martha Maxine** $2.40, 2.20; **Ideal Nectarine** $9.40

EXACTA (6-2) $68.60. TRIFECTA (6-2-4) $656.60. $1 PICK 3 (6-7-6) $558.80.

PORTSFANCY tucked early, picked up the very live cover of big favorite MARTHA MAXINE, tipped for the drive, kicked into gear and surged past for the upset. The latter was snatched up at the start and was reserved, ame uncovered with a prolonged grind, reached the leader turning home, took the lead but was outfinished. IDEAL NECTARINE tucked third, saved ground, got clear up the rail and finished with a good rally. DARLINS ELIGHT gapped at the rear, came out final turn and was going well to the wire, but too late. MIND BOGGLING raced third over and lacked a serious late kick. IDEAL WEATHER yielded to the quarter, sat the pocket trip with tle to offer late. CHANCEY LADY left well, drove on to the front, rated the half, picked up the pace significantly in the turn as pressure came and succumbed early stetch. GO ON BB lagged and was never a threat. CUZ HE CAN sat jammed in traffic and never factored in the outcome.

m 5 by Sportsmaster, Finish Firstfancy by Life Sign

wners: 1. Larry Baron,Horsham,PA, 2. Ervin Miller Stb Inc,Springfield,IL;T P Alagna,Sorrento,FL;Brittany Fms,Versailles,KY, 3. D R Van Witzenburg,Crest Hill,IL, 4. White Birch Farm,Allentown,Nj, 5. Let It Ride Stables Inc,Delray each,FL;Mentally Stable Inc,Delray Beach,FL, 6. S Burke,Frdrcktwn,PA;L Karr,Rndlph,NJ;Weaver Bruscemi,Cnsbrg,PA;Jjk Stbs,Frt Ldrdl,FL, 7. Niele A Jiwan,Burnaby,BC, CA, 8. Frank D Baldachino,Clarksburg,NJ, 9. Bulletproof nterprises,Boca Raton,Fl.

Sure enough, Brian Sears put a perfect drive on Sportsfancy, and that got my pick four off to a roaring start. I did hit the pick four that night and it returned over $1,000 for a $40 wager. I had it, and anybody who listened to me on TVG could have had it as well.

Here's another example of a horse that simply offered odds too high to pass up, and it came in an elimination race for none other than the Hambletonian.

Red	**ATOMIC HALL**			b c 3, by Self Possessed, Audra Hall by Garland Lobell							1:54.0 M1	08 13	1 1 2	$97,418		
				Leif Alber,Soborg 2860,DE							1:59.2 In1	07 6	1 4 0	$81,053		
1	Eric Goodell (165) (0-0-0-0 .000)			Tr.Trond Smedshammer(105-11-17-9 .105)						Last 6 Sts-$21,425	3 1:54.0 (1)		Lifetime	$178,471		
	7-11^{08} M1	1 fst 28^2 57	1.25^3 1.53^2	SDancerFnl-D	350000 7	10^{12} $76\frac{3}{4}$	$89\frac{1}{2}$	7^{11}	$69\frac{3}{4}$	28	1.55^2	63.00 GoodellE	Dwychtmnhw^3,ClbrtyScrt$\frac{3}{4}$	imprvd ins,mild late
	7-4^{08} M1	1 fst 28^2 56^1	1.25^1 1.54	SDancerElm-D	35000 10	$98\frac{1}{4}$ $99\frac{3}{4}$	$8°5\frac{3}{4}$	6^3	$43\frac{1}{2}$	28^1	1.54^3	38.00 GoodellE	ClbrtyScrt^1,AcHghHll$\frac{3}{4}$	fllw winner,mild late
	6-20^{08} M1	1 fst 27^4 56^2	1.25^1 1.54	NJSS Fnl-D	175000 1	$64\frac{1}{2}$ 86	$95\frac{3}{4}$	$94\frac{3}{4}$	5^2	28	1.54^2	5.00 SearsB	ClbrtyScrtnk,FlMyMscls$\frac{1}{2}$	buried,angled,plenty
	6-12^{08} M1	1 fst 28^2 57^1	1.26^2 1.54^3	NJSS 3YO	30900 2	$4°3\frac{3}{4}$ $11\frac{1}{2}$	1nk	$2x1\frac{1}{4}$	8^{15}	31^1	1.57^3	7.30 SmedshmrT	ClbrtyScrt1$\frac{3}{4}$,OverRuldnk	brush,press,wknd,brk
6-1	6-5^{08} M1	1 fst 29^2 57^4	1.25^4 1.54^4	NJSS 3YO	30300 4	$54\frac{3}{4}$ 55	$6°5\frac{1}{2}$	4^6	$2\frac{1}{2}$	28	1.54^4	2.50 SearsB	NatclNtn$\frac{1}{2}$,AtomcHll2$\frac{1}{2}$	dull cover,charging
	5-22^{08} M1	1 sly 28^3 59^1	1.29^2 1.57	Qua 3YO	4	$56\frac{1}{2}$ $55\frac{1}{4}$	$5°4\frac{1}{4}$	56	$25\frac{3}{4}$	28	1.58^1	nb SearsB	Napoleon5$\frac{3}{4}$,AtomcHll1$\frac{1}{2}$	good rally

---

There's a reason that driver Eric Goodell is nicknamed the King of the Longshots, and Atomic Hall also fit several different angles that can produce good payoffs.

First, Atomic Hall was trained by a guy that won the 2004 Hambletonian, Trond Smedshammer. Every 3-year-old trotter trained by Smedshammer is pointed for one race: the Hambletonian.

If you examined the colt's recent races a bit more closely, you realized he had absolutely no realistic chance to win any of his last three starts. Goodell was quoted as saying just that in the pre-race press notes. Atomic Hall was getting post-position relief, starting from the pole after being stuck in posts 7 and 10 in his last two tries. In the July 4 start from post 10, he was actually very good at odds of 38-1, finishing only a few lengths behind Celebrity Secret, his main rival on this day. With that said, I started Atomic Hall at a respectable 6-1 in the morning line and picked him second in my race review, explaining that he had no shot recently and it was about time he stepped up with more. I didn't suspect that he would be completely ignored in the wagering and end up going off at 22-1.

From the rail, Goodell figured to have his colt in a good, ground-saving, stalking spot, and when they turned for home Goodell swung Atomic Hall out with a strong and powerful kick to charge by Celebrity Secret and win his first race as a 3-year-old. The payoff was a staggering $46.80 and because Atomic Hall won the elimination, Goodell and Smedshammer would be able to pick their own post for the $1.5 million final. Not bad for them, and not bad for anyone who recognized the ridiculous overlay on a horse that had a chance. This instance exemplifies the importance of watching morning lines and horses that are far above their "true" prices.

10

HANDICAPPING TROTTERS

I've always felt that you handicap a trot race a lot differently from a pacing event. There are so many more things that must be considered with trotters, and I've tried to find a few examples that illustrate my theory.

Perhaps one of the most significant equipment changes with trotters is the addition or subtraction of trotting hopples. By now, you should all know that 99 percent of pacers wear hopples, which are the straps wrapped around their legs to keep them on the correct gait. Many years ago, trainer Ken Shand developed the trotting hopples, which look different, but the premise is the same. It keeps a trotter more balanced and lessens the chance that he will go offstride. It doesn't work for every horse, but it works a lot more often than not.

Let's take a look at a talented young filly named Margarita Momma and her program past performances from July 2, 2008.

Gray	‡MARGARITA MOMMA		b f 2, by Yankee Glide, Sheena Hall by Conway Hall						1:54.1 Lx1	08 12 6 0 3	$235,780
			Jorgen Jahre Jr,3201 Sandefjord,NO;Jan E Johnson,Lighthouse Point,FL							07 0 0 0 0	-
8	Jan Johnson (130) (0-0-0-0 .000)		Tr.Jan Johnson(28-4-2-4 .143)						Last 6 Sts-$1,937	2 1:54.1 (1)	Lifetime $235,780
	6-18⁰⁸ M1	1 gd 29¹ 1.00¹ 1.31 1.59⁴ NJSS 2YO F	38750 2	x8¹⁷ 8¹¹ 8⁵¾ 8⁵¾ 5⁶¾	29	2.01¹	2.70 JohnsonJ	DreamPnk1½,BeMyBaby2¾			brk 1st turn,gd finish
	6-11⁰⁸ M1	1 fst 31 1.04 1.33⁴ 2.02 Qua 2YO F	2	1½ 1½ 1² 1² 1²¾	28¹	2.02	nb JohnsonJ	MrgrtMmm2¾,CurliCue15¼			top,rated,cruised

8-1

At this stage of the year, almost all 2-year-olds are just getting started. Margarita Momma had only one "baby race" before heading to the gate in a real stakes race on June 18. Her qualifier on June 11 was exceptional, as she flashed strong speed, rated comfortably, and then sprinted home handily to win at first asking in a fairly decent time of 2:02. That's pretty quick for a first start out of a freshman trotting filly.

Unfortunately, she followed up that dazzling debut with a typical mistake on June 18, going offstride soon after the start at the low odds of 5-2. Trainer Jan Johnson has probably forgotten more about good trotters than I know, so for him to put the hopples on this promising filly without even another qualifier told me he had the answer.

Since she drew post 8 against a quality stakes field, and showed that break, I felt we'd get a decent price on a filly that, to me, looked best. I also felt the price wouldn't be short due to the fact that the 57-year-old Johnson was again driving her. He doesn't win too many races driving nowadays, but it made perfect sense for him to steer her with first-time trotting hopples. After a good tussle for the early lead, Margarita Momma wound up winning easily, and returned a square $8.20. The filly went on to have a solid stakes season the rest of the year, many times being driven by Ron Pierce. It's important to recognize the talent of a young horse, let the trainer do his or her job, and then hop on board when the time is right.

Another example of how to spot a good-looking young trotter with ability came up in the form of Crazed on Father's Day, June 15, 2008.

Yellow	‡CRAZED					br c 3, by Credit Winner, Mary Lou Hall by Mr Lavec								1:52.2 M1		08 14 8 2 2 $1,057,79
6	Frank Antonacci (160) (0-0-0-0 .000)					Lindy Rcg Stb,Enfield,CT;G N & E S Hoffman,FL;R A Rudolph,NJ								1:57.0 Lx1 Q		07 5 1 0 0 $5,26
						Tr.Frank Antonacci,Jr.(17-4-2-3 .235)								Last 6 Sts-$5,266	3 1:52.2 (1)	Lifetime $1,063,05
	6-5⁰⁸ M1	‡ 1 fst 30³ 1.00² 1.30² 1.591	Qua 3YO			6	4⁴¾	4⁵½	4°3¼	3¹¾	2½	28¹ 1.59¹	nb AntonacciF	ClbrtyClssc½,Crazed1¾		steady rall
	5-29⁰⁸ M1	‡ 1 fst 294 59² 1.294 1.574	Qua 3YO			8	7¹¹	7¹³	6°9	68¾	4¹¹	28² 2.00	nb AntonacciF	KajanKkr9¼,AndvrsSnⁿk		late,beat wea
	11-24⁰⁷M1	‡ 1 fst 284 571 1.281 1.57²	CrownFnl-D	650000	9	65½	66	95½	88	78½	294 1.59	125.00 LachanceM	Dwychtmnhw¹,ClbrtyScrt²		no move
	11-16⁰⁷M1	‡ 1 fst 291 1.00¹ 1.314 1.59	CrownElm-D	25000	7	33¼	34¼	43	46¼	46¼	274 2.00¹	32.70 LachanceM	Dwychtmnhw³,ClbrtyScrt³		tuck,sat,outkicke
3-1	11-3⁰⁷ DD ⅝	‡ 1 fst 27³ 57² 1.26² 1.56³	Matron-E	37338	8	7°9	7°7	6°3	59	57¾	311 1.58¹	25.50 LachanceM	LearJetta,Waterstne,DiManggio		
	10-18⁰⁷VD ⅞	‡ 1 fst 28² 58³ 1.28³ 1.58¹	NW1	2800	1	12	12	12¼	16	19¼	29³ 1.58¹	*1.10 MAntoncciFr	Crazed,PmbrkGngr,MalarkyT		

At first glance, Crazed doesn't exactly have the look of a killer just yet. Little would anyone know that just six weeks later, Crazed would end up in the Hambletonian, finishing a strong second for trainer Frank Antonacci and Tim Tetrick. In fact, Crazed ended his sophomore season with eight wins, a few stakes tallies, and over $1 million in earnings.

Several things about Crazed suggested that he might be something special. First, he made five starts at age 2. He had only one miscue and then the hopples went on. He performed admirably in the season-ending Breeders Crown, but he just hadn't fully matured yet. That would come. The connections, the Antonacci family, had been associated with some of the sport's top trotters, including several Hambletonian winners.

So, how do you lock on to a horse that looks like this in June? You watch him qualify!

Crazed had his first qualifier at the end of May and just toured the track with a fairly decent finish. Look at his last quarter of 28$\frac{2}{5}$. It's not easy for a young trotter to do that in only his first start back at age 3. Then look at the progression to the second qualifier a week later. Antonacci was slightly more aggressive, putting his colt into the race on the final turn, and they finished up smartly again, charging home in 28$\frac{1}{5}$, missing by less than a length.

This was clearly the case of a horse going in the right direction, and when he made his sophomore debut on June 15, I felt all systems were on go.

Ironically, trainer Antonacci ended up driving himself that day, as his listed pilot, Ryan Anderson, scratched off his nine programmed drives. If only he'd known what he was missing. Antonacci piloted flawlessly to an effortless 1:57$\frac{3}{5}$ triumph, ending up as the 2-1 second betting choice. He wasn't even the favorite.

A side benefit for those who had been following Crazed was that his victory came in a key good race. It produced next-out winner Rustyaholic, who was profiled in Chapter 2—another example of how paying close attention can yield a double dip of good results.

11

HANDICAPPING
2-YEAR-OLDS

Over the years, I've had some success and a lot more failure trying to figure out the 2-year-olds. The nature of training the Standardbred freshman has changed dramatically over the years, as some barns like to get them ready early and others prefer to wait until the season's second half. Handicapping harness racing is very comparable to the Thoroughbred guessing game when it comes to 2-year-olds, and I don't feel I have a total handle on it. At that age, the Standardbreds are also maturing daily and weekly and their performance can change dramatically over a short time frame.

One thing I can tell you is that it takes even more work to try and analyze the 2-year-olds. By the second week of June at the Meadowlands, it's typical for there to be 15 or 20 baby races going on, and they qualify twice a week for the rest of the meet, which lasts until August. In other words, it's incredibly time-consuming, and what you see in the morning doesn't always translate to what you'll see at night.

I did manage to latch on to a pair of winners toward the end of the 2008 meet that I felt stood out, but these were few and far between for me. The first example of a horse I liked a lot was Stunning Delight from June 18. Her name should have been Stunning Debut, because that's what was coming.

Green											

STUNNING DELIGHT

br f 2, by Windsongs Legacy, Armbro Stunning by Victory Dream
Jason E & Douglas W & Ronald L Allen,Southampton,NJ
Tr.Randy Beeckman(15-3-3-0 .200)

4											

David Miller (167) (0-0-0-0 .000)

2:00.0 M1   08 5 1 1 0 $35,300
            07 0 0 0 0   -
Last 6 Sts-$0 2 2:00.0 (1)   Lifetime $35,300

| 6-11⁰⁸ M1 | 1 fst 30¹ 1.02¹ 1.34² 2.02³ Qua 2YO F | 1 | 44 | 45½ | 2°1½ | 1nk | 1¹⅜ | 28 | 2.02³ | nb MillerDv | StnnngDlght¹⅜,BeMyBaby¹⅜ | unc,chall,right by |
| 6-4⁰⁸ M1 | 1 sly 32⁴ 1.04¹ 1.35 2.03 Qua 2YO F | 4 | 12½ | 12½ | 2nk | 22 | 22¼ | 28² | 2.03² | nb MillerDv | NwHmpshrGrl2¼,StnnngDlght⅜top,rtd,prs,gv way,hld |

7-2

With just two past-performance lines to look at, I guess I couldn't blame anybody for not wanting to bet too seriously on these races. It's just not that easy, but the key to this filly was watching her qualify in those baby races. Even though she finished second in her first attempt, the effort was a high-quality one and a race that went pretty fast. I know that sounds funny, but 2-year-old trotting fillies don't usually go much faster than 2:03 in their debuts.

The second qualifier was the real eye-catcher, however. Driver Dave Miller got a good feel for her in the first race and then he changed the tactics up a bit in the second qualifier. He tipped her to the outside and the filly just ate up the ground, inhaling the leader and drawing away under no urging whatsoever. No doubt, this was a filly with some extreme talent—although the only way for you to know that would have been to watch the qualifier yourself, read the qualifier comments from *Harness Eye*, or check out my race review in the official program or on the Meadowlands website.

As it turned out, we weren't going to get rich on this one either. Despite being very careful with her early, Dave Miller shook free of stretch traffic and flew home to an easy win. The only problem was the price . . . a mere $5.20. With the availability of race replays and things like that, you just don't get the value that was once available.

Another example of a horse that was ready to win came up on July 31 with In The Game. This is also an example of "knowing the game" and who the players are. Take a look at In The Game's past performances from that night.

IN THE GAME					b f 2, by I Am A Fool, Elena Blue Chip by Magical Mike					1:54.1 M1	08 7 3 0 2			$82,042
					Bulletproof Enterprises,Boca Raton,Fl						07 0 0 0 0			-
John Campbell (150) (0-0-0-0 .000)					Tr.Paul Reid					Last 6 Sts-$3,250	2 1:54.1 (1)		Lifetime	$82,042
7-21^{08} PcD$\frac{5}{8}$(A) 1 fst 28^4 58 1.27^1 1.56 NW1 FM					6500 7	1no 3$^2\frac{3}{4}$	2^{o1}	3^3	1$^1\frac{1}{2}$	28^3 1.56	5.70 ReidP		InTheGame,Snapper,Prettoty	
7-16^{08} M1 1 fst 29^2 1.00^1 1.30^4 1.57^4 Qua 2YO F					7	5$^8\frac{1}{2}$ 5$^6\frac{1}{2}$	3$^o3\frac{1}{2}$	4$^4\frac{1}{4}$	3$^4\frac{3}{4}$	27^2 1.58^4	nb JohanssonM		CheapMtl$\frac{1}{2}$,FrnksDrm4$\frac{1}{4}$	out final,evenly
3 7-9^{08} PcD$\frac{5}{8}$ 1 fst 29^4 1.00^4 1.30^1 1.59 Qua2yo					8	5^5 5$^5\frac{3}{4}$	6^7	4^{10}	3^{12}	29^4 2.01^2	nb SimonsM		Warsaw,PrincessDare,InTheGame	

Several things stand out about the potential for In The Game in this spot. She was entered in a minor stakes race, the Kindergarten Classic, which is designed for some fillies that might not be ready for the top level of stakes action.

In The Game was clearly improving for her new trainer, Paul Reid, who took over in mid-July. Her win at Pocono Downs was a standout, multiple-move effort, and she was switching drivers to John Campbell. Campbell is a master with young horses and this would be the perfect situation to find out just how good she was. Best of all was the fact that she probably wouldn't be the favorite. Here's what I wrote in the program that night, hinting that she was sitting on a big effort.

RACE 3 REVIEW Thursday, July 31, 2008 *By David Brower*

1 **KISS ME KATE** - Filly by Real Artist has been good in all starts so far. Facing another good one in #2 and it should be good battle at some point.

1A **PERFECTIONIST** - Complements her entrymate nicely, except for the bad post. Might have to soften up #2 to have best chance. That won't be easy.

2 **ANNIE MAC** - Has looked super so far and she catches a big break with the pole draw. Can dictate the action and she is still the one to beat here.

3 **CELEBRITY ZELDA** - Stopped last two, so I have to pass for now.

4 **IN THE GAME** - Showed up sharp at Pocono and this barn has uncorked a few surprises here in the past. Don't be shocked if she goes very well.

5 **GORDYYY'S PET** - Still acting greenly and I cannot endorse at the moment. Not quite as fast, or as sharp as the inside ones. Not for me.

6 **PRETTY LADY** - Homebred is on the right track, as she continues to get faster. Unfortunately, she's running into a few faster foes. Tough spot.

7 **JK CAMEO** - Scratched out of a sires stakes up at Vernon. She's shown little early zip so far, but I must point out that Pierce ends up on this one.

TOP CONTENDERS 4-2-1-7

By this point, I probably don't have to tell you what happened, but here it is anyway. In The Game pulled first over and just crushed the field by almost two lengths under a confident Campbell drive. As I suspected, she was not the favorite, and returned a generous $8.20 considering all that I had mapped out.

THIRD RACE: MEADOWLANDS, JUL. 31-1 Mile Pace. The Kindergarten Classic. 2 Year Old Fillies. Purse $10,000.

7-21-6PcD	In The Game	Jo.Campbell 3	4$1\frac{1}{2}$	3°1	2°1	1$\frac{1}{2}$	1$1\frac{3}{4}$	29	29	28^3	27^3	1.54^1	P.Reid	3.10
7-10-2M1	Annie Mac	Y.Gingras 1	2$2\frac{1}{4}$	2$\frac{3}{4}$	3$1\frac{1}{2}$	3$3\frac{1}{2}$	2$1\frac{1}{2}$	28	29^4	29	27^4	1.54^3	L.Toscano	*1.30
7-16-6ChD	Kiss Me Kate	B.Sears 5	6$\frac{3}{4}$	7°2	6°1	4$1\frac{1}{4}$	3$1\frac{1}{2}$	29^2	29^2	28^4	27^1	1.54^4	J.Takter	e1.90
7-19-2TgD	Perfectionist	G.Grismore 8	1$1\frac{1}{2}$	1$1\frac{1}{2}$	1nk	2nk	4$5\frac{1}{4}$	27^4	29^4	29	28^3	1.55^1	J.Takter	e1.90
7-25-qM1	Jk Cameo	G.W.Sholty 7	7$^{o}\frac{3}{4}$	5$^{o}1\frac{1}{4}$	4$^{o}1\frac{1}{2}$	5$3\frac{3}{4}$	5$\frac{1}{2}$	29^3	28^3	29	29	1.56^1	L.Toscano	8.50
7-23-1M1	Gordyyys Pet	A.Miller 4	5$1\frac{1}{4}$	6^1	7$\frac{3}{4}$	7$6\frac{3}{4}$	6^3	29^1	29^2	29^1	28^3	1.56^2	R.Siegelman	36.20
7-19-5TgD	Pretty Lady	M.Lachance 6	8	8	8°	6$\frac{3}{4}$	7dis	29^4	29^2	28^4	29	1.57	L.Rathbone	19.80
7-16-5ChD	Celebrity Zelda	B.Connor 2	3^2	4nk	5nk	8	8	28^3	29^3	29^2	34^3	2.02^1	S.Lind	34.60

e-Kiss Me Kate & Perfectionist - J. Takter trained entry.
Off: 7:59 Time: 0:27.4, 0:57.3, 1:26.3, 1:54.1. Mutuel Pool: $165,794. Temp. 83°
MUTUELS: **In The Game** $8.20, 3.40, 2.60; **Annie Mac** $3.20, 2.20; **Kiss Me Kate** $2.10; **Perfectionist** $2.10
EXACTA (4-2) $23.80. TRIFECTA (4-2-1) $29.90. PICK 3 (8-6-4) $101.20.

IN THE GAME was flushed uncovered just before the half, moved into striking position final turn, took over in the lane and drew off while drifting for the score. ANNIE MAC sat a pocket trip, angled in the lane with dead aim but was easily outkicked to the wire. KISS ME KATE was out third over, angled in down the lane and came with a good late flurry. PERFECTIONIST left to the front, rated out easy fractions, faced pressure final turn and gave way willingly. JK CAMEO blew the first turn trying to leave, worked out a live cover trip, gapped badly final turn and held the weak for a small share. GORDYYYS PET was completely shuffled out final turn, angled free in the lane but flattened out after a short burst. PRETTY LADY was out from the back final turn but never fired. CELEBRITY ZELDA sat a three-hole and quit badly final turn.

b f 2 by I Am A Fool, Elena Blue Chip by Magical Mike

Owners: 1. Bulletproof Enterprises,Boca Raton,FL, 2. Stake Your Claim 10,Secaucus,NJ, 3. Christina Takter,E Windsor,NJ;John D Fielding,ON;R A W Equine Inc,ON, 4. Brittany Farms,Versailles,KY, 5. 3 Brothers Stables,New York,NY;Steve Jones,Montgomery,NY, 6. Lessee-The Cheyenne Gang LLC,Port Washington,NY, 7. M&L Of Delaware Inc,Wilmington,DE, 8. Celebrity Farms,New York,NY.

While I have decreased my wagering on 2-year-olds substantially, there is still the odd situation that demands a bet—but you must be selective and get all the best of it. By that, I mean you must have solid reasons for liking the horse, and you must get proper betting value. I don't want any favorites in 2-year-old races, because they just aren't consistent enough to warrant the risk.

12

IMPROVING FORM/ CLASS DROPS

IMPROVING FORM

One of the things most handicappers forget is that we're dealing with real, living, breathing animals. Horses are not machines, and they often drift in and out of form on a regular basis. It is critical that good handicappers recognize the hints that lead to improved form, or even regressing form.

Sometimes, it's something as simple as a renewed burst of speed. Sometimes, it's a pattern of racing from off the pace for a few weeks, and then a gas-pedal blast-out effort. I've also seen horses that usually show speed benefit from a change of tactics and do better racing from the back of the pack.

An ideal example of a horse that was clearly about to improve her form was Striptease Hall from April 4, 2008.

reen **STRIPTEASE HALL** | **b m 4, by Artiscape, St Anne Hall by Blissfull Hall** | **1:53.1 M1** | **08 30 2 5 3 $50,025**
S Burke,Frdrcktwn,PA;Weaver Bruscemi,Cnsbrg,PA;J Koechlin | **1:52.3 ID1** | **07 25 5 6 1 $57,205**
4 **Yannick Gingras (150) (0-0-0-0 .000)** | **Tr.Mickey Burke(329-31-52-32 .094)** | **Last 6 Sts-$14,455** | **3 1:52.3 (1)** | **Lifetime $139,097**

	3-28 08	M1	1	fst	27^2	56^2	1.26^1	1.54^3	NW10000FM	23500	2	4^4	$4^{\circ 3\frac{1}{4}}$	$2^{\circ\frac{3}{4}}$	$1^{1\frac{1}{4}}$	2^{hd}	28^1	1.54^3	★1.80 GingrasY	Menwyltr^{hd},StrptsHll^2	uncvrd,caught late
	3-20 08	M1	1	fst	26^4	56^3	1.25^1	1.52^2	JerseyGirls	20000	10	10^{12}	$9^{4\frac{1}{2}}$	$12^{\circ 8\frac{3}{4}}$	10^8	$9^{7\frac{1}{4}}$	26^4	1.53^4	e1.70 MillerA	RelVlcty^1,MarttHll^{hd}	too far,mildly
	3-13 08	M1	1	fst	27^4	56^1	1.24^4	1.52^3	JerseyGirls	20000	3	$7^{9\frac{3}{4}}$	10^{10}	$10^{\circ 11}$	8^{13}	7^{16}	28^4	1.55^4	e★.30 SearsB	RelVlcty$^{2\frac{1}{4}}$,PopDiva^{hd}	out,best rest
	3-6 08	M1	1	fst	28^1	56^2	1.25^1	1.54^3	Qua		2	6^{12}	$6^{7\frac{1}{2}}$	$6^{5\frac{1}{2}}$	7^5	$4^{3\frac{1}{2}}$	29	1.55^1	nb CampbellJo	Pnclfndrpls$^{1\frac{3}{4}}$,Phyleon$^{1\frac{1}{2}}$	mild bid,evenly
8-1	2-15 08	M1	1	fst	27^3	56^4	1.26^4	1.53^2	NW12500FM	26000	9	9^{11}	$9^{6\frac{3}{4}}$	$7^{\circ\circ 2\frac{3}{4}}$	3^2	2^3	26^3	1.54	6.30 GingrasY	LfOfLxryN^3,StrptsHll$^{2\frac{1}{4}}$	too far,plenty
	2-8 08	M1	1	fst	27^4	55^4	1.24	1.52^4	NW12500FM	26000	6	7^{10}	$8^{9\frac{1}{4}}$	8^7	$8^{7\frac{1}{4}}$	$4^{2\frac{1}{2}}$	27^4	1.53^1	15.40 GingrasY	Smstrsfrthpn^{nk},DlghtflHp^{nk}	saved,mild late

Here's a mare that goes in and out of form frequently, as you can see by her erratic pattern of starts. I'm sure she's a difficult horse to train, even in the care of the nation's top stable, the Burkes.

Going into this race, Striptease Hall was already 0 for 7 on the year, having shown very little speed and having been crushed in two tries of the Jersey Girls series. However, if you watched her race on March 28, you saw a Herculean effort, considering her recent drubbings. She fought tenaciously despite a difficult, grinding trip and lost a photo to perfect-trip-sitter Menowyoulater. Yes, she was a beaten favorite, but that means somebody liked her, an example of tote-board action on that particular evening.

One week later, Striptease Hall showed up in a race for nonwinners of $15,000 last six; she had earned exactly $14,455 in her last six. She barely fit the condition of the race, but it was also a decent class hike from her prior loss. Because of the class hike, her 0-for-7 record in 2008, and the strength of this bunch, I felt she would offer good value and made her 8-1 on the morning line. It also helped that the favorites were stuck out in posts 9 and 10, respectively.

After a hotly contested pace, driver Yannick Gingras swung Striptease Hall wide from a third-over position in the outer tier and they burst home to win going away. The mare won her first race of the season and returned $17.60, just a fraction below my 8-1 morning line. Since it was the sixth race of the night, this was a chance to get started in a high-value pick four, or any other exotic wager, provided the $17.60 wasn't enough.

Another perfect example of a mare that was ready to win was Marnie Hall from July 11.

White	MARNIE HALL(L)				b m 6, by Blissfull Hall, Meggie Mo by Jate Lobell										1:50.1 M1	08 19 3 5 1	$147,735
					Daniel Plouffe,Bedford-Jean C Dessureault,Candiac,Qc										1:50.3 M1	07 17 3 3 2	$186,831
3	Daniel Dube (150) (0-0-0-0 .000)				Tr.Mark Silva(273-37-31-27 .136)								Last 6 Sts-$13,975		4 1:49.0 (1)		Lifetime $1,212,585
	7-4₀₈ M1	1 fst 27² 56	1.23⁴ 1.51	NW17000FM	29500 1	4⁵	3°1¾	2°½	2½	2nk	27¹ 1.51 L	4.20 DubeD	OmenHnvrnk,MarniHll¹¾	long unc,cldn't reach
	6-27₀₈ M1	1 fst 27¹ 54⁴	1.23 1.50⁴	W20001 FM	35000 4	8⁹	9⁷½	10⁷¼	10⁶¾	10⁸¾	28¹ 1.52³ L	14.20 McCarthyA	StreetDancer,Guestimate	trailed
	6-13₀₈ M1	1 fst 27² 56³	1.24¹ 1.51	LibertyFnl-D	250000 4	9⁶¾	8³¼	7⁴¾	8⁴	11⁷	27¹ 1.52² L	34.00 DubeD	LifeOfLuxuryN,DarlinsDelight	nothing
	6-6₀₈ M1	1 fst 27¹ 54²	1.22⁴ 1.49⁴	NW27500FM	37500 8	6⁸½	6°7½	6°3½	6²¾	7⁵¼	27² 1.50⁴ L	5.30 DubeD	Tdwtrdrgnfly1½,BrnStrytllr1¼	3rd over,tired
3-1	5-30₀₈ M1	1 fst 26² 53⁴	1.22¹ 1.49³	W25001 FM	42000 7	7¹⁰	7⁹½	7⁴	7²	5⁴¼	27² 1.50² L	9.20 DubeD	JadahRsA1¾,StrtDncr¹	lag,beat tired,mildly
	5-23₀₈ M1	1 fst 26³ 55⁴	1.24¹ 1.51	NW27500FM	37500 8	8¹³	6⁵½	5³	5²¾	3²	26³ 1.51² L	26.10 DubeD	RileyRos1½,MsMaggie½	imprvd ins 2x,mild

Marnie Hall was a classy mare and had earned over $1 million in her career, but her form up to that point in 2008 was quite suspect until she delivered a key-race effort on July 4. If you'll notice, Omen Hanover won that event, and I used her as an example in Chapter 8. Here's how you get a double dip of good karma from just one race. Not only did we cash with Omen Hanover that night, but I also couldn't wait for Marnie Hall's next start, based on what I saw. She fought Omen Hanover in ultra-gutsy fashion all the way to the wire. Omen Hanover really had to dig down to earn that win and it showed that Marnie Hall was back to her old self and was ready to win.

On July 11, I installed Marnie Hall as the 3-1 favorite and explained in my race review that she woke up in her prior race and that she had a huge post advantage over the second choice in the race, Ideal Weather from post 10. I had the ultimate confidence in Marnie Hall, but knew deep down that we weren't going to get rich; sometimes, you just have to take what they give you. Marnie Hall delivered as expected, digging in gamely to win by a neck and paying just $5.20.

CLASS DROPS

Theoretically, the flip side of an improvement in form is a horse who is dropping in class, and it is always one of the most powerful angles in handicapping harness racing. The key to learning its power is defining when a class drop is a good thing and when it is not. That takes a little more practice. It's not always easy to realize that a horse dropping in claiming price just isn't sharp and is therefore not a good play. But there are also times when that drop will pose a great betting opportunity. If you can learn to figure out which trainers are crafty and excellent in these situations, you will latch on to a lot of winners.

When a horse wins a race, he is usually forced up in class, especially in any of the conditioned races that are based on earnings over a horse's past five or six starts. That horse will then be "buried" against tougher company for anywhere from a few weeks to a month. When he or she is allowed to drop back down in class, that's what we are looking for. It's an angle that doesn't always produce the big prices, but when you can spot what you think is a sure winner, it opens the door to many money-making possibilities via the gimmicks. I've picked out three examples of perfect class drops that led to fairly decent payoffs.

Let's start with Thanks For Stoppin, who went to the gate in the second race on May 21, 2008, from post 1.

Red **THANKS FOR STOPPIN** — b g 3, by Real Artist, Pacific Wildfire by Pacific Fella — 1:52.1 M1 — 08 18 3 0 3 $32,423
Patricia M Hogan,Cream Ridge,NJ — 07 4 0 2 0 $5,000
1 George Brennan (150) (0-0-0-0 .000) — Tr.Edward Lohmeyer(44-7-1-7 .159) — Last 6 Sts-$10,159 — 4 1:51.2 (1) — Lifetime $90,173

	5-9 08	Mw 5/8	1	sly	27^{4}	55^{3}	1.22^{4}	1.51^{1}	D-PASS3YOC&G	42552	6	7^{11}	9^{13}	9^{23}	8^{20}	8^{25}	28^{4}	1.56^{1}	32.40	WilderWM	SandShotr,FirstRate,KysNautls	
	5-1 08	ChD 5/8	1	fst	27^{2}	56^{3}	1.23^{3}	1.52^{2}	D-PASS 3YOCG	35661	5	5^{6}	$6^{4\frac{1}{2}}$	$6^{3\frac{1}{2}}$	$5^{2\frac{3}{4}}$	$3^{2\frac{1}{2}}$	28^{3}	1.52^{4}	10.10	ManziCa	Atochia,EgyptnAr	closed steadily
	4-23 08	ChD 5/8	1	fst	27^{4}	57	1.24^{2}	1.53	NW2PMCdHG	11000	3	$3^{2\frac{1}{2}}$	$5^{3\frac{1}{2}}$	5^{4}	$5^{3\frac{1}{2}}$	$4^{1\frac{3}{4}}$	28^{1}	1.53^{2}	6.00	ManziCa	MagicShw,CBKHnv	dead cover,evenly
	4-15 08	ChD 5/8	1	fst	29^{1}	58^{4}	1.27^{3}	1.56^{2}	Qua		1	4^{3}	$4^{2\frac{1}{2}}$	3^{o1}	$2^{\frac{1}{2}}$	$2^{\frac{3}{4}}$	28^{4}	1.56^{3}	nb	ManziCa	FirstRat,ThnksFrS	live cover, gamely
3-1	4-8 08	ChD 5/8	1	gd	30^{3}	1.00^{1}	1.29^{2}	1.58^{1}	Qua		1	$3^{2\frac{3}{4}}$	$3^{3\frac{3}{4}}$	$2^{1\frac{1}{2}}$	$2^{\frac{3}{4}}$	$1^{\frac{1}{4}}$	28^{3}	1.58^{1}	nb	ManziCa	ThanksFrS,FirstRate,TheFitstr	
	8-2 07	M1	1	fst	28	57	1.25^{2}	1.54^{2}	NW1 2YO	10000	2	$3^{3\frac{3}{4}}$	4^{3}	$5^{2\frac{1}{2}}$	5^{1}	$2^{1\frac{1}{2}}$	28^{4}	1.54^{3}	23.80	BrennanG	$TradEdtr^{1\frac{1}{2}}$,ThnksFrStppn	sat,ang,trot

Here's a 3-year-old gelding conditioned by a great horseman in Eddie Lohmeyer, and owned by his wife, the famed equine surgeon Dr. Patty Hogan. Thanks For Stoppin had only raced three times on the season, all in the state of Pennsylvania, with two of those starts coming in restricted Pennsylvania sire stakes. Those are high-class races, and the last one in particular contained a top colt in Sand Shooter, one of the best 2-year-olds from the previous year. Thanks For Stoppin was still a maiden and drew an outside post at the Meadows for that start, so in reality, he had no chance.

Anybody familiar with trainer Lohmeyer knows that his horses usually improve with experience, and at this point, the gelding was about ready to deliver a quality effort. The switch back to the mile track would be no problem, because he'd raced over the Meadowlands strip the prior summer. Experience counts, and I'm guessing Lohmeyer had this maiden-race spot in mind all along after Thanks For Stoppin was speed-tightened in those stakes races.

Thanks For Stoppin delivered the effort I expected and won easily in $1{:}52^{1}/_{5}$, breaking his maiden, but returned only $5. Unfortunately, the morning-line favorite in the race was scratched and that reduced our potential for greater profit. Sometimes, those things happen.

The night of July 18 at the Meadowlands gave us two ideal examples of the class drop working to perfection. It would have made for a great parlay!

In the first race that night, Western Smoocher was taking a big and suspicious-looking drop in claiming price. That's one way to look at it, but I felt that trainer Rick Bilach was simply trying to steal a race and pray that his horse didn't get claimed.

WESTERN SMOOCHER — **b g 4, by Western Ideal, Sugar Kissed by Direct Scooter** — **1:49.1 M1 08 35 11 4 4 $186,680**
Larry Baron,Horsham,PA — **1:52.2 PcD 5/8 07 23 3 3 4 $31,523**
Daniel Dube (150) (0-0-0-0 .000) — **Tr.Richard Bilach** — **Last 6 Sts-$37,675 4 1:49.1 (1) Lifetime $275,553**

$7\text{-}6_{08}$	ChD $\frac{5}{8}$	1	fst	27^{3}	55	1.23^{3}	1.51^{1}	4YO Open	35000	1	$4^{4\frac{1}{2}}$	4^{5}	$3^{\circ 1\frac{3}{4}}$	$3^{1\frac{1}{2}}$	$4^{1\frac{1}{4}}$	27^{2}	1.51^{2}	8.50	DubeDa	Alilblty,CndrlaGy	2nd over,driving
$6\text{-}28_{08}$	M1	1	fst	27^{1}	54^{4}	1.23	1.50	Open 4YO	32000	9	10^{11}	10^{11}	$10^{5\frac{3}{4}}$	$10^{5\frac{1}{2}}$	$9^{7\frac{3}{4}}$	27^{2}	1.51^{3}	31.10	PlanoL	$NoblFlcn^{\frac{1}{2}}$,$WonThWst^{1\frac{1}{2}}$	trailed,no shot
$6\text{-}14_{08}$	M1	1	sly	27^{1}	54^{2}	1.22^{2}	1.50^{3}	50000 4YO	27500	9	9^{13}	9^{11}	$9^{9\frac{1}{2}}$	9^{8}	$5^{3\frac{1}{2}}$	27	1.51^{1}	*2.00	DubeD	StLdsKngpn,*TjsIdel	trailed,angled,too far
$6\text{-}7_{08}$	M1	1	fst	26^{3}	54^{4}	1.24	1.50^{4}	50000 4YO	27500	2	5^{5}	$8i^{4\frac{3}{4}}$	$7^{\circ\circ 3\frac{1}{2}}$	$5^{1\frac{1}{4}}$	$1^{\frac{1}{2}}$	26^{1}	1.50^{4}	*1.20	DubeD	$WstrnSmchr^{\frac{1}{2}}$,$IdelVntg^{1\frac{3}{4}}$	widest,flying
$5\text{-}31_{08}$	M1	1	fst	26	52^{3}	1.21	1.49^{1}	50/60000	33000	1	6^{9}	$6^{\circ 9}$	$6^{\circ\circ 4}$	$4^{\frac{1}{2}}$	1^{hd}	27^{2}	1.49^{1}	7.40	DubeD	$WstrnSmchr^{hd}$,$MchllsGmstn^{1}$	3rd over,wide,surged
$5\text{-}24_{08}$	Fhd	1	fst	27	56^{1}	1.24^{1}	1.52^{3}	Prf	13000	6	$6^{6\frac{1}{4}}$	$6^{\circ 6\frac{1}{4}}$	$4^{\circ 2\frac{1}{4}}$	$5^{3\frac{1}{4}}$	$2^{1\frac{1}{4}}$	28^{1}	1.52^{4}	7.30	DubeDa	DreamPrf,WstnSmch	2nd over,3 wide,rally

Here was a gelding that had been on some kind of roll. Nine wins on the year, with well over $130,000 earned. Why was he in for just a $40,000 base tag, when he won for a $50,000 tag five weeks earlier? The horse was returning from a start at Harrah's Chester against open company and he actually picked up a check in that start. The open level is a much stronger race than a $40,000 claimer.

Two things came to mind. First of all, consider the date. July 18 is late in the meet at the Meadowlands, so there would be only a few more opportunities for Western Smoocher to race on the big track. If he won the race and got claimed, that would be another $61,000 earned, on top of the $130,000 he already had for the season. Not bad for a horse that made just $31,000 as a 3-year-old. Also, some trainers have that mystique about them where other trainers won't claim their horses. Both of these factors were in play on that night. Here's what I wrote in my race review:

RACE 1 REVIEW Friday, July 18, 2008

By David Brower

1 **REAL TOWN** - Retains longshot status after seeming a bit overmatched at this level so far. Has the pole, but would need to find a lot more stamina.

2 **POKER HAT** - Never really made a move upon return. He should be better than that, and he will offer a big, square price for anybody wanting to try.

3 **BE BAD BILL** - He's had some moments here in the past, but not off layoff.

4 **ULOOKMATTVELOUS** - Suffered the Med shuffle last time and has now had a few races to get acclimated. I think it's time to pull trigger, take shot.

5 **ROMAN SHARK** - Stopped last two, so that usually means he's tailing off. I will hop off the bandwagon now and see if he improves at all. A big maybe.

6 **BEST MAGIC** - Has to be considered with these. Rallied nicely behind a strong winner last time and only needs similar journey and bigger kick.

7 **MAJOR IDEAL** - Post 10 killed him last time. The 54 halves killed him before that. Overdue for a luckier kind of break. The one to fear in here.

8 **YANKEE STARDOM** - Up from Chester and Pocono where his form was good, but this will be a much tougher test in my opinion. Bad post hurts.

9 **WESTERN SMOOCHER** - He's beaten better than this several times this season. The drop is a big one and he's overcome bad post. One to beat.

10 **NO ROAD PARKING** - Endured a difficult, grinding trip last time. Stuck with brutal post once again and note Sears sticks with again That's positive.

TOP CONTENDERS 9-2-7-6

The only knock here was the post, and you can see that Western Smoocher isn't exactly the world's fastest horse out of the gate. I felt that didn't matter, because if he was anywhere in the same zip code by the three-quarter pole, he was going to steamroll the field, and that's exactly what he did. And the best news of all for Bilach was that he wasn't claimed.

RST RACE: MEADOWLANDS, JUL. 18-1 Mile Pace. $40,000 Clm. Alw. 4 Year Olds. Purse $22,000.

6-12ChD	Western Smoocher	D.Dube 9	8°1½	7°1¾	6°°hd	3^2	1¼	28^1	27	28^2	26^4	1.50^2	R.Bilach		★1.10
11-8M1	Best Magic	E.Goodell 6	7¼	5°1¼	3°°hd	2no	2nk	28	26^4	28^3	27^1	1.50^3	D.Pinkney,Jr.		4.00
11-8M1	Poker Hat	Ti.Tetrick 2	41¾	1°1	11¾	1½	32½	27^1	27^1	28^2	27^4	1.50^3	Ri.Norman	L	12.60
11-8M1	Roman Shark	Dv.Miller 5	2nk	4hd	4^1	51½	43¼	26^4	28	28^3	27^4	1.51^1	K.Rucker	L	13.10
11-8M1	Real Town	Y.Gingras 1	11½	2½	2^1	4hd	51¼	26^3	28	28^3	28^3	1.51^4	B.Saunders	L	18.00
11-8M1	No Road Parking	B.Sears 10	91¾	8°2¼	8°°1½	6nk	62¾	28^3	26^4	28^2	28^1	1.52	A.Montini		16.00
8-qM1	Be Bad Bill	C.Manzi 3	51½	6no	71¼	72¾	7^3	27^2	27^4	28^2	29	1.52^3	J.Hndrtpfnd,Jr.		49.90
4-7M1	Major Ideal	M.Lachance 7	10	9dis	9dis	8nk	85¼	29	27	28^1	29	1.53^1	P.Fusco	L	10.40
11-8M1	Ulookmattvelous	A.Miller 4	61¼	3°1	5°nk	9dis	9dis	27^4	26^4	29	30^3	1.54^1	J.Dunning	L	5.80
2-11ChD	Yankee Stardom	Jo.Campbell 8	3x°1	x10x	10	10	10	27	36				Ji.Campbell	L	22.50

asix: Poker Hat, Roman Shark, Real Town, Major Ideal, Ulookmattvelous, Yankee Stardom.

Off: 7:06 Time: 0:26.3, 0:54.2, 1:22.4, 1:50.2. Mutuel Pool: $168,235. Temp. 87°

MUTUELS: **Western Smoocher** $4.20, 2.80, 2.80; **Best Magic** $4.00, 3.20; **Poker Hat** $4.40

EXACTA (9-6) $15.60. TRIFECTA (9-6-2) $52.90.

VESTERN SMOOCHER was third over down the backside in a dull flow, moved wide with cover final turn, took dead aim in the lane and went by under a confident drive. BEST MAGIC was stuck behind a clogger final turn, noved wide for stretch aim but was outkicked to the wire. POKER HAT brushed to the front after the action settled, took them through the turn on own terms but gave way in the lane once confronted. ROMAN SHARK left for n early spot, sat to the lane, angled with aim and came with a belated charge. REAL TOWN showed good speed to the front, yielded for a pocket, was sucked out in the brutal pace and tired in the lane. NO ROAD ARKING followed the winner wide final turn but lacked stretch rally. BE BAD BILL sat contently along the cones, angled in the lane and should be better next out. MAJOR IDEAL sat in and never made a play. ILOOKMATTVELOUS was left uncovered down the backside, never placed a bid and grinded the outer flow to a halt final turn. YANKEE STARDOM was clearly going to be parked on the rim and broke off the turn.

g 4 by Western Ideal, Sugar Kissed by Direct Scooter

Claiming Prices: 1. $50,000, 2. $50,000, 3. $50,000, 4. $50,000, 5. $50,000, 6. $50,000, 7. $50,000, 8. $50,000, 9. $50,000, 10. $50,000.

Owners: 1. Richard R Annunziata,Mahopac,NY, 2. Ralph Carnevale,Cream Ridge,NJ;Frank L Eagan Jr,Creamridge,NJ, 3. David H Mc Duffee,Nashua,NH, 4. Niss Allen Inc,Fair Lawn,NJ, 5. Frank J Bellino,Bronxville,NY, 6. Albina Montini,Acton,ON, CA;Nikolas R Drennan,Burlington,ON, CA, 7. Gty Stable,Englishtown,NJ, 8. Bramdeo Singh,Yonkers,NY, 9. Ian P Fromowitz,Richmond Hill,ON, CA;John D Fielding,Toronto,ON, CA, 10. Emposimato Stables,Holmdel,NJ;Juniper Ii LLC,River Vale,NJ.

The next example came up a little later in the evening. Yankee Lance was showing an incredible form spree for trainer Scott Rollins. Keep in mind that his last several starts came against the top-priced claimers we have at the Meadowlands. They're usually grouped in the $75,000/$100,000 range, and Yankee Lance was very competitive in those events. So, why was he entered this night for just $40,000?

ack **YANKEE LANCE(L)** — **b g 5, by Bettor's Delight, Lovin Yankee by On The Road Again** — **1:49.0 M1 08 22 6 2 0 $105,605**

5 **Ron Pierce (160) (0-0-0-0 .000)** — **Dave Clayville, Lightning 5 Racing Stable & Meadow Vernon Stable** — **1:49.4 M1 07 26 5 2 6 $86,284**

Tr.Scott Rollins — **Last 6 Sts-$45,900** — **5 1:49.0 (1)** — **Lifetime $216,574**

	$7\text{-}5_{08}$	M1	1 gd	26^2	54^3	1.23	1.49^4	75/100000	37500	3	5^8	5°4½	4°3	52¼	5^3	26^4	1.50^2	L	3.10 PierceR	OtOnABndr1½,JKCuLatrnk	live cover,mildly
	$6\text{-}28_{08}$	M1	1 fst	26^1	54^2	1.22	1.49^1	75/100000	39500	2	44¾	63½	74¼	6^4	45¾	27^3	1.50^2	L	4.10 BerryP	AllstrBlJn3½,Bllvllghtnng¾	buried,late pace
	$6\text{-}21_{08}$	M1	1 fst	26^1	53^3	1.22^4	1.50	75/100000	39500	4	79¼	7°5½	7°°3¾	74½	54¾	27^2	1.51	L	3.10 GoodellE	DreamPrf1¼,AllstrBlJn1¾	3d ovr,fllw wide,too far
0,000	$6\text{-}14_{08}$	M1	1 sly	27^1	53^4	1.22	1.50^4	75/100000	39500	2	77¼	8°9¼	8°6¼	6^5	1^1	27^3	1.50^4	L	2.70 PierceR	YankeLnc1,DreamPrfhd	5th ov,wd str,charged
-2	$6\text{-}7_{08}$	M1	1 fst	26^2	54	1.22^1	1.49	50/60000	33000	5	8^{11}	8°7½	7°°3¾	71½	1^1	26	1.49	L	★1.40 PierceR	YankeLnc1,MchllsGmstn¾	widest,driving
	$5\text{-}31_{08}$	M1	1 fst	26	52^3	1.21	1.49^1	50/60000	33000	3	9^{12}	9^{12}	7^4	81½	41¼	27^3	1.49^2	L	3.10 PierceR	WstrnSmchrhd,MchllsGmstn1	saved,ang,belated

Again, a few things came to my mind when handicapping his chances. It was nearing the end of the meet and Yankee Lance was a horse that always needed a big-size track. When the Meadowlands closed just a few weeks later, there wouldn't be any place for him to race. It had already been a successful season, with five wins and over $90,000 banked in earnings. So, if Yankee Lance won and got claimed, that would tack on another $53,000 to the account. That's not bad.

As handicappers, most of us don't really care about who gets claimed—we just want winners! Yankee Lance won by two lengths in 1:50²/₅, paying only $4.20, but he did get claimed. So it was a good news, bad news situation for the connections. Overall, I think they had a successful season with a veteran claimer and Rollins knew that he could get one more win before the meet ended.

13

FIRST-TIME LASIX

Lasix, or the anti-bleeding medication furosemide, has been legal in New Jersey racing for a couple of decades now, but the angle of first-time Lasix still intrigues me to this day. It doesn't work as consistently as some of the other angles discussed earlier in this book, but it's still powerful if you can get the right price. Don't fall for the horses that are overbet, but do recognize the few that offer true value.

Let's take a look at Haverford Hanover in the eighth race from May 3, 2008. Since this was late in the night on Kentucky Derby Day, I think the fans just missed the boat on this one, or were too tired from betting all day.

What made this horse so attractive on this night was going to be the price, because he was bound to be ignored with a couple of other high-profile horses in the race. Splendid Kisser was in there, off a roaring win in the SportsNet NY series final, and so was Big Heart, with three straight out-of-town wins from the powerful combination of trainer George Teague and driver Brian Sears. However, they had posts 9 and 10, respectively, which would only hinder their chances. I also have a rule I try to follow: I will almost never play a short-priced favorite after a victory in a series final. That summed up Splendid Kisser in this situation.

Haverford Hanover delivered nothing but top-quality efforts from January up until April 19, when he stopped on the lead for no apparent reason. He was also claimed that night by trainer Mark Kesmodel and was facing a different class on May 3, nonwinners of four races. If the added Lasix was the answer to that last clunker, then we were on to something here, and the value would be incredible.

I started Haverford Hanover at 6-1 in the morning line, knowing that I was going to pick him on top in my race review. Despite all that, take a look below at the result and the payoff.

EIGHTH RACE: MEADOWLANDS, MAY 3-1 Mile Pace. Non-winners of 4 ext. pari-mutuel races or $135,000 lifetime. 4 Year Olds & Under. Purse $26,000.

4-19-11M1	Haverford Hanover	Dv.Miller	8	$1^{\circ 1\frac{1}{4}}$	$2^{1\frac{1}{4}}$	$1^{1\frac{1}{4}}$	$1^{\frac{1}{2}}$	$1^{\frac{1}{2}}$	27^3	27	28	27^3	1.50^1	M.Kesmodel	L 15.00
4-17-5M1	Major Suit	A.Miller	5	$2^{1\frac{1}{2}}$	$3^{1\frac{3}{4}}$	2^1	$2^{2\frac{1}{2}}$	$2^{1\frac{1}{2}}$	27^4	27	28	27^2	1.50^1	K.Rucker	L 23.60
4-26-9M1	Lennon Blue Chip	R.Pierce	6	$7^{1\frac{1}{2}}$	$7^{1\frac{1}{4}}$	$6^{\frac{3}{4}}$	5no	3^2	29^2	26^3	27^2	27^1	1.50^3	S.Elliott	*1.60
4-19-8M1	Dont Fool Me Now	M.Lancaster	2	3^1	4^{nk}	$4^{\frac{1}{2}}$	$3^{\frac{3}{4}}$	$4^{\frac{1}{2}}$	28^1	27	28	27^4	1.51	G.Anthony	78.00
4-17-5M1	Free De Vie	Ty.Buter	3	$8^{1\frac{1}{2}}$	$8^{\circ 2}$	$i7^{\circ\circ\frac{3}{4}}$	4^{nk}	5^{nk}	29^3	26^3	27^1	27^3	1.51	J.Howard	L 5.60
4-25-7M1	Art At Heart	G.W.Sholty	7	$9^{1\frac{1}{2}}$	$9^{2\frac{1}{4}}$	$8^{\circ\frac{1}{2}}$	8^1	$6^{\frac{3}{4}}$	30	26^3	27	27^3	1.51^1	G.W.Sholty	L 34.40
4-26-6M1	Artstreos	D.Dube	4	$5^{1\frac{3}{4}}$	$5^{\circ 2}$	$5^{\circ\circ\frac{1}{2}}$	$6^{\frac{1}{2}}$	7^{hd}	28^3	26^3	28	28	1.51^1	C.Porcelli,Jr.	L 29.40
4-10-10DD	Big Heart	B.Sears	10	10	10	10	9^{19}	$8^{4\frac{3}{4}}$	30^1	26^4	27	27^1	1.51^1	G.Teague,Jr.	7.00
4-17-5M1	Captain Cambest	Jo.Campbell	1	$4^{\circ 1\frac{3}{4}}$	$1^{\circ hd}$	$3^{\circ\frac{1}{2}}$	7^{hd}	9^{dis}	28^2	26^1	28^2	29^1	1.52^1	Ka.Williams	L 13.40
4-17-5M1	Splendid Kisser	Y.Gingras	9	$6^{1\frac{3}{4}}$	$6^{\circ 1\frac{1}{2}}$	$x9x^{\circ 1}$	x10	10	29	26^3	28^1	38^4	2.02^3	Jf.Stafford	2.30

Lasix: Haverford Hanover, Major Suit, Free De Vie, Art At Heart, Artstreos, Captain Cambest.

Off: 9:38 Time: 0:27.3, 0:54.3, 1:22.3, 1:50.1. Mutuel Pool: $400,627. Temp. 53°

MUTUELS: **Haverford Hanover** $32.00, 10.20, 6.60; **Major Suit** $16.60, 8.00; **Lennon Blue Chip** $3.00

EXACTA (8-5) $417.20. TRIFECTA (8-5-6) $1,116.50.

HAVERFORD HANOVER left and was parked to the lead at the opening quarter, made the top, faced a backside bid going to the half, refused to give in and kept that one hung out to dry, rated the pace while on a speed mission and dug in gamely in the lane under mild urging to keep MAJOR SUIT at bay. The latter left right to the front, yielded to the winner at the quarter, sat the pocket trip as the leader got locked up in a speed duel, loomed larger as the race went on, looked poised and ready to strike, angled out for the stretch drive, took dead aim and was held off while having no excuse. LENNON BLUE CHIP sat on the rail and saved ground the whole way, angled out around the final turn, ducked back in, found clearance towards the finish, angled out again and closed steadily. DONT FOOL ME NOW sat a three hole trip, got boxed, made no moves and weakened under whip urging. FREE DE VIE lagged at the rear, pulled out at the half, got bothered by a breaking rival before three quarters while making a bold move, fanned widest around the final turn under whip urging and flattened out. ART AT HEART sat next to last past two calls, edged off the rail at three quarters, angled wide and beat tired rivals. ARTSTREOS pulled to the outside, picked up parked out cover, tipped wide and tired. BIG HEART trailed the field and had no shot. CAPTAIN CAMBEST was on the go past the opening quarter, attacked first over on the rim and looked to brush by the leader, got repelled going to the half, kicked out the earplugs and pressed on under urging, had enough and threw in towel after a brutal trip. SPLENDID KISSER tucked sixth, was following third over at the half, attempted a three wide move before the third marker, made a costly break and kissed his chances goodbye.

b g 4 by The Panderosa, Hattie by Abercrombie

Owners: 1. Joseph & Laurie Davino,Clarksburg,NJ, 2. Rucker Stb & D Van Witzenburg,IL;Panhellenic Stb Corp,NY;Sheffield Stb,PA, 3. Rodney Mitchell Inc,Dover,DE, 4. Darryl O Gombert,Rutherford,NJ;Hankook Stable,Fort Lee,NJ, 5. Sandra E Sokol,Belle Vernon,PA;Bernie Horabik,Grindstone,PA, 6. J M L Stables,Heathrow,FL;Sholty Stable Inc,Lexington,KY, 7. Ralph Katz,Burr Ridge,IL;Carl J Porcelli Jr,Crete,IL, 8. Teague Inc,Harrington,DE, 9. Sbk Stbs,E Rutherford,NJ;M&M Hrns Rcg LLC,Nanuet,NY;Vip Internet Stb LLC,Piscataway,NJ, 10. White Birch Farm,Allentown,NJ.

How about that price on a horse that was completely ignored in the betting and had only one clunker over a four-month span?

In the interest of fairness, I will now show you one that got away, and I can freely admit a mistake after I make it.

On Meadowlands Pace Night 2008, the fourth race of the night brought us a fresh face from Delaware—and boy, do I wish I'd looked a little closer, because in retrospect, it was easy to see why Kamwood Warrior had a great chance.

Blue-Red **KAMWOOD WARRIOR N(L)** — **b g 5, by Courage Under Fire, Kamwood Las by New York Motoring** — 1:51.0 M1 — 08 10 4 4 1 $42,665

10 — **Brian Sears (145) (0-0-0-0 .000)** — **J&E Stable Inc,Hartly,DE;Bob Stevenson Inc,Hartly,DE** — 07 14 0 4 1 $5,601

Tr.Robert Stevenson — **Last 6 Sts-$14,395** 5 1:51.0 (1) — **Lifetime $81,149**

	$7\text{-}3_{08}$	Har	1	fst	28	58^{3}	1.27	1.55^{2}	NW4	8500	7	$6^{7\frac{1}{4}}$	$7^{\circ 5\frac{1}{4}}$	$3^{\circ\circ 2\frac{1}{4}}$	$3^{1\frac{1}{2}}$	2no	28	1.55^{2}	6.10 DavisEdJr	FxvSosa,KamwdWarr,CaspinPce	
	$6\text{-}26_{08}$	Har	1	fst	29^{2}	59^{4}	1.29^{2}	1.57^{3}	Qua		2	1^{1}	$1^{1\frac{1}{2}}$	1^{1}	1^{1}	$1^{1\frac{1}{2}}$	28^{1}	1.57^{3}	nb DavisEdJr	KamwdWarr,NobleTess,CaspinPce	
	$5\text{-}29_{08}$	Har	1	fst	27^{4}	56^{3}	1.25^{4}	1.55^{4}	NW4	9000	scr	sk				scr					scratched-sick
	$5\text{-}22_{08}$	Har	1	fst	28^{4}	57	1.26^{1}	1.54^{2}	NW4	9000	7	7^{10}	$7^{9\frac{3}{4}}$	$3^{\circ 2\frac{3}{4}}$	$3^{3\frac{1}{4}}$	$2^{3\frac{1}{4}}$	28^{1}	1.55	16.80 DavisEdJr	QuckThnkr,KamwdWarr,MsqteHeat	
15-1	$5\text{-}1_{08}$	Har	1	fst	28^{3}	58	1.26^{1}	1.55^{2}	NW4	9000	7	6^{9}	$6^{5\frac{3}{4}}$	$4^{\circ 4\frac{3}{4}}$	$5^{4\frac{1}{2}}$	2^{1}	28^{2}	1.55^{3}	14.90 DavisEdJr	Calibratr,KamwdWarr,MsqteHeat	
	$4\text{-}24_{08}$	Har	1	fst	29^{2}	58^{1}	1.27^{4}	1.57^{1}	Qua		5	$3^{\circ 3}$	2^{3}	2^{3}	2^{5}	$2^{5\frac{1}{2}}$	29^{4}	1.58^{1}	nb DavisEdJr	GlasPack,KamwdWarr,stsky	

At first glance, it was probably pretty easy to just eliminate the 5-year-old recent import from New Zealand. He'd only raced three times in North America and those races were on the half-mile track at Harrington. He didn't win any of them, but he was second all three times. Bobby Stevenson trained him down in Delaware, and Bob is a veteran of the Big M racing wars. He knows what it takes to win a race at the Meadowlands. The gelding was sent north for this race by Bob's daughter, Janet, and his son-in-law, Eddie Davis Jr.—and he was getting Lasix for the first time.

Now, maybe they just wanted to come up and see the $1 million Meadowlands Pace, and have a horse to race at the same time, but look at who they asked to drive: Brian Sears. That, folks, is another sign of positive intent, especially after the horse drew the dreaded 10 hole.

The field he faced contained no killers, and a suspect favorite that hadn't won a race all year. The only problem was post 10. Sears, being the absolute precisionist that he is, knew exactly what to do. He floated the gelding out for a seat in the middle of the pack. He pulled Kamwood Warrior to grind up on the outside and he overpowered the field in an amazing 1:51. The payoff wasn't bad either ($12), but far from my bad morning line of 15-1.

So folks, this is one that I really missed. It's always easy to see after the fact and that's why I want you to learn from my mistake. This was a prime chance to get a nice price with several solid handicapping angles working in your favor. Maybe next time, I won't let Kentucky Derby fever affect my home-track handicapping.

14

WARM-UPS

Every once in a while, if you pay attention, a good situation will present itself if you are diligent enough to watch horses warm up. Most Standardbreds come out between races, usually about an hour before their own event, to warm up. As you get more familiar with horses warming up, you will eventually know what they're supposed to look like. It's actually easier than it sounds, but it does require a bit of work. A simple note on your program as you're watching the warm-ups between races will help you keep track of what you've seen. You will learn which horses always look good and which ones always look bad, or lazy, or just sloppy-gaited. There are many types.

Certain trainers, such as Ron Burke, always warm up their horses the right way of the track and try to sprint at the end of the mile. He feels this sharpens them up and gets them on their game. Other trainers, or sometimes grooms, will just let horses jog a few miles the wrong way of the track simply to stretch their legs and start the warm-up process. Those horses will usually get a more aggressive score-down with their driver after the post parade.

Getting to know the patterns of trainers and individual horses is crucial. Why? Because once in a while you will see something out of the ordinary, and you'd better be paying attention. That 3-5 shot in the fourth-race trot might not look so hot tonight, so it could become a wonderful betting opportunity against him or her. Or, that 15-1 shot that has post 10 in the eighth race usually just jogs a few miles, and tonight, he's turning and going a trip. That's always a sign of positive intent.

The situation I picked out to explain this occurred at Harrah's Chester on their biggest day of racing in 2008. August 17 was Battle of Brandywine Day in the Delaware Valley. The track played host to several stakes races, and one of them in particular made my day. The $350,000 Valley Forge Stakes was the ninth race on the card and it appeared to be a great matchup between Tug River Princess and Thong. They had been rivals all summer long, and a big race like that could easily determine who would gain command in the race for the division champion.

Tug River Princess had been super all season for her trainer, Ross Croghan, but was coming off a disappointing seventh in the Mistletoe Shalee on Hambletonian Day. Thong was in the same race and also tired badly, eventually finishing ninth. Basically, the two fillies sizzled each other in the August heat of Hambo Day.

Two weeks later, the rematch was on with Tug River Princess starting from post 2 and Thong in post 3.

9

1 MILE PACE
PURSE $350,000
Sunday, August 17, 2008
HARRAH'S CHESTER

The Valley Forge
E.C. No. 4
3 Yr. Old Fillies

EXACTA-TRIFECTA
SUPERFECTA
PICK 3 (9-10-11)

PLEASE ASK FOR HORSE BY PROGRAM NUMBER

RED **ERIC GOODELL** (35) wh-r blu-l blu (2,084-262-284-277-.246)

Tr-JOSH GREEN (638-168-117-76-.405)
b f 3 by Artiscape-Party Animal-The Panderosa
Leonard R Hubbard,Cambridge,MD

2008	16	3	2	3	$147,661 1:52⁴Chst⅝ ft
2007	9	2	1	0	$74,775 1:55²M1 ft
Life	25	5	3	3	$222,436 3, 1:52⁴Chst⅝ ft

Br- Perretti Farms,NJ

1 **CARTNIVEROUS**

10-1

LAST 6 STARTS-$107,299

Date	Trk	Purse	FL Tc	U/D Tmp	Det Med Clm	Class	Dis	Leader's Time 1/4	1/2	3/4	Time	PP	1/4	1/2	3/4	Str	Fin	Ind 1/4	Ind Time	1/4 Odds	Ind Drv	Tm	Order of Finish First Second Third	St
8- 9	08 3PcD⅝	56415	ft	75	D	ADIOO VOLO		27^{2}	56	123^{1}	152^{2}	5	$8^{\circ 6\frac{3}{4}}$	$5^{\circ 3\frac{3}{4}}$	$6^{\circ 4}$	$7^{7\frac{1}{2}}$	$7^{14\frac{3}{4}}$	31^{2}	155^{2}	*1.50	ErGoodell	JoGreen	UpFBethan,IdlNctme,AlicsRstr	-8
7-31	08 6Chst⅝	17000	ft	83	▼	NW6PMCdFM		27^{1}	56	123^{2}	152^{4}	7	$4^{4\frac{1}{4}}$	$4^{\circ 3\frac{1}{2}}$	$1^{1\frac{1}{2}}$	1^{2}	1^{3}	29^{2}	152^{4}	*.60	ErGoodell	JoGreen	Cartnivrs,TmlsArtst,PageTurnr	-8
7-18	08 3M1	56700	ft	87	D	TarportHap		25^{4}	54^{3}	122^{3}	149^{2}	4	$6^{11\frac{1}{4}}$	$6^{\circ 7}$	$7^{\circ 5\frac{3}{4}}$	$7^{7\frac{1}{4}}$	$5^{7\frac{1}{4}}$	27	150^{4}	17.10	ErGoodell	JoGreen	HapyDremr,TugRvrPrn,CuzSheCan	-7
6-27	08 1M1	68110	ft	81	D	Ladyship		27^{1}	55^{4}	124	151^{2}	4	$6^{5\frac{3}{4}}$	$4^{\circ 3\frac{1}{2}}$	$2^{\circ hd}$	1^{1}	$4^{2\frac{3}{4}}$	28	152	3.80	ErGoodell	JoGreen	KnockThrT,CheryBomb,Haunted	-7
6-20	08 4M1	175000	ft	76	D	3yrF NJSS		28^{2}	58	125^{4}	152^{4}	5	$8^{\circ 8\frac{1}{2}}$	$5^{\circ 3}$	$4^{\circ 1\frac{1}{4}}$	$2^{\frac{1}{2}}$	$1^{\frac{3}{4}}$	26^{4}	152^{4}	17.10	ErGoodell	JoGreen	Cartnivrs,KnockThrT,IdlNctme	-1
6-13	08 3M1	37700	ft	77		3yrF NJSS		27	54^{4}	123^{1}	151^{1}	7	$1^{\circ\frac{1}{2}}$	$2^{1\frac{3}{4}}$	$3^{1\frac{1}{4}}$	$5^{2\frac{1}{4}}$	$4^{3\frac{1}{2}}$	28^{2}	151^{4}	7.20	ErGoodell	JoGreen	ChyneTrsh,ChclteArt,GodNwsLdy	-7
6- 6	08 6M1	38300	ft	69		3yrF NJSS		27^{2}	56^{1}	124^{2}	152^{1}	8	$7^{\circ 10\frac{1}{2}}$	$7^{\circ 4\frac{1}{2}}$	$6^{\circ 4\frac{1}{2}}$	$5^{3\frac{1}{2}}$	$5^{2\frac{3}{4}}$	27^{3}	152^{4}	3.40	ErGoodell	JoGreen	ChyneTrsh,JkGetpngo,ChclteArt	-8
5-31	08 6M1	200000	ft	73	D	Miss NJ		27	55	123^{1}	151^{4}	9	$3^{1\frac{1}{4}}$	$4^{4\frac{1}{4}}$	$2^{\circ 1}$	$3^{2\frac{1}{4}}$	5^{3}	29	152^{2}	13.50	ErGoodell	JoGreen	KnockThrT,IdealNwtn,GodNwsLdy	-1
5-23	08 2M1	20000	ft	65	D	Miss NJ		27^{2}	57^{1}	124^{4}	151^{3}	5	$1^{1\frac{1}{2}}$	$1^{1\frac{1}{2}}$	$2^{1\frac{1}{4}}$	$3^{1\frac{1}{2}}$	3^{1}	26^{4}	151^{4}	14.00	ErGoodell	JoGreen	IdealNwtn,KnockThrT,Cartnivrs	-8
5-16	08 2M1	38900	sy	48		3yrF NJSS		27^{4}	55^{2}	124^{2}	152^{1}	1	$5^{3\frac{1}{2}}$	$4^{\circ 3\frac{3}{4}}$	$1^{\circ hd}$	$1^{\frac{3}{4}}$	$3^{5\frac{1}{4}}$	28^{4}	153^{1}	13.40	ErGoodell	JoGreen	KnockThrT,BestPlace,Cartnivrs	-9
5-10	08 12Fhld	55850	ft	61		HelnDancer		27^{3}	57	126	155^{2}	7	$8^{10\frac{1}{2}}$	8^{9}	$7^{\circ\circ 4\frac{1}{2}}$	7^{3}	5^{3}	29^{1}	156	72.00	DaMiller	JoGreen	FrStzHorn,Thong,PrncsJina	-8
5- 1	08 10Har	8000	ft	62		FMNW3LTCD		29	58^{4}	128^{2}	157^{3}	2	$1^{1\frac{1}{2}}$	$1^{1\frac{1}{2}}$	$1^{1\frac{1}{2}}$	$1^{1\frac{1}{2}}$	$1^{1\frac{3}{4}}$	29^{1}	157^{3}	*.05	AMorgan	JoGreen	Cartnivrs,Indeman,MomsToy	-8

2

LUE

JOHN CAMPBELL (53) wh-c red-l blu (907-123-100-97-.233)

TUG RIVER PRINCESS

Tr-ROSS CROGHAN (530-90-84-67-.300)
b f 3 by Badlands Hanover-Aucryifiwanto-Au Crombie
Let It Ride Stbs,Dlry Bch,FL;Robert Cooper Stbs,Bc Rtn,FL;
J Silva,Lng Bch,NY

2008	12	8	1	2	$269,829	1:51¹Moh⅞ ft
2007	5	5	0	0	$21,000	1:56 Har ft
Life	17	13	1	2	$290,829	3, 1:51¹Moh⅞ ft

Br- Bobby Mills & Michael L Tait,DE

5-2

LAST 6 STARTS-$154,979

8-2	08	5M1	407400	gd81	D	M Shalee	26³ 53⁴	122² 151	8	2°1½	1¹	5⁴	85½	78½	29² 152⅜E°0.30	JCampbell	RoCroghan	StylishAr,GodNwsLdy,MisScartt-10
7-25	08	6M1	25000	ft 82	D	M Shalee	26² 54³	122⁴ 150	8	5°6½	5°4¼	5°3	4¹½	3nk	26³ 150 E°0.40	JCampbell	RoCroghan	McartsNCr,DesrblCnd,TugRvrPrn-11
7-18	08	3M1	56700	ft 87	D	TarportHap	25⁴ 54³	122³ 149²	2	3⁴	1¹½	1¹½	1½	2nk	26⁴ 149²	.60	JCampbell	RoCroghan	HapyDremr,TugRvrPrn,CuzSheCan -7
7-10	08	1M1		ft 80		Qua	27⁴ 57⁴	127² 153³	7	1¹½	1¹½	4¹1½	1¹	2ns	26¹ 153³	NB	JCampbell	RoCroghan	HapyDremr,TugRvrPrn,ANGscnfsn -9
7-3	08	9M1		ft 85		Qua	28¹ 56¹	124² 152²	4	38½	3°7½	3°7½	2⁷	2¹0½	28⁴ 154³	NB	JCampbell	RoCroghan	TengePage,TugRvrPrn,KisngBndt -5
6-14	08	5Mohi	718370	ft 73		D-FANHANOV	28¹ 56⁴	123⁴ 151¹	1	4⁴	4°	4°	3²½	3¹½	151³	.50	JCampbell	DaMcCall	ChncyLady,Artimttsl,TugRvrPrn-10
6-7	08	3Mohi	34300	ft 84		D-FANHANOV	27¹ 55³	123³ 151¹	1	5	5⁴	4°	1½	1³½	151¹	.35	JCampbell	DaMcCall	TugRvrPrn,CuzSheCan,ImJstSpcl -9
5-30	08	5Mohi		ft 46		QUA	28⁴ 58¹	126¹ 153⁴	7	1	2	2	2¹	1²½	153⁴	NB	DaMcCall	DaMcCall	TugRvrPrn,VoelzHnv,StnAppeal -7
5-22	08	1M1		ft 53		Qua	28³ 59	128⁴ 155¹	7	3³¼	3³¼	1¹½	1¹½	2nk	26² 155¹	NB	JCampbell	RoCroghan	HapyDremr,TugRvrPrn,SandFthrs -7
4-16	08	3M1	,68900	ft 60		Blossom	29³ 57²	126² 153	4	1°1½	1¹½	1¹	1¹	1³½	26³ 153	.05	JCampbell	RoCroghan	TugRvrPrn,ChyneTrsh,ErmaLaEm -6
4-10	08	8DDⁱ	100000	ft 62		DSBF FINAL	26	55²	123¹ 151²	1	3⁵	3°1½	2°½	15	28¹ 151²	.05	JCampbell	TrWarwick	TugRvrPrn,DoverDoly,BdndsPwr -8
4-2	08	3M1	22500	ft 44		Blossom	29	59²	128³ 155	2	2½	1½	1¹	13	12½	26² 155	.10	JCampbell	RoCroghan	TugRvrPrn,ChyneTrsh,Cartnivrs -5

3

HITE

TIM TETRICK (26) grn-yel-wh (2,761-624-443-372-.360)

THONG

Tr-KEVIN LARE (213-39-20-27-.278)
b f 3 by Western Hanover-Bikini Line-Artsplace
Jerry Silva, Long Beach,NY;North State Street Stable, Dover,DE

2008	9	6	1	1	$290,069	1:50⁴M1 ft
2007	11	3	2	2	$332,857	1:53⁴Moh⅞ ft
Life	20	9	3	3	$622,926	3, 1:50⁴M1 ft

Br- Stonegate Stdbred Fms Inc,NJ

2-1

LAST 6 STARTS-$250,715

8-2	08	5M1	407400	gd81	D	M Shalee	26³ 53⁴	122² 151	2	42½	2°¹	42½	95½	913½	30⁴ 153⁴E°0.30	TiTetrick	KeLare	StylishAr,GodNwsLdy,MisScartt-10
7-25	08	7M1	25000	ft 82	D	M Shalee	27² 55	123³ 150²	1	4³	4°3½	2°½	1½	1¹½	26³ 150²	1.70	TiTetrick	KeLare	Thong,ANGscnfsn,GodNwsLdy-10
7-18	08	4M1	57700	ft 87	D	TarportHap	27	54²	123¹ 150²	7	3°1½	1¹½	1½	1½	1nk	27¹ 150²	.70	TiTetrick	KeLare	Thong,DesrblCnd,LvngCrime -9
7-5	08	8YR	325230	ft 72		LISMOREFIN	28² 57	124⁴ 153³	6	44½	4°3	2°nd	2¹½	1½	28⁴ 153³	1.10	TiTetrick	KeLare	Thong,GodNwsLdy,ChyneTrsh -8
6-27	08	6YR	20000	ft 84		LISMORE	28¹ 57	125 153¹	4	2°ns	1¹½	1¹½	1¹	1¹½	28¹ 153¹	1.70	StBouchard	KeLare	Thong,Hanahisbl,IdealNwtn -6
6-14	08	10Mohi	73500	ft 73		FAN HANOVE	28¹ 56¹	124 151²	6	4	4°	2°	12½	14½	151²	1.50	TiTetrick	KeLare	Thong,ImJstSpcl,Ladycino-10
6-7	08	6Mohi	34300	ft 84		D-FANHANOV	27¹ 55²	123 151²	7	1°	2	2	24½	32½	152	1.45	PaMacdonell	KeLare	ANGscnfsn,SprigHnv,Thong -7
5-17	08	9Meai	42552	ft 62	D	PASS 3YOF	27¹ 56³	123⁴ 152¹	8	1°1	1¹½	1²	1²	12½	28²152¹	.60	DaPalone	KeLare	Thong,PaviaHnv,ReNstyWs -9
5-10	08	12FHoi	55850	ft 61		HelnDancer	27³ 57	126 153³	8	1¹1½	1½	1½	1½	2hd	29²155²	2.50	JCampbell	KeLare	FrStzHorn,Thong,Prncs,Jina -8
5-1	08	4M1		ft 60		Qua	29¹ 59	127³ 155	1	33½	33½	2⁴	2½	1¹½	26³ 155	NB	JCampbell	KeLare	Thong,HapyDremr,GodNwsLdy -7
4-24	08	4M1		ft 76		Qua	29³ 100	129³ 156²	5	77½	6°¾	4°4½	3¼	1²	26² 156²	NB	JCampbell	KeLare	Thong,HapyDremr,GodNwsLdy -7
11-10	07	12DDⁱ	231650	ft 43		MATRON-F	26³ 55⁴	123² 152¹	4x	5⁷	65½	66½	54½	5³	28⁴153²	20.40	ATLynchJr	ATLynchJr	HapyDremr,StylishAr,RedyToWin -8

4

REEN

YANNICK GINGRAS (29) h grn-wh-go (1,747-223-253-203-.247)

RESPECTABLE (PA)

Tr-STEVE ELLIOTT (215-41-39-24-.329)
b f 3 by Blissfull Hall-Hawaiian Beachlady-Jenna's Beach Boy
Bulletproof Enterprises, Boca Raton,FL

2008	9	4	2	0	$129,993	1:52 PcD⅝ ft
2007	5	2	0	0	$8,963	1:53 PcD⅝ ft
Life	14	6	2	0	$138,956	3, 1:52 PcD⅝ ft

Br- John P Hurtgen,PA

5-1

LAST 6 STARTS-$120,368

7-31	08	8Mear	51890	ft 80	▼D	PASS3YOF	27³ 55³	124 154²	7	2°¹	1½	2¹	73½	78½	31⁴ 156	1.10	RaTharps	StElliott	TwnOksTes,Makerbark,RivenHnv -8
7-25	08	7M1	25000	ft 82	D	M Shalee	27² 55	124 154¹	4	5	89	8°8½	9°°6	84½	811½	27⁴ 152³	YaGingras	StElliott	Thong,ANGscnfsn,GodNwsLdy-10
7-14	08	7Chsti	51891	ft 74	D	PASS 3YOF	27² 56⁴	125² 153³	8	4°4	1¹½	11	1½	1¹½	28¹ 153³	7.50	YaGingras	StElliott	Respctble,Panitarim,RivenHnv -8
6-24	08	13PcDⁱ	42552	ft 72	D	PaSS 3YOF	27² 56²	125 153³	9	55	1¹	1hd	1½	12½	27³ 152²	.40	YaGingras	StElliott	Respctble,RivenHnv,FddleRose -9
6-7	08	9PcDⁱ	20899	ft 92	D	JmLynchFnl	26⁴ 54³	122 150²	6	52½	4°3¼	2°¹	2hd	2½	28¹ 150²	6.50	YaGingras	StElliott	IdeaNwtn,Respctble,LightnngG -9
5-17	08	9PcDⁱ	42552	ft 62		JmLynchElm	27⁴ 54¹	122⁴ 152	4	54½	5°3½	3°1½	2¹	1½	28¹ 152	6.50	YaGingras	StElliott	Respctble,LightnngG,SandFthrs -9
5-29	08	4Chsti	14300	ft 71	▼	NW4FMCdFM	27² 57³	125¹ 153⁴	2	4⁷	3°1½	2°½	31	2½	28³153⁴	.40	TiTetrick	StElliott	BonMot,Respctble,LadyDgn -8
5-17	08	6Meai	42152	ft 62	▲D	PASS 3YOF	27⁴ 554	124 154	1	3⁴	3³	2°¹	4x3	x4xp62½	29³154²	7.50	DaPalone	StElliott	DragonfLn,HShowbiz,PmbrkeLil -8
5-1	08	2Chsti	12100	ft 59	▼	NW2FMCdFM	27³ 58	126¹ 153⁴	5	32½	3°2½	1¹	1¹	14½	27⁴154²	2.70	TiTetrick	StElliott	Respctble,RdsAshlee,LadyDgn -7
4-15	08	6SGR1		ft 60		QUA	29⁴ 58⁴	124 156	3	5³	54	35	27½	27⁴156¹	NB	PaWReid	StElliott	FakeOnroN,Respctble,Staley -5
4-1	08	5SGR1		ft 72		QUA	30² 101³	128² 156	5	2½	1½	1½	31	33½	27⁴156¹	NB	PaWReid	StElliott	PopZPop,SegndoHnv,Respctble -4
10-3	07	4Lex1	96500	ft 80	D	F2vo-Stk	28¹ 55	123⁴ 151	1	SCR VET - Sick						RoDinges		BechyGirl,KnockThrT,FlpForLve -7

5

LACK

GREG GRISMORE (38) wh-red-blk (1,573-197-203-219-.243)

GOOD NEWS LADY

Tr-JIMMY TAKTER (207-42-45-29-.370)
b f 3 by Western Ideal-Whats New-Falcon Seelster
Brittany Farms, Versailles,KY; Val D'Or Farms, Millstone,NJ;
Christina Takter, East Windsor,NJ

2008	10	0	3	3	$242,977	
2007	12	4	0	3	$231,474	1:52³Lex1 ft
Life	22	4	3	6	$474,451	2, 1:52³Lex1 ft

Br- Brittany Farms,KY;Val D'Or Farms,NJ

6-1

LAST 6 STARTS-$206,293

8-2	08	5M1	407400	gd81	D ·	M Shalee	26³ 53⁴	122² 151	5	7°4½	7°3½	2°¹	2¹½	2½	28³1511	24.30	GrGrismore	JiTakter	StylishAr,GodNwsLdy,MisScartt-10
7-25	08	7M1	25000	ft 82	D	M Shalee	27² 55	123³ 150²	5	1½	2¹½	3¹	4¹½	3¹½	26⁴ 150¹	17.20	GrGrismore	JiTakter	Thong,ANGscnfsn,GodNwsLdy-10
7-18	08	3M1	56700	ft 87	D	TarportHap	25⁴ 543	123 149²	7	7¹3½	7⁸	54⁴	44½	44½	26⁴ 150¹	17.20	GrGrismore	JiTakter	HapyDremr,TugRvrPrn,CuzSheCan-7
7-5	08	6YR	325230	ft 72		LISMOREFIN	28² 57	124⁴ 153³	7	78½	76½	73½	64	2¹½	28³ 154	33.50	GrGrismore	JiTakter	Thong,GodNwsLdy,ChyneTrsh -8
6-27	08	6YR	20000	ft 84		LISMORE	28¹ 57	125 153¹	5	54½	66	54½	56½	45½	28³ 154²	21.50	GrGrismore	JiTakter	Thong,Hanahisbl,IdealNwtn -6
6-20	08	4M1	175000	ft 76		3vrF NJSS	28² 58	125⁴ 154	2	78½	7°4½	6°2½	52½	45½	27 153¹	6.50	AnMiller	JiTakter	Cartnivrs,KnockThrT,JdNctme-10
6-13	08	4M1	37700	ft 77		3vrF NJSS	27	54⁴	123¹ 151¹	1	44½	46	2°1½	1¹½	33	28²1514	1.30	AnMiller	JiTakter	ChyneTrsh,ChclteAr,GodNwsLdy -7
5-31	08	4M1	200000	ft 73		Miss NJ	27	56	123 151²	3	44½	46	2°¹½	42½	3½	28¹ 152	5.60	AnMiller	JiTakter	KnockThrT,AdeanEs,GodNwsLdy -7
5-23	08	4M1	20000	ft 65		Miss NJ	27³ 57	125³ 153	4	44½	4°4½	1°°¹	42½	3¹½	27⁴154¹	1.10	AnMiller	JiTakter	ErmaLaEm,GodNwsLdy,McartsNCr -6
5-8	08	12M1	39500	sy 48		3vr F NJSS	28	57	126 153	7	73½	73½	8¹1½	44	27⁴154³	4.00	AnMiller	JiTakter	ChyneTrsh,ErmaLaEm,GodNwsLdy -7
5-8	08	12M1		ft 60		Qua	28	5⁷¹	126³ 154	7	6¹°3½	5°4½	4°°1½	1½	1½	27³1542	NB	BrSears	JiTakter	YankeLovr,GodNwsLdy,TmisArtist -8

6

ELLOW

STEPHANE BOUCHARD (41) grn-wh (1,803-318-303-238-.314)

ARTIMITTATESLIFE

Tr-EDWARD HART (205-38-27-28-.304)
b f 3 by Art Major-Oven Mitt-Albert Albert
Robert B Young, Guelph,ON, CA; Paul A Gazzola, Guelph,ON, CA;
Brian K Barton, Carlisle,ON, CA

2008	9	6	1	1	$295,547	1:52 Moh⅞ ft
2007	7	2	3	2	$98,284	1:55 TgDn⅝ ft
Life	16	8	4	3	$393,831	3, 1:52 Moh⅞ ft

Br- R B Young & P A Gazzola & B K Barton,ON

9-2

LAST 6 STARTS-$267,447

8-6	08	2PcDⁱ		ft 72		QUA	29¹ 58	125³ 153⁴	5	1hd	2²	2¹½	2³	2³	28³154⁴	NB	StBouchard	EdHart	5rsreKepr,Artimtts,FrStzHorn -5
7-27	08	5TgDnⁱ	40147	ft 82		3YO F NYSS	28¹ 57¹	124⁴ 152²	1	1¹½	1¹½	1¹	1¹½	1³½	28³152²	.60	StBouchard	EdHart	Artimtts,Ladycino,AwayWeGo -7
7-15	08	9YR	48807	ft 81		3YR F NYSS	28¹ 57	124⁴ 152²	6	1¹½	1¹½	1¹½	1½	1⁴	27³152²	.45	StBouchard	EdHart	Artimttsl,OnlsdeghtflDi -8
7-5	08	7Gosh	15000	gd76-1		3YR F NYSS	27² 58²	127 156²	4	1°1½	1¹½	1½	1½	14	29²156²	NB	StBouchard	EdHart	Artimttsl,slalsbla,MryLynLee -7
6-22	08	7Stga	37459	ft 64		3YR F NYSS	28	57³	126³ 154	2	12	1½	1½	12	1²	27⁴154³	.05	StBouchard	EdHart	Artimttsl,WonNghtSt,RvrbnkHnv -7
6-14	08	5Mohi	718370	ft 73		D-FANHANOV	28¹ 564	123⁴ 151¹	3	6°	5°	54	1511	10.90	BrSears	RoBYoung	ChncyLady,Artimttsl,TugRvrPrn-10
6-7	08	8Mohi		ft 60		Qua	28¹ 56³	124 152	5	7°	5°	2²	1½	152	7.55	BrSears	RoBYoung	Artimttsl,AFstyAr,CruznIny1 -9
5-25	08	7TgDnⁱ	270625	ft 72	D	EBC 3YO F	26⁴ 55¹	123¹ 152	6	78½	52½	6°5	52½	4½	28²154²	15.30	StBouchard	EdHart	MadamCnts,WomanRbis,FirstDraw -9
5-18	08	8TgDnⁱ	12500	gd48-1		EBC 3YO F	27⁴ 562	124⁴ 154³	3	44½	1¹¹	1½	1¹½	1½	29³154³	.80	StBouchard	EdHart	RvrbnkHnv,Artimttsl,EngrtsGl -7
5-10	08	9GeoDⁱ	9900	ft 51		F-NW3R5000	27	55²	124³ 154	2	2	1½	1½	1²	1²	29²154	*1.35	DaBoughton	EdHart	Artimttsl,CrfeDuHrs,KllynRose+ -9
5-3	08	1GeoDⁱ		ft 50-1		QUA	28	58³	128 158	5	1¹	1½	1½	1½	1½	30 158	NB	RoBYoung	RoBYoung	Artimttsl,WhsprTrce,TinyTears -5
9-15	07	4YR	150000	ft 66		NYSS 2YOF	28⁴ 58	124⁴ 156²	3	43½	3°2½	2°¹½	1¹½	29²156³	4.90	StBouchard	EdHart	KisngBndt,Artimttsl,JkMajorte -8

PINK **GEO. NAPOLITANO JR** (42) red-wh-grn (990-148-138-118-.267) **Tr-ROSS CROGHAN** (530-90-84-67-.300)

7 **KNOCK THREE TIMES**(L) — b f 3 by Western Ideal-Deer Valley Miss-Artsplace

Mentally Stable Inc,Delray Beach,FL;
Robert Cooper Stables LLC,Boca Raton,FL

2008	10	4	2	1	$231,750	1:51²M1 ft
2007	11	1	3	2	$163,874	1:55¹M1 sy
Life	21	5	5	3	$395,624	3, 1:51²M1 ft

Br- Melvin P Segal,NC

12-1

LAST 6 STARTS-$100,778

8-8	08 11PcD$\frac{5}{8}$	16100	sy 63-2	L	NW8850L5FM	28	57^1	124^4	154^3	1	$4^{3\frac{3}{4}}$	$3^{\circ 2\frac{1}{4}}$	$1^{1\frac{1}{2}}$	1^{hd}	$4^{1\frac{3}{4}}$	30^1	155	*.80	ErGoodell	RoCroghan	TwnOksTes,DelaCreme,Cinderela -
7-25	08 7M1	25000	ft 82	DL	M Shalee	27^2	55	123^3	150^2	9	$10^{\circ 12}$	$10^{\circ 9\frac{3}{4}}$	$10^{\circ 7\frac{1}{4}}$	$10^{5\frac{1}{2}}$	$7^{6\frac{1}{4}}$	26^3	151^3	18.40	ErGoodell	RoCroghan	Thong,ANGscnfsn,GodNwsLdy-1
7-18	08 5M1	56700	ft 87	DL	TarportHap	27^4	55^3	123^3	150^4	5	$6^{8\frac{1}{2}}$	$4^{\circ 4\frac{1}{2}}$	$1^{\circ ns}$	1^{hd}	$5^{6\frac{3}{4}}$	28^3	152^1	*.90	DaMiller	RoCroghan	TengePage,BechyGirl,Expresive -
6-27	08 1M1	68110	ft 81	DL	Ladyship	27^1	55^4	124	151^2	7	7^7	$6^{\circ 4\frac{3}{4}}$	$4^{\circ 1\frac{1}{4}}$	2^1	$1^{\frac{3}{4}}$	27^1	151^2	*1.20	DaMiller	RoCroghan	KnockThrT,CheryBomb,Haunted -
6-20	08 4M1	175000	ft 76	DL	3yrF NJSS	28^2	58	125^4	152^4	3	$5^{\circ 6\frac{1}{2}}$	$1^{\circ\frac{3}{4}}$	$1^{\frac{1}{4}}$	$1^{\frac{1}{2}}$	$2^{\frac{3}{4}}$	27^1	153	*1.30	DaMiller	RoCroghan	Cartnivrs,KnockThrT,IdlNctme-1
6-13	08 5M1	37700	ft 77	L	3yrF NJSS	28	56^4	124^4	152^2	1	4^5	$4^{4\frac{3}{4}}$	$3^{\circ 1\frac{1}{2}}$	2^{ns}	1^{nk}	27^2	152^2	*.40	DaMiller	RoCroghan	KnockThrT,IdlNctme,ErmaLaEm -
5-31	08 6M1	200000	ft 73	DL	Miss NJ	27	55	123^1	151^4	4	$8^{\circ 8\frac{1}{2}}$	$6^{\circ 6}$	$4^{\circ\circ 1\frac{1}{2}}$	2^1	1^{hd}	28^1	151^4	E*0.80	BrSears	RoCroghan	KnockThrT,IdealNwtn,GodNwsLdy-1
5-23	08 2M1	20000	ft 65	DL	Miss NJ	27^2	57^1	124^4	151^3	7	4^5	$3^{\circ 2\frac{1}{4}}$	$1^{1\frac{1}{4}}$	$1^{1\frac{1}{4}}$	2^{nk}	26^4	151^3	*.60	DaMiller	RoCroghan	IdealNwtn,KnockThrT,Cartnivrs -
5-16	08 2M1	38900	sy 48	L	3yrF NJSS	27^4	55^2	124^2	152^1	8	9^{10}	$9^{7\frac{3}{4}}$	$7^{\circ\circ 3\frac{1}{2}}$	$3^{\frac{3}{4}}$	$1^{3\frac{1}{4}}$	27^1	152^1	9.80	DaMiller	RoCroghan	KnockThrT,BestPlace,Cartnivrs -
5-10	08 7Fhld	54350	ft 61	L	HelnDancer	27	56	125^2	155	6	$6^{6\frac{1}{4}}$	$6^{6\frac{1}{4}}$	$4^{\circ 1\frac{3}{4}}$	$3^{3\frac{1}{4}}$	$3^{6\frac{1}{4}}$	30^2	156^1	43.30	DaMiller	RoCroghan	CuzSheCan,WldWstShw,KnockThrT -
4-30	08 3Fhld		ft 50	L	Qua	29^4	101^1	131^1	159^4	6	$1^{\circ 1\frac{1}{4}}$	$1^{1\frac{1}{2}}$	1^2	$1^{1\frac{1}{4}}$	$1^{3\frac{1}{4}}$	28^3	159^4	NB	BrDickens	RoCroghan	KnockThrT,GloriaGrl,KelysAngl -
4-23	08 2Fhld		ft 67	L	Qua	30^2	101^2	131^3	200	6	$3^{3\frac{1}{4}}$	3^3	$3^{\circ 3}$	2^2	1^{nk}	27^4	200	NB	BrDickens	RoCroghan	KnockThrT,Ladycino,SgnOfAqrs -

GRAY **BRIAN SEARS** (40) wh-br (1,666-345-227-208-.324) **Tr-MONTE GELROD** (48-11-6-5-.333)

8 **STYLISH ARTIST** — b f 3 by Artsplace-Honey Bunny-Precious Bunny

Mark E Steacy,ON;R Peter Heffering,ON;
Dr Malcolm G Man Son Hing,BC;David K Reid,ON

2008	8	1	1	2	$218,856	1:51 M1 gd
2007	11	5	2	1	$498,634	1:52⁴DD⅝ ft
Life	19	6	3	3	$717,490	3, 1:51 M1 gd

Br- M E Steacy & R Peter Heffering & D K Reid,ON

10-1

LAST 6 STARTS-$218,856

8-2	08 5M1	407400	gd 81	D	M Shalee	26^3	53^4	122^2	151	6	$8^{\circ 6}$	$9^{\circ 5}$	$3^{\circ 2\frac{1}{2}}$	$2^{\frac{3}{4}}$	$1^{1\frac{1}{2}}$	28^1	151	72.90	ErGoodell	MoGelrod	StylishAr,GodNwsLdy,MisScarlt-1
7-25	08 7M1	25000	ft 82	D	M Shalee	27^2	55	123^3	150^2	11	$5^{4\frac{1}{2}}$	$5^{\circ 4\frac{3}{4}}$	$4^{\circ 2}$	$3^{1\frac{1}{4}}$	$4^{1\frac{3}{4}}$	26^4	150^4	23.50	JJamieson	MoGelrod	Thong,ANGscnfsn,GodNwsLdy-1
7-18	08 4M1	57700	ft 87	D	TarportHap	27	54^2	123^1	150^2	5	$7^{\circ 6}$	$6^{\circ 5\frac{1}{2}}$	$4^{\circ\circ 1\frac{1}{4}}$	$4^{1\frac{1}{2}}$	7^3	27^3	151	12.70	YaGingras	MoGelrod	Thong,DesrblCnd,LvngCrlne -
7-11	08 6Moh$\frac{7}{8}$	27440	ft 75		3YR-F-COND	27	57^1	125^2	152^1	1	2	2	2	$2^{1\frac{1}{4}}$	2^{hd}		152^1	7.50	JaMoiseyev	MaSteacy	ImJstSpcl,StylishAr,VoelzHnv -
7-4	08 3Moh$\frac{7}{8}$	27720	ft 78		3YR-F-COND	27^2	56^3	125^3	152^1	4	1	2	2	$2^{2\frac{1}{4}}$	$3^{2\frac{1}{4}}$		152^3	3.80	JaMoiseyev	MaSteacy	SprigHnv,ShipsBkni,StylishAr -
6-27	08 9Moh$\frac{7}{8}$	24750	ft 77		F-NW4R1000	28^4	57^4	126^1	153	2	2	2	3	3^2	$3^{2\frac{1}{4}}$		153^2	6.90	JaMoiseyev	MaSteacy	SprigHnv,DremfrEtr,StylishAr -
6-20	08 8Moh$\frac{7}{8}$	26730	ft 60		F-NW25000L	27^3	56^2	124	151	8	10°	10	10	$10^{12\frac{1}{2}}$	$9^{14\frac{1}{4}}$		153^4	38.70	ShSteacy	MaSteacy	PinkKngro,SgyBrtchs,MnhtnKln-1
6-6	08 11Moh$\frac{7}{8}$	23520	ft 84		F-NW22500L	27^2	56	124^2	151^2	scr	sk				scr						ElusivPry,FrcklySra,KgDelight -
5-30	08 10Moh$\frac{7}{8}$	25250	ft 53		3YR-F-COND	27^2	57^2	125	153	8	8	8°	8°	8^5	8^9		154^4	6.45	JaMoiseyev	MaSteacy	MaeveHnv,HasAnAttd,CuzSheCan -
5-23	08 1Moh$\frac{7}{8}$		ft 53		QUA	29^1	58^4	127^2	156^1	1	1	1	1	1^4	$1^{4\frac{1}{2}}$	28^4	156^1	NB	JaMoiseyev	MaSteacy	StylishAr,StonbrdgN,GoNative -
5-16	08 1Moh$\frac{7}{8}$		ft 50		QUA	27^4	58^2	128^2	156^1	4	2	2	2	$2^{1\frac{3}{4}}$	2^1		156^2	NB	MaSteacy	MaSteacy	ShakThtJn,StylishAr,GoGetHer -
11-24	07 1M1	650000	ft 35-1	D	BreedersCr	27^2	56	125^1	153	1	$1^{1\frac{1}{2}}$	$2^{1\frac{1}{2}}$	$2^{1\frac{1}{4}}$	$4^{\frac{1}{2}}$	$1^{1\frac{1}{2}}$	27^3	153	4.70	GeBrennan	MaSteacy	StylishAr,UpFBethan,Dragonfst-1

TRACKMAN SELECTIONS: 3-2-6-5

OWNER ENTRIES UNCOUPLED PER PHRC DEPUTY DIRECTOR

NO.4 IDEAL NEWTON SCRATCHED LAM

But, here's the rub. If you watched Thong during her tremendous run of races from June through July, she would always look lively during her warm-ups and score-downs. That was not the case at Chester. When she came onto the track about an hour before the race, you knew you were looking at a tired horse. She had a slight head-nod and just didn't have the spark that she normally would. Trainer Kevin Lare tried to get her to roll through that warm-up mile, but folks, it just wasn't there that day.

That meant that Tug River Princess from a nice, inside post was just about a lock. I am always hesitant to use that word, but that day it was true. Here's what happened.

NINTH RACE: HARRAHS CHESTER, SUN., AUG. 17-1 Mile Pace. CLASS: VALFORGE. Purse: $350,000

Tug River Princess	J.Campbell	2	$45\frac{3}{4}$	$3°3$	$11\frac{1}{2}$	1^2	$13\frac{1}{4}$	*1.70
Good News Lady	G.Grismore	5	$22\frac{1}{2}$	$21\frac{1}{2}$	3^3	2^2	$23\frac{1}{4}$	6.80
Artimittateslife	S.Bouchard	6	3^4	$43\frac{1}{4}$	$44\frac{1}{2}$	4^5	3^5	6.60
Respectable	Y.Gingras	4	$710\frac{1}{4}$	$65\frac{3}{4}$	6^7	5^7	4^6	32.90
Cartniverous	E.Goodell	1	$68\frac{3}{4}$	$7°6\frac{3}{4}$	$7°°7\frac{1}{2}$	$67\frac{3}{4}$	$58\frac{1}{2}$	25.60
KnockThreeTimes	G.Napolitano,Jr	7	8^{12}	$88\frac{1}{4}$	8^9	$79\frac{1}{4}$	$68\frac{3}{4}$	28.80
Stylish Artist	B.Sears	8	$12\frac{1}{4}$	$11\frac{1}{2}$	$21\frac{1}{2}$	$33\frac{1}{2}$	$711\frac{3}{4}$	6.20
Thong	T.Tetrick	3	$57\frac{1}{4}$	$5°4\frac{3}{4}$	$5°5\frac{1}{2}$	$813\frac{1}{4}$	$814\frac{3}{4}$	1.80

Track: Fast, Temp: 84-0 Time:26.1 55.4 1:22.4 1:50.2 .

Now, these situations are few and far between, especially with such high-profile stakes horses, but it does happen and you want to be in on it when it does. Just a little bit of watching warm-ups will put you onto a lot of winners, and take you off a lot of losers. Isn't that why we're here?

15

READING BETWEEN THE LINES/ HAMBLETONIAN DAY

READING BETWEEN THE LINES

This category might be a little hard to explain. You've probably heard the phrase "Know the game." You should always know the players involved and try and figure out why they do what they do. I like to call it "Read between the lines," because there's often a tale to be told by just thinking about the logic behind certain decisions.

In the interview with Brian Sears that kicked off this book, he talked about some of the difficult decisions that he has to make. Some of them are incredibly complex, and undoubtedly cause him to agonize about making the right choice. He also said that most of the time, he will pick the horse that has the best chance to win that night—not always, but most of the time. The night of May 14, 2008, provides the perfect example of such a choice. Take a look at Expressive, a well-bred filly coming off a qualifier where she was driven by Sears.

Yellow **EXPRESSIVE** — b f 3, by Artsplace, Clear Copy by Jate Lobell — Brittany Farms,Versailles,KY

6 Brian Sears (145) (0-0-0-0 .000) — Tr.Edward Lohmeyer(44-7-1-7 .159) — Last 6 Sts-$8,700

1:52.4 Lx1	08	11	3 0 1		$25,570
1:56.4 ChD 5/8	07	3	1 1 1		$8,700
3 1:52.4 (1)				Lifetime	$34,270

	$5\text{-}8^{08}$	M1	1 fst	28^2	57	1.26^1	1.54^1	Qua 3YO F		6	1^3	$1^{2\frac{1}{2}}$	$1^{1\frac{1}{2}}$	1^2	1^1	28	1.54^1	nb SearsB	Expressv^1,$\text{JkGetpng}^{1\frac{3}{4}}$	tiring,safe
	$5\text{-}1^{08}$	M1	1 fst	28^4	57^4	1.27	1.55^3	Qua 3YO F		8	7^{10}	$5^{\circ 5\frac{1}{4}}$	$4^{\circ 2\frac{3}{4}}$	$4^{1\frac{3}{4}}$	5^2	28^2	1.56	nb SearsB	LkShrDrv^{nk},$\text{AshlysGm}^{\frac{3}{4}}$	cover,gap,flattened
	$5\text{-}1^{08}$	M1	1 fst	28^4	57	1.25^3	1.55^1	Qua 3YO F		x6x	7^{35}	dnf						nb SearsB	$\text{OnThCtwlk}^{3\frac{3}{4}}$,$\text{BbbsJcyB}^{nk}$	broke bef start,plld up
	$11\text{-}8^{07}$	ChD $\frac{5}{8}$	1 fst	28	57^1	1.26^1	1.55^4	NW3PMCD FM	10000	1	$4^{4\frac{1}{4}}$	$1^{1\frac{1}{2}}$	$1^{\frac{3}{4}}$	$1^{\frac{3}{4}}$	$2^{\frac{3}{4}}$	29^4	1.56	2.00 ManziCa	GeorgnBay,Expresive,ILuvIt	
3-1	$11\text{-}1^{07}$	ChD $\frac{5}{8}$	1 fst	28^3	58^1	1.26	1.55^3	NW3PM FM	10000	5	$5^{6\frac{1}{2}}$	$7^{7\frac{1}{4}}$	$6^{\circ 4}$	4^3	$3^{2\frac{1}{4}}$	29^1	1.56	3.70 ManziCa	CntrsDaug,RealGmblr,Expresive	
	$10\text{-}25^{07}$	ChD $\frac{5}{8}$	1 gd	28^1	57^1	1.27^1	1.56^4	NW3PM FM	10000	4	$7^{7\frac{3}{4}}$	$7^{\circ 7\frac{1}{2}}$	$5^{\circ 3}$	$3^{\frac{1}{4}}$	$1^{\frac{1}{2}}$	29	1.56^4	42.70 ManziCa	Expresive,Artexpres,Alouette	

Here's trainer Eddie Lohmeyer again and this filly is the real deal, because she's got it all. She has a big-time pedigree and she showed some serious speed at age 2. This would be her first start back as a sophomore, and that last qualifier was a dazzler. She was on cruise control for Sears just about the whole way around, striding out nicely at the end with a big last quarter. Earlier, I also discussed what to look for in a qualifier like this.

Now, here's the problem. Entered against Expressive was a filly named Classic Star, who was making her racing debut for trainer Steve Elliott and owners Jeff Snyder and Lothlorien Equestrian Centre. Now, that may mean absolutely nothing to you, but trust me, it means a lot to Sears. He raced the 2006 Horse of the Year, Rocknroll Hanover, for those very owners, so this was a tough choice to make for a supposedly simple maiden race. He chose Expressive, and here's what I wrote in my race review.

RACE 8 REVIEW Wednesday, May 14, 2008 *By David Brower*

1   **LAKE SHORE DRIVE** - Inexperience cost her from post 10 last time. Just toss that and you might have a live longshot in here. Sits in and stalks.

2   **WAFFLESICECREAM** - It's not easy to rate her interesting set of qualifiers. She's done it all, but her last wasn't particularly good. I want to watch one.

3   **HEAVENLY HELEN** - Tossed in a clunker last try, but fillies will do that from time to time. Liable to bounce back big and upset the applecart.

4   **WILLING HEART** - In from Balmoral where she was just fair. The competition here is tougher and she must prove her heart is worthy.

5   **UPBID HANOVER** - Also just fair down at Chester. Back on big track where she had a few tries. I'm not ready to hop into her corner just yet.

6   **EXPRESSIVE** - Absolutely cruised in last qualifier. It was a standout and Sears chose her over #7. That's the clincher. She's ready for this. Bet.

7   **CLASSIC STAR** - So far, most of the Elliott trainees that ship in from elsewhere have needed a start. I will go with that theory for now. Wait.

8   **SHAYNA BABY** - I still CANNOT believe she got caught last time. That was her best chance to break maiden. With that said, use underneath.

9   **BUBBAS JOICEY B** - Her qualifiers were good, but this post is bad. #8 is a guaranteed blast out, just inside. That makes the task a lot tougher.

10   **HAUNTED** - Sears off and Silva on. That's a pass for tonight in this post.

TOP CONTENDERS 6-8-3-1

For Sears to give up the drive on Classic Star, he had to love the quali-fier that Expressive turned in. Maybe he made a phone call to the own-ers or trainer Steve Elliott to ask about Classic Star's readiness. Obviously, we don't know that and frankly, we don't own either filly, so we don't care. We just want to know who's most likely to win on the night of May 14.

Let's just say that I felt pretty confident stepping up to the window to bet on Expressive, and she rewarded my faith with an easy, come-from-behind win by more than a length over Classic Star. The win payoff was only $6.40, but if you had the exacta (which I didn't), it paid a healthy $24.

HAMBLETONIAN DAY

Hambletonian Day is the biggest day of racing in the sport, and usually one of my toughest days of work. In the past, it's been the last day of my work year, and although sometimes it seems like the day that never ends, it truly is a thrill to be involved. There is nothing quite like the feel you get when there are 25,000 people at the track, most of them overlooking the apron outside, where we go on the air.

We broadcast internationally over a span of eight hours. The first race usually starts at 11:00 a.m., and there are always 15 or more races that day, including the $1.5 million Hambo. Keep in mind, it's August in New Jersey and the temperature is about 100 degrees and we are under steam-ing studio lights on our set outside, sitting in suits and ties, sweating by 10:00 a.m. Add to that the countless well-wishers and friends who come by the set to offer opinions, say hello, get autographs, and ask for a win-ner!

You can't get any more pressure than that, so I feel compelled to come up with at least one solid play during the day to give out to all my friends. The races are so competitive and so good that day, the task is sometimes impossible. In 2008, however, I knew I had at least one sure winner, but he wasn't running until the 13th race that day.

Pink	**TIZ A MASTERPIECE**										**b c 3, by Western Hanover, Trulyawork Of Art by Artsplace**								**1:49.0 M1**	**08 16 5 1 0**	**$200,769**
											Kentuckiana Racing Stable,Lexington,Ky								**1:58.1 Lx1 Q**	**07 0 0 0 0**	**-**
7	**Andy Miller (160) (0-0-0-0 .000)**										**Tr.Blair Burgess(3-1-1-0 .333)**							**Last 6 Sts-$81,020**	**3 1:49.0 (1)**	**Lifetime**	**$200,769**
	7-19$_{08}$ M1	1	fst	26	51^4	1.19^1	1.47	MdwindsFnl-D	1100000	9	9^{10}	9^{12}	9^9	$8^{9\frac{3}{4}}$	$6^{6\frac{1}{2}}$	27^1	1.48^1	60.80 MillerA	ArtOffcl^{nk},Smbchsmwhr^5		passed tired foes
	7-12$_{08}$ M1	1	fst	27^3	54^4	1.22^3	1.50^2	MdwindsElm-D	50000	3	$5^{\circ 4\frac{1}{4}}$	$5^{\circ 5}$	$5^{\circ\circ 2\frac{1}{2}}$	2^1	$2^{\frac{3}{4}}$	27^3	1.50^3	32.60 MillerA	ShrThDlght$^{\frac{3}{4}}$,TzAMstrpc^1		loop,cvr,wd,gd rally
	6-28$_{08}$ HoP $\frac{7}{8}$	1	fst	27	55^1	1.23^3	1.51^1	Hoosier Cup	500000	10	$5^{5\frac{3}{4}}$	$5^{4\frac{3}{4}}$	$5^{\circ 3\frac{1}{2}}$	$4^{6\frac{1}{2}}$	$4^{6\frac{1}{4}}$	28^1	1.52^2 B	30.60 DillanderJa	ArtOficil,Dali,Beeeyouuu		
	6-23$_{08}$ Mhk $\frac{7}{8}$	1	sly	26^3	55^4	1.23^3	1.51^4	NW2	20000	6	$5^{8\frac{1}{4}}$	$4^{5\frac{3}{4}}$	$2^{\circ 3}$	2^3	$1^{2\frac{1}{4}}$	27^3	1.51^4	★.65 BrewerJs	TzAMstrpc,LglLtgtr		tucked,unc,drew off
5-2	6-16$_{08}$ Mhk $\frac{7}{8}$	1	fst	27^4	55^4	1.24^3	1.52^4	NW3	20000	7	7^{12}	$7^{\circ 9\frac{3}{4}}$	$5^{\circ 4\frac{1}{4}}$	5^2	$1^{\frac{1}{2}}$	27^2	1.52^4	2.40 BrewerJs	TzAMstrpc,LittlThf		trail,cvr,stormed by
	6-8$_{08}$ Mhk $\frac{7}{8}$	1	fst	27	55^3	1.23^2	1.53	NW16000Lcd	17640	8	9^{17}	$7^{\circ 13}$	$6^{\circ 7\frac{1}{2}}$	2^1	$1^{1\frac{3}{4}}$	28^1	1.53	★1.75 BrewerJa	TzAMstrp,Dnrtrtsp		long rally,sharp

Tiz A Masterpiece hadn't raced since his post 9 performance in the $1 million Meadowlands Pace. On Hambo Day, we traditionally run a 3-year-old stakes race called the Oliver Wendell Holmes, named after a former governor of New Jersey. It doesn't always attract the top colts, who are getting a rest after the Med Pace and moving on to their next serious stakes engagement.

If you look closely at the lines of Tiz A Masterpiece, he's got a lot of things going for him. He's trained by a master of 3-year-olds, Blair Burgess, and he is clearly a colt on the improve. His race in the Meadowlands Pace was completely overshadowed by the world-record time and incredible performance of upset winner Art Official, who just nipped eventual Horse of the Year Somebeachsomewhere.

When I watched the replay closely, however, I observed Tiz A Masterpiece flying up the pylons late from an impossible spot. He was very good that night, even though his past-performance line shows him finishing sixth, beaten almost seven lengths. I know that it appears unimpressive, but in reality, it was the colt's best career race to date.

When he showed up in the Holmes, against a less than stellar group of colts, I thought he was an absolute cinch. Here's what I wrote in the program.

RACE 13 REVIEW Saturday, August 2, 2008

By David Brower

1 **LIS DEO** - We haven't seen this colt yet, so I don't know what we're dealing with. He's 5-7 and capable of 25 quarters. Is he this good? We'll find out.

2 **HARLEY D HANOVER** - Been sneaky good all season. Got a touch of needed rest recently and he fits here. I wouldn't be shocked by big one.

3 **WEEKEND GAMBLER** - Adds Lasix now after a few clunkers of late. He's yet to prove himself a true stakes horse. I have to see it first.

4 **SPACE WALK** - Down from Canada and into barn of Lachance. This is aiming a bit high, but he did keep up well in Cup consolation. A big maybe.

5 **FRANKYLUVSMEATBALS** - Earned a hard-fought and well-deserved win here last week. Back to the tougher stakes grind now. He's got lot to prove.

6 **MCCEDES** - The NJ Classic champ is back. Now on Lasix and off a good, rallying qualifier. If the Lasix solves the problem, he's the one to fear again.

7 **TIZ A MASTERPIECE** - Loved his try in the Pace elim and had a LOT of pylon pace in the final from impossible spot. Paced much faster too!

8 **COLD CAPE COD** - Not in a good spot out here, needless to say. I don't think he can blast and I don't think he can outfinish these. Not for me.

TOP CONTENDERS 7-6-2-1

I make very few bets on Hambletonian Day, because it's such an incredibly busy time for me, and I will freely admit my betting history on that day over the years has been poor. I try not to get too excited about betting, I just concentrate on my work and the great day of racing and fun. On Hambletonian Day 2008, the first thing I did when I got to the track that morning was bet on Tiz A Masterpiece. It was the only bet I made all day.

Thankfully, Tiz A Masterpiece performed as expected, brushing to the lead and cruising away from the field by two lengths in a time of 1:49. That is still his lifetime-best mark. He only paid $3.60, but on a day when it's so hard to come up with winners, I thought that was the best bet of the day. I can only hope that all the faithful still had some money left by the 13th race!

CONCLUSION

The process of handicapping harness races can be as easy or as difficult as you make it. The people that do their homework and analyze the races thoughtfully will always be more successful. To be a winning gambler requires patience and fortitude, a few things that I lack most of the time.

While researching and writing this book, I've learned a lot about myself and my abilities as a handicapper, and I know it will only help me in the future. I need to be more patient and wait for the situations to present themselves. The game is always changing, and adapting to the changes is not easy—but it's almost always fun! Even when I'm pulling my hair out after a missed opportunity or a lost photo finish, I know I enjoyed trying to figure it out. That's why we do it.

I hope I've passed along some of the things to look for when you get to the track and open up that program. The answers are there, provided you know what to look for. It's a great game and there's no feeling in the world that can compare to cashing a ticket on a harness race.

As Paul Newman's character, Eddie Felson, said in *The Color of Money*, "Money won is twice as sweet as money earned." If you can find a truer statement than that, I'd like to hear about it.

HOW TO READ THE PAST PERFORMANCES

Courtesy of Harness Eye

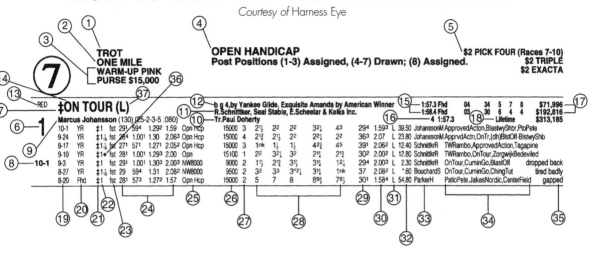

1 - Type of race
2 - Distance of today's race
3 - Warm-up color of saddle pads
for this race and purse
4 - Race conditions
5 - Wagering information
6 - Betting number
7 - Denotes the horse will be racing with trotting
hobbles or freelegged
8 - Morning-line odds
9 - Today's driver, his weight, total starts, win,
place and show totals and win percentage
10 - Horse's trainer - Total starts, win, place and
show totals and
win percentage (when available)
11 - Horse's owner
12 - Horse's color, sex, age, sire,
dam and dam's sire
13 - Horse's saddle-pad color
14 - Horse's name
15 - Horse's best win time for the current and
previous year
16 - Age and time of the horse's fastest winning
effort
17 - Horse's individual statistics from the current
and previous year; including total starts, top
three finishes and yearly earnings
18 - Horse's lifetime earnings
19 - Date of past performances

20 - Track where horse competed; (A) denotes that
the race was contested in the afternoon
21 - Denotes hobbled trotter
or freelegged pacer
22 - Distance of race
23 - Track condition
24 - Quarter, half, three-quarters
and final time of the winning horse
25 - Type of race
26 - Purse of race
27 - Horse's starting post position
in previous races
28 - Horse's quarter, half, three-quarters, stretch
and finish calls with lengths behind the leader
29 - Horse's individual final fractional time
30 - Horse's final time
31 - Denotes which medication (if any) the horse
used in each start
32 - Horse's post-time odds
in previous races
33 - Driver for previous races
34 - Top three finishers in horse's
previous races
35 - Performance comment
36 - Denotes field contained a horse that started
from the second tier
37 - Denotes horse will race with
Lasix (L) today

GLOSSARY OF TERMS

Courtesy of Harness Eye

ACROSS THE BOARD A bet on a horse to win, place and show. If the horse wins, the player collects three ways; if second, two ways; and if third, one way, losing the win and place bets.

ALSO-ELIGIBLE A horse officially entered, but not permitted to start unless the field is reduced by scratches below a specified number.

ALSO-RAN A horse who finishes out of the money.

BACKSTRETCH The straight area of the track between the turns. Also, the stable area.

BANDAGE Strips of cloth wound around the lower part of a horse's legs for support or protection against injury.

BELATED Indicates a horse that finishes well but too late.

BLANKET FINISH Horses finishing so closely together they could be covered by a blanket.

BLINDSW Abbreviation for blindswitched. When a horse is trapped between horses on the outside.

BOX If you have two or more horses that you think will finish in the top spots, but you are not sure of the order, you can box them. Example: an exacta box on horses #3 and #6. You win if #3 wins and #6 places OR #6 wins and #3 places. The same method can be applied to boxing a trifecta or a superfecta.

BREAK To go offstride. The horse loses natural trotting or pacing rhythm and starts galloping.

BRIDLE Horse's headgear, which includes the bit, reins, and may include blinkers, or "blinds."

BRUSH When a horse makes a fast quick move.

BUTE (BUTAZOLIDIN) Trade name for phenylbutazone, an analgesic permitted for use on horses in some racing jurisdictions.

CHALK (CHALK PLAYER) Horse favored in a race. Bettors who wager on favorites.

CLAIMING RACE Race in which horses are entered subject to being purchased for a specified price.

CHART CALLER Person who records the positions of all the horses in the race at designated points of call.

CLOSER A horse who runs best in the latter part of the race, coming from off the pace.

CLUBHOUSE TURN Generally, the turn closest to the clubhouse.

COLORS Outfit worn by each driver so they can be easily recognized.

COLT Male horse age 3 or younger.

COUPLED Two or more horses running as an entry in a single betting unit.

DAILY DOUBLE Type of wager calling for the selection of winners of two consecutive races, usually the first and second.

DAM Mother of a horse.

DEAD HEAT Two or more horses finishing in a tie at the wire.

DISQUALIFICATION Change in order of finish by officials for an infraction of the rules.

DREW OFF Refers to the winner pulling clear from the field.

GLOSSARY

DRIVING Strong urging by a driver in a race.

DULL COVER When a horse follows another horse on the outside he is said to be behind cover. Dull (bad) cover occurs when a horse follows another horse that is not keeping up well.

EASED A horse pulled up before the finish of a race, usually due to injury.

ENTRY Two or more horses owned by the same stable or (in some cases) trained by the same trainer and thus running as a single betting unit.

EQUIVALENT ODDS The mutuel price horses pay for each $1 bet.

EQUIPMENT Gear worn by a horse in a race.

EXACTA A wager in which the first two finishers in a race, in exact order of finish, must be picked.

FIELD The horses in a race.

FIELD HORSE (or MUTUEL FIELD) Two or more starters running as a single betting unit, when there are more entrants than positions on the tote board.

FILLY Female horse age 3 or younger.

FIRST-OVER The first horse to make a move on the leader in a race, moving up on the outside.

FRACTIONAL TIME Intermediate time recorded in a race, as at the quarter, half, three-quarters, etc.

FREE-LEGGED A pacer that races without wearing hobbles (hopples).

FRONT-RUNNER A horse who usually leads (or tries to lead) the field for as far as he can.

GAPPED When a horse does not keep up with the other horses.

GATE Starting mechanism.

GELDING Castrated male horse.

GRIND When a horse gradually progresses on the outside.

HANDICAPPER One who makes selections based on past performances.

HANDLE The total amount of money wagered into wagering pool.

HANGING When a horse has a clear chance at gaining ground but fails to gain.

HARNESS The gear that is used to attach the sulky to a horse, to carry the hobbles, and to enable the driver to steer the horse.

HEAD OF THE STRETCH Beginning of the straight run home.

HOBBLES/HOPPLES The straps that connect the front and rear legs on the same side of a horse. Most pacers wear hobbles to help balance their stride and maintain a pacing gait. There are also trotting hobbles that work through a pulley system to help trotters maintain their gait.

HOOD/EYE HOOD A material or mesh covering that usually allows a horse to see less of his surroundings. It is designed to relax the horse and there are many different kinds of hoods and blinkers.

HORSE An ungelded male horse age 4 or older.

IN When a horse goes from the outside to the rail.

IN THE MONEY Finishing first, second or third.

INQUIRY An announcement by the judges that they are going to review the race more carefully before posting it as "official."

JOGGED An easy victory.

LASIX Trade name for furosemide, a diuretic medication used in the treatment of bleeders.

LENGTH The measuring distance between horses. One horse equals one length.

LOCK Slang for a "sure thing" winner.

LOOPED A horse that goes for the lead but is passed by a horse to his outside is said to have been looped.

MAIDEN A horse or driver that has yet to win a race.

MAIDEN RACE A race for nonwinners.

MARE Female horse age 4 or older.

MORNING LINE A linemaker's estimate of what the final odds will be in a race, made before betting begins.

MUDDER A horse who races well on a muddy track.

NO PACE (TROT) A horse that displayed a very poor effort.

NOSE Smallest advantage a horse can have at the finish.

OBJECTION Claim of foul lodged by a driver.

ODDS-ON A horse whose odds are less than even money. A horse whose odds are 4-5 is said to be odds-on.

OFFICIAL Sign displayed when result is confirmed. Also a racing official.

ON THE BOARD Finishing among the first three; sometimes the first four.

ON THE NOSE Betting a horse to win only.

OUT When a horse moves off the rail, he is out.

OVERLAY A horse going off at a higher price than he appears to warrant based on his past performances.

OWN CLIP A horse that is allowed to set his own fractions.

PACE Relative rate of early movement in a race. Also, the gait of a horse (pacer).

PACING A horse's gait in which the front and rear legs on the same side move in unison. Approximately 80 percent of Standardbreds in competition are pacers.

PADDOCK Structure or area where horses are saddled and kept before post time.

PARIMUTUEL PAYOFF The posted amount each bettor will receive for a winning mutuel ticket.

PAST PERFORMANCES A compilation in *Harness Eye* (or the track program) of a horse's record.

PHOTO FINISH A result so close it is necessary to use a finish-line camera to determine order of finish.

PICK THREE A wager in which the bettor must correctly select the winners of three consecutive races on one card, betting all three at once. The same principle applies to pick fours and pick sixes.

PLACE Finished second in a race.

PLACE BET Wager on a horse to finish second or better.

POCKET A horse in a pocket sits directly behind the leader in a race. Sometimes, he is unable to obtain a clear run because he has other horses in front, behind, and to the side of him.

POST PARADE Horses parading in front of the stands to be viewed by the patrons/judges.

POST POSITION Position behind the starting gate from which a horse starts.

POST TIME Designated time for a race to start.

PURSE Prize money distributed to owners.

PYLONS (ON THE PYLONS) Pylons are the traffic-cone objects that replaced the inner-hub rail of years ago. They mark the inside boundary of the track.

QUALIFIER (QUA) A nonbetting race in which a horse attempts to finish in a required time. A qualifying race is required whenever a horse misses an extended period of time.

QUARTER MOVE Used to describe a horse that makes a quick move to the front at the quarter call.

RATED Used to describe a horse that is being purposely restrained by his driver to reserve energy for later.

ROUGH When a pacer or trotter does not keep a smooth stride.

SCORE-DOWN The score-down is the final warm-up procedure in the minutes before the race. It comes after the post parade and is designed to either loosen a horse up or encourage him to be on his toes.

SCRATCH To be withdrawn from a race.

SHADOW ROLL A lambswool-covered noseband positioned halfway up a horse's face to keep him from seeing shadows on the ground.

SHOW Finishing third in a race.

SHOW BET Wager on a horse to finish in the money; third or better.

SHUFFLED When a horse loses ground along the rail because of many lead changes.

SIMULCAST Televising a race to other tracks, OTB branches, or other outlets for the purpose of wagering.

SIRE Father of a horse.

STARTING GATE The vehicle the horses follow before the race begins.

STATE-BRED A horse bred in a particular state and thus eligible to compete in special races restricted to state-breds.

STEWARDS (JUDGES) Track's top officials responsible for enforcing the rules.

STRETCH CALL Position of the horses when they exit the final turn of the race.

STRONG Describes a horse that won with an exceptional effort.

SULKY Also known as the cart or racebike, the sulky is attached to the harness and carries the driver.

SUPERFECTA A bet selecting the first four finishers in exact order.

TAKEOUT The percentage of tax taken from each betting pool and distributed according to state law among the state, horsemen (purses), and racetrack.

TOTE BOARD Lighted display board that shows odds. Also displays betting pools, minutes to post, fractions, final times, order of finish, and payoffs.

TOUT One who gives tips on racehorses, usually with expectation of some personal reward in return; to give tips.

TRIFECTA A bet selecting the first three finishers in exact order.

TRIP The path the horse takes during the race.

TROT A horse's gait in which the front and rear legs move diagonally in tandem; left front with right rear, etc.

TWO MOVES Used to describe a horse that made two successful attempts at getting the lead.

UNDERLAY A betting situation in which a horse's chance of winning does not justify his low odds—that is, the horse is too short a price.

WHIP (STICK) Equipment used by the driver to encourage the horse to accelerate.

WIRE The finish line. It's an imaginary line running between the poles.

YIELD A horse gives up the lead when he yields.

USTA TRACKS

Provided by: United States Trotting Association

CALIFORNIA
Cal-Expo
1600 Exposition Blvd.
Sacramento, CA 95815
(916) 263-3000
http://www.calxharness.com/

DELAWARE
Dover Downs
1131 N. DuPont Highway
Dover, DE 19901
(302) 674-4600 or 800-711-5882
http://www.doverdowns.com/

Harrington Raceway
15 West Rider Rd.
Harrington, DE 19952
(302)398-7223
http://www.harringtonraceway.com/

FLORIDA
Pompano Park Harness
1800 SW 3rd St.
Pompano Beach, FL 33069
(954) 972-2000
http://www.theislepompanopark.com/

ILLINOIS
Balmoral Park
26435 South Dixie Highway
Crete, IL 60417
(708) 672-1414
http://www.balmoralpark.com/

Du Quoin State Fair
655 Executive Drive
Du Quoin, IL 62832
(618) 541-1515

Hawthorne Racecourse
3501 S. Laramie Ave.
Cicero, IL 60804
(708) 780-3700
http://www.hawthorneracecourse.com/

Maywood Park
8600 W. North Ave.
Melrose Park, IL 60160
(708) 343-4800
http://www.maywoodpark.com/

Springfield, Ill. State Fair
801 East Sangamon Avenue
Springfield, IL 62794-9281
(217) 782-4231

INDIANA
Hoosier Park
4500 Dan Patch Circle
Anderson, IN 46013
(765) 642-7223
http://www.hoosierpark.com/

Indiana Downs
4200 N. Michigan Rd.
Shelbyville, IN 46176
(317) 421-0000
http://www.indianadowns.com/

Indiana State Fair
1202 E. 38th St.
Indianapolis, Indiana 46205-2869
(317) 927-7500

IOWA
Prairie Meadows
One Prairie Meadows Drive
Altoona, IA 50009
(515) 967-1000
http://www.prairiemeadows.com/

KENTUCKY
Player's Bluegrass Downs
150 Downs Drive
Paducah, KY 42001
(270) 444-7117

The Red Mile
1200 Red Mile Rd.
Lexington, KY 40504
(859) 255-0752
http://www.theredmile.com/

Thunder Ridge
164 Thunder Rd.
Prestonsburg, KY 41653
(606) 886-7223

MAINE
Bangor Raceway
100 Dutton St.
Bangor, ME 04401
(207) 947-6744
http://www.bangorraceway.net/

Scarborough Downs
90 Payne Rd.
Scarborough, ME 04070
(207) 883-4331
http://www.scarboroughdowns.com/

MARYLAND
Ocean Downs
10218 Racetrack Rd.
Berlin, MD 21811
(410) 641-0600
http://www.oceandowns.com/

Rosecroft Raceway
6336 Rosecroft Dr.
Fort Washington, MD 20744
(301) 567-4000
http://www.rosecroft.com/

MASSACHUSETTS
Plainridge Racecourse
301 Washington St.
Plainville, MA 02762
(508) 643-2500
http://www.prcharness.com/

MICHIGAN
Hazel Park
1650 E. Ten Mile Rd.
Hazel Park, MI 48030
(248) 398-1000
http://www.hazelparkraceway.com/

Jackson Harness Raceway
200 W. Ganson St.
Jackson, MI 49204
(877) 316-0283
http://www.jacksonharnessraceway.com/

Northville Downs
301 S. Center St.
Northville, MI 48167
(248) 349-1000
http://www.northvilledowns.com/

Sports Creek Raceway
4290 Morrish Rd.
Swartz Creek, MI 48473
(810) 635-3333
http://www.sportscreek.com/

MINNESOTA
Running Aces Harness Park
15201 Zurich St. NE
Columbus, MN 55025
(651) 925-4600
http://www.runningacesharness.com/

NEW HAMPSHIRE
Rockingham Park
Rockingham Park Blvd. (I-93 exit 1)
Salem, NH 03079
(603) 898-2311
http://www.rockinghampark.com/

NEW JERSEY

Freehold Raceway
130 Park Avenue
Freehold, NJ 07728
(732) 462-3800
http://www.freeholdraceway.com/

The Meadowlands
50 State Route 120
East Rutherford, NJ 07073
(201) 843-2446
http://www.thebigm.com/

NEW YORK

Batavia Downs
8315 Park Rd.
Batavia, NY 14020
(585) 343-3750
http://www.batavia-downs.com/

Buffalo Raceway
5600 McKinley Parkway
Hamburg, NY 14075
(716) 649-1280
http://www.buffaloraceway.com/

Historic Track-Goshen
44 Park Place
P.O. Box 192
Goshen, NY 10924
(845) 294-5333
http://www.goshenhistorictrack.com/

Monticello Raceway
204 Route 17B
Monticello, NY 12701
(845) 794-4100
http://www.monticelloraceway.com/

Saratoga Gaming and Raceway
342 Jefferson St.
Saratoga Springs, NY 12866
(518) 584-2110
http://www.saratogaraceway.com/

Tioga Downs
2384 West River Rd.
Nichols, NY 13812
(607) 946-8464
http://www.tiogadowns.com/

Vernon Downs
4229 Stahlman Rd.
Vernon, NY 13476
(315) 829-6825
http://www.vernondowns.com/

Yonkers Raceway
810 Yonkers Ave.
Yonkers, NY 10704
(914) 968-4200
http://www.yonkersraceway.com/

OHIO

Delaware, OH Fair
236 Pennsylvania Ave.
P.O. Box 1278
Delaware, OH 43015
(800) 335-3217
http://www.littlebrownjug.com

Northfield Park
10705 Northfield Rd.
Northfield, OH 44067
(330) 467-4101
http://www.northfieldpark.com/

Raceway Park
5700 Telegraph Road
Toledo, OH 43612
(419) 476-7751
http://www.racewayparktoledo.com/

Scioto Downs
6000 S. High St.
Columbus, OH 43207
(614) 491-2515
http://www.sciotodowns.com/

PENNSYLVANIA
Harrah's Chester
Casino and Racetrack
777 Harrah's Blvd.
Chester, PA 19013
(484) 480-8020
http://www.harrahs.com/

The Meadows
Race Track Rd.
Meadow Lands, PA 15347
(724) 225-9300
http://www.themeadowsracing.com/

Mohegan Sun at Pocono Downs
1280 Hwy 315
Wilkes-Barre, PA 18702
(570) 831-2100
http://www.poconodowns.com/

VIRGINIA
Colonial Downs
10515 Colonial Downs Parkway
New Kent, VA 23124
(804) 966-7223
http://www.colonialdowns.com/

SIRE STATS

Sire stats provided by: United States Trotting Association

Leading Money-Winning Sires in 2008
All-Age Trotters

Sire Name	Foals	Starters	Earnings
MUSCLES YANKEE	824	261	$ 9,794,458
ANGUS HALL	740	350	$ 8,368,373
CREDIT WINNER	449	208	$ 7,333,227
CONWAY HALL	709	242	$ 7,196,680
STRIKING SAHBRA	855	264	$ 6,329,823
S J'S PHOTO	753	192	$ 6,279,936
YANKEE GLIDE	679	220	$ 6,056,808
ANDOVER HALL	318	154	$ 5,094,623
MALABAR MAN	630	170	$ 4,551,934
LINDY LANE	872	188	$ 3,995,861
DREAM VACATION	378	144	$ 3,860,520
SELF POSSESSED	338	105	$ 3,835,521
LIKE A PRAYER	265	126	$ 3,752,824
KADABRA	191	118	$ 3,466,044
SJ'S CAVIAR	406	158	$ 3,372,439
VALLEY VICTOR	451	156	$ 3,299,137
BALANCED IMAGE	1111	115	$ 3,228,746
MR LAVEC	927	208	$ 3,218,264
BROADWAY HALL	199	118	$ 3,175,522
CANTAB HALL	110	70	$ 2,452,208

*Foals of Racing Age (2-14) Updated: 04/02/2009

Leading Money-Winning Sires in 2008
All-Age Pacers

Sire Name	Foals	Starters	Earnings
WESTERN HANOVER	1713	484	$ 15,481,537
CAMLUCK	1654	537	$ 15,087,375
THE PANDEROSA	715	383	$ 12,439,268
BETTOR'S DELIGHT	404	275	$ 11,279,391
DRAGON AGAIN	551	319	$ 10,698,742
WESTERN IDEAL	443	235	$ 10,577,746
ARTISCAPE	794	389	$ 10,037,544
CAM'S CARD SHARK	1308	384	$ 9,479,989
CAMBEST	1383	393	$ 8,904,818
REAL ARTIST	615	330	$ 8,814,161
ARTSPLACE	1572	353	$ 8,602,919
BLISSFULL HALL	618	356	$ 8,334,378
BADLANDS HANOVER	514	288	$ 8,273,750
ART MAJOR	249	184	$ 8,167,053
ASTREOS	730	394	$ 8,134,198
SPORTSMASTER	1326	376	$ 7,071,587
MACH THREE	259	177	$ 6,659,756
GRINFROMEARTOEAR	632	276	$ 6,421,854
KEYSTONE RAIDER	1000	308	$ 6,351,045
REAL DESIRE	344	215	$ 6,113,665

*Foals of Racing Age (2-14) Updated: 04/02/2009

Leading Sires Average Earnings per Foal in 2008

*minimum 15 registered foals in 2006

2-Year-Old Pacers

Sire Name	2006 Foals	Starters	Earnings	Avg Earnings
NO PAN INTENDED	54	35	$ 1,440,625	$ 26,678
WESTERN IDEAL	94	58	$ 2,414,893	$ 25,690
ART MAJOR	112	75	$ 2,218,037	$ 19,804
WESTERN HANOVER	139	99	$ 2,533,700	$ 18,228
SPORTSMASTER	63	43	$ 1,032,210	$ 16,384
TWIN B CHAMP	37	11	$ 563,299	$ 15,224
COLE MUFFLER	79	48	$ 1,182,639	$ 14,970
REAL DESIRE	100	59	$ 1,456,987	$ 14,570
JATE LOBELL	31	13	$ 410,942	$ 13,256
BETTOR'S DELIGHT	90	61	$ 1,169,939	$ 12,999
DREAM WORK	27	19	$ 342,857	$ 12,698
APACHES FAME	30	15	$ 369,976	$ 12,333
ALLAMERICAN NATIVE	90	62	$ 1,089,994	$ 12,111
WESTERN TERROR	129	66	$ 1,391,360	$ 10,786
BADLANDS HANOVER	117	65	$ 1,169,530	$ 9,996
I AM A FOOL	119	60	$ 1,130,887	$ 9,503
REAL ARTIST	104	69	$ 969,495	$ 9,322
ARTSPLACE	106	59	$ 940,114	$ 8,869
MCARDLE	72	49	$ 625,237	$ 8,684
THE PANDEROSA	115	70	$ 985,547	$ 8,570

Updated: 04/02/2009

Leading Sires Average Earnings per Foal in 2008

*minimum 15 registered foals in 2006

2-Year-Old Trotters

Sire Name	2006 Foals	Starters	Earnings	Avg Earnings
MALABAR MAN	46	28	$ 1,526,322	$ 33,181
CANTAB HALL	110	70	$ 2,452,208	$ 22,293
MUSCLES YANKEE	108	60	$ 2,406,818	$ 22,285
STRIKING SAHBRA	73	43	$ 1,382,359	$ 18,936
ANDOVER HALL	81	47	$ 1,460,794	$ 18,034
CREDIT WINNER	75	47	$ 1,234,977	$ 16,466
CR COMMANDO	54	32	$ 802,947	$ 14,869
WINDSONG'S LEGACY	114	53	$ 1,688,971	$ 14,816
YANKEE GLIDE	93	48	$ 1,344,506	$ 14,457
BROADWAY HALL	112	71	$ 1,576,136	$ 14,073
LIKE A PRAYER	77	41	$ 1,008,749	$ 13,101
PSYCHIC SPIRIT	17	9	$ 203,934	$ 11,996
ANGUS HALL	112	66	$ 1,332,987	$ 11,902
CONWAY HALL	98	66	$ 1,123,587	$ 11,465
TOM RIDGE	62	34	$ 682,600	$ 11,010
IN CONCHNITO	17	11	$ 176,383	$ 10,375
AMIGO HALL	55	27	$ 525,302	$ 9,551
KADABRA	77	41	$ 717,046	$ 9,312
PLESAC	16	5	$ 143,717	$ 8,982
SOUTHWIND LUSTRE	20	3	$ 172,814	$ 8,641

Updated: 04/02/2009

Leading Sires Average Earnings per Foal in 2008

*minimum 15 registered foals in 2005

3-Year-Old Pacers

Sire Name	2005 Foals	Starters	Earnings	Avg Earnings
MACH THREE	76	59	$ 3,671,255	$ 48,306
ART MAJOR	137	109	$ 5,949,016	$ 43,423
BETTOR'S DELIGHT	87	72	$ 3,481,363	$ 40,016
THE PANDEROSA	106	87	$ 3,942,745	$ 37,196
BADLANDS HANOVER	109	77	$ 3,707,369	$ 34,013
WESTERN IDEAL	83	61	$ 2,719,983	$ 32,771
MCARDLE	86	66	$ 2,594,730	$ 30,171
REAL ARTIST	125	97	$ 3,587,076	$ 28,697
ALLAMERICAN NATIVE	74	57	$ 2,107,859	$ 28,485
CAMLUCK	140	115	$ 3,915,599	$ 27,969
WESTERN HANOVER	134	97	$ 3,498,172	$ 26,106
DRAGON AGAIN	132	98	$ 3,282,950	$ 24,871
ALLAMERICAN INGOT	75	61	$ 1,615,868	$ 21,545
ARTISCAPE	118	89	$ 2,373,939	$ 20,118
CAM'S CARD SHARK	82	64	$ 1,632,066	$ 19,903
REAL DESIRE	104	74	$ 2,042,798	$ 19,642
ARTSPLACE	106	77	$ 2,001,688	$ 18,884
NO PAN INTENDED	133	93	$ 2,509,587	$ 18,869
USHER HANOVER	22	15	$ 399,362	$ 18,153
RIVERBOAT KING	38	33	$ 643,955	$ 16,946

Updated: 04/02/2009

Leading Sires Average Earnings per Foal in 2008

*minimum 15 registered foals in 2005

3-Year-Old Trotters

Sire Name	2005 Foals	Starters	Earnings	Avg Earnings
CREDIT WINNER	88	55	$ 3,952,274	$ 44,912
CONWAY HALL	107	75	$ 3,879,708	$ 36,259
MUSCLES YANKEE	136	77	$ 4,508,016	$ 33,147
KADABRA	114	77	$ 2,748,998	$ 24,114
ANDOVER HALL	117	73	$ 2,774,202	$ 23,711
S J'S PHOTO	70	42	$ 1,644,444	$ 23,492
YANKEE GLIDE	94	55	$ 2,011,041	$ 21,394
STRIKING SAHBRA	98	74	$ 1,991,154	$ 20,318
LIKE A PRAYER	88	53	$ 1,761,082	$ 20,012
DUKE OF YORK	59	27	$ 1,130,045	$ 19,153
ANGUS HALL	144	101	$ 2,657,888	$ 18,458
BROADWAY HALL	87	47	$ 1,599,386	$ 18,384
LINDY LANE	89	51	$ 1,605,719	$ 18,042
CR COMMANDO	45	27	$ 796,245	$ 17,694
SELF POSSESSED	59	32	$ 991,861	$ 16,811
DREAM VACATION	79	43	$ 1,319,556	$ 16,703
MALABAR MAN	52	36	$ 763,326	$ 14,679
CR EXCALIBUR	44	32	$ 599,919	$ 13,635
PEARSALL HANOVER	27	16	$ 318,908	$ 11,811
KEYSTONE NORDIC	52	35	$ 604,038	$ 11,616

Updated: 04/02/2009

ABOUT THE AUTHOR

DAVE BROWER has been a harness-racing fan since his childhood, growing up five minutes from the Meadowlands Racetrack in Passaic, New Jersey. A 1991 graduate of St. John's University with a B.S. in journalism, he is currently the morning-line oddsmaker and track handicapper at the Meadowlands. He also hosts the track's nightly television show, *Racing from the Meadowlands* on SportsNet New York, and is a regular guest on TVG's Friday-night *Drive Time*, providing on-site analysis and interviews.

CONTRIBUTORS

KEITH GISSER, the publicity director at Northfield Park in Ohio, is also the track's on-air handicapper. He is the author of *Northfield Park: Images of Sports*, a history of the colorful oval known as the Home of the Flying Turns.

DERICK GIWNER is the editor of *Harness Eye*, the only daily newspaper devoted to the sport. In addition to covering harness racing as a writer/handicapper, he participates as an owner and in the sulky as an amateur driver. He has also served as both a track announcer and chart caller.